Space Story

Fiona Ostby

WEST
MARGIN
PRESS

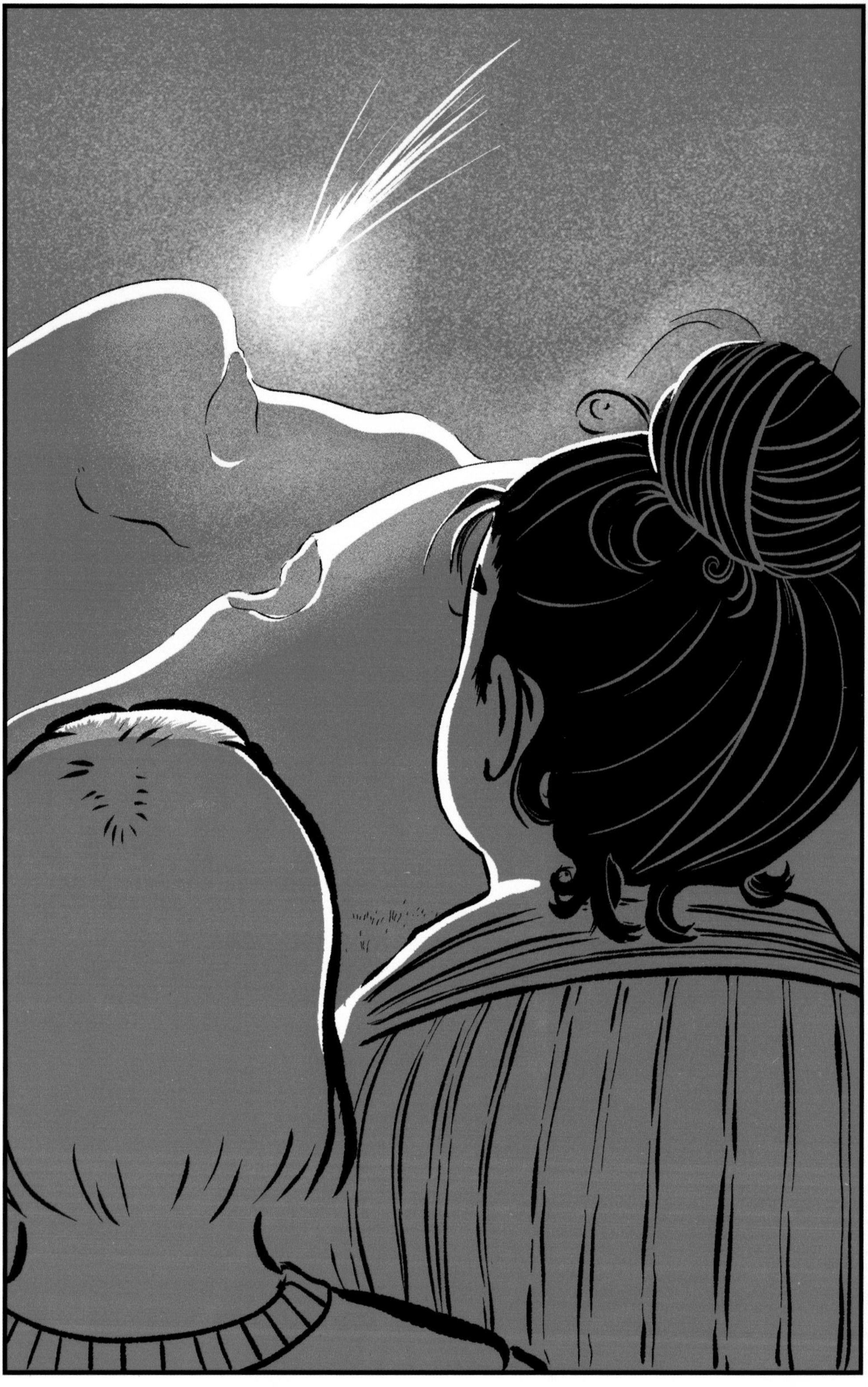

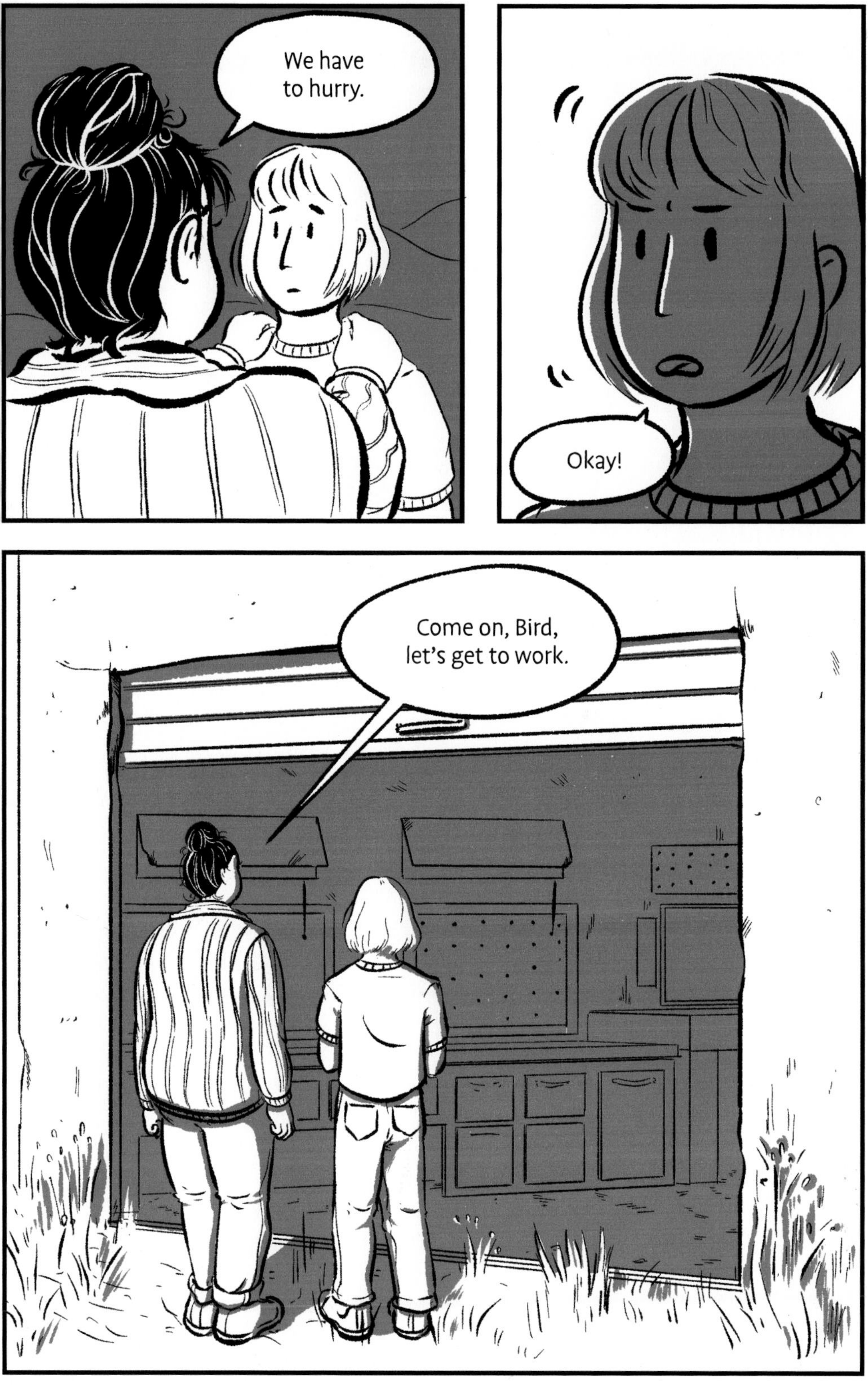
We have to hurry.
Okay!
Come on, Bird, let's get to work.

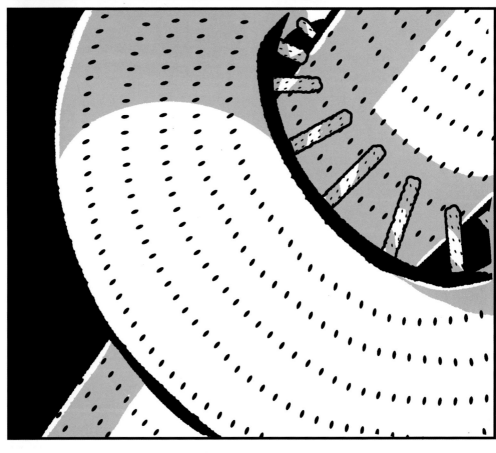

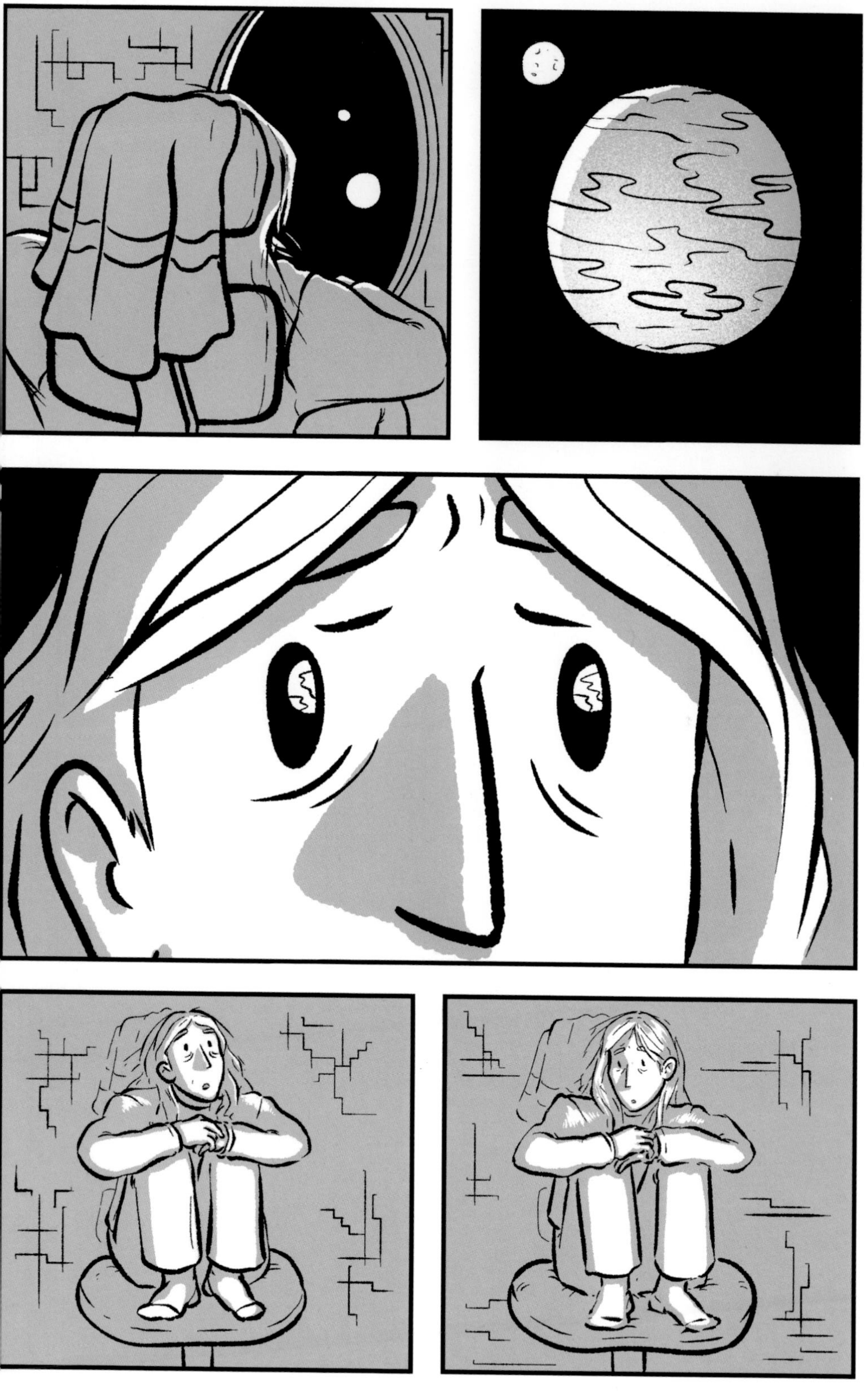

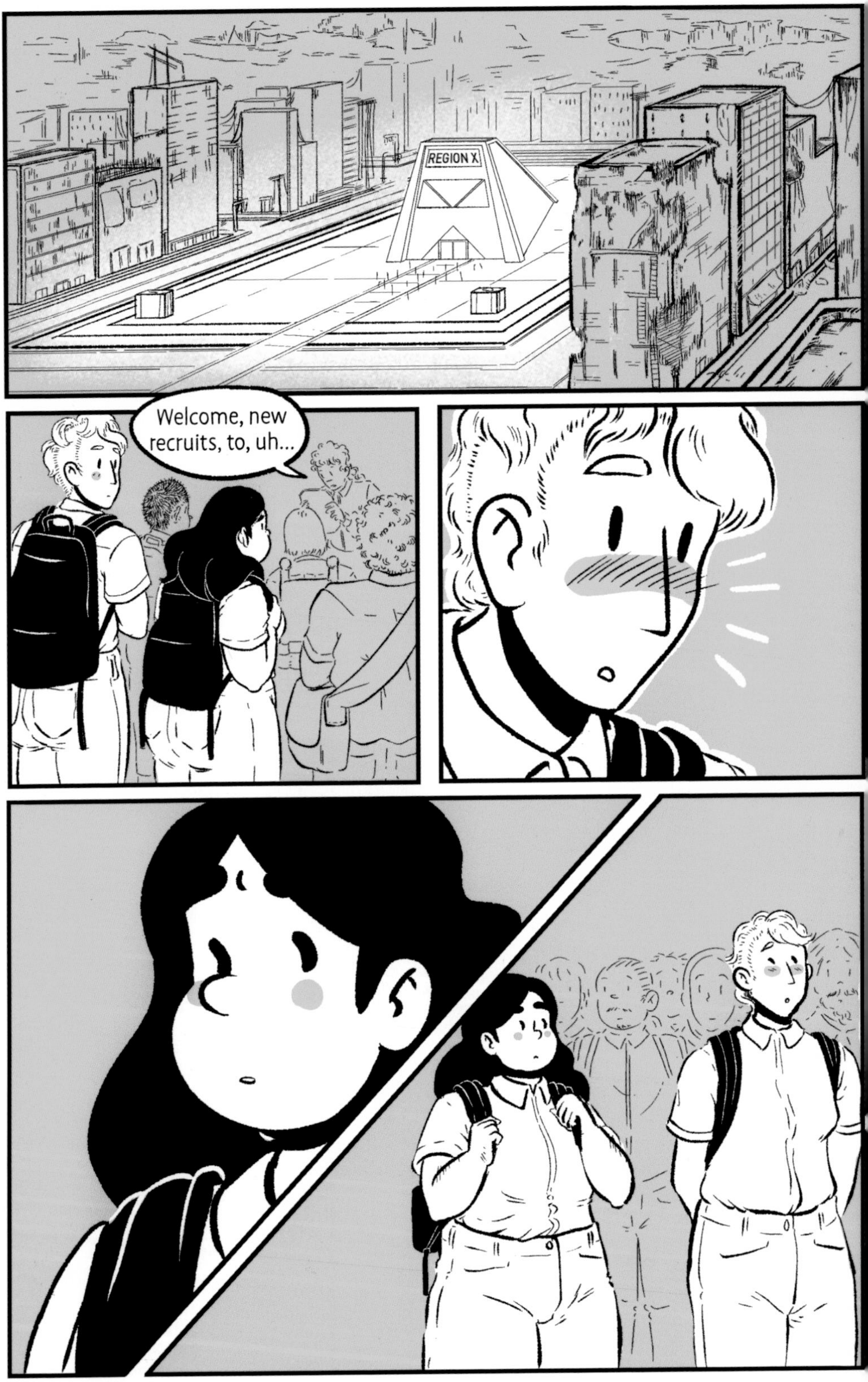
REGION X
Welcome, new recruits, to, uh...

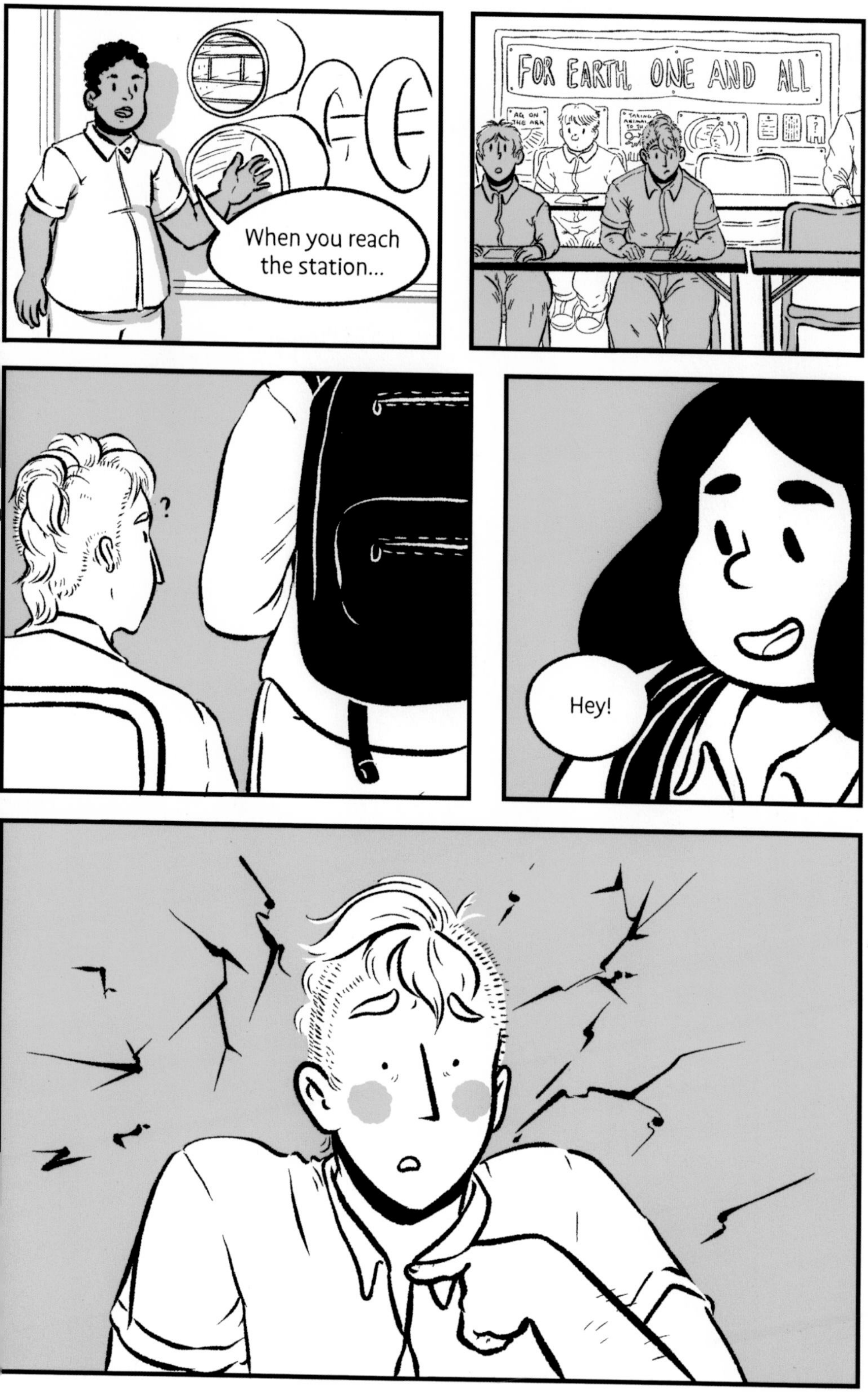
When you reach the station...
FOR EARTH, ONE AND ALL
AG ON THE ARK
?
Hey!

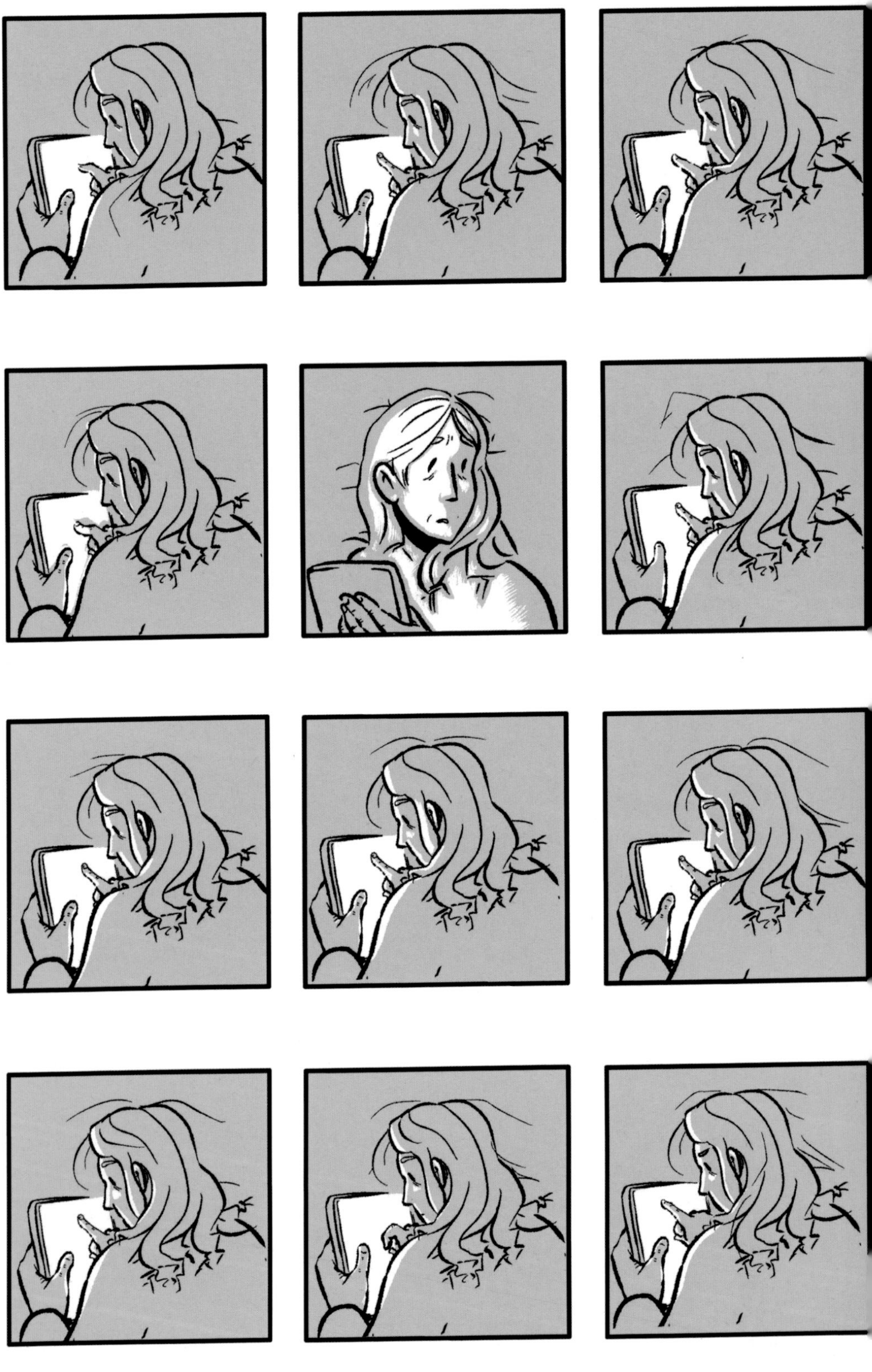

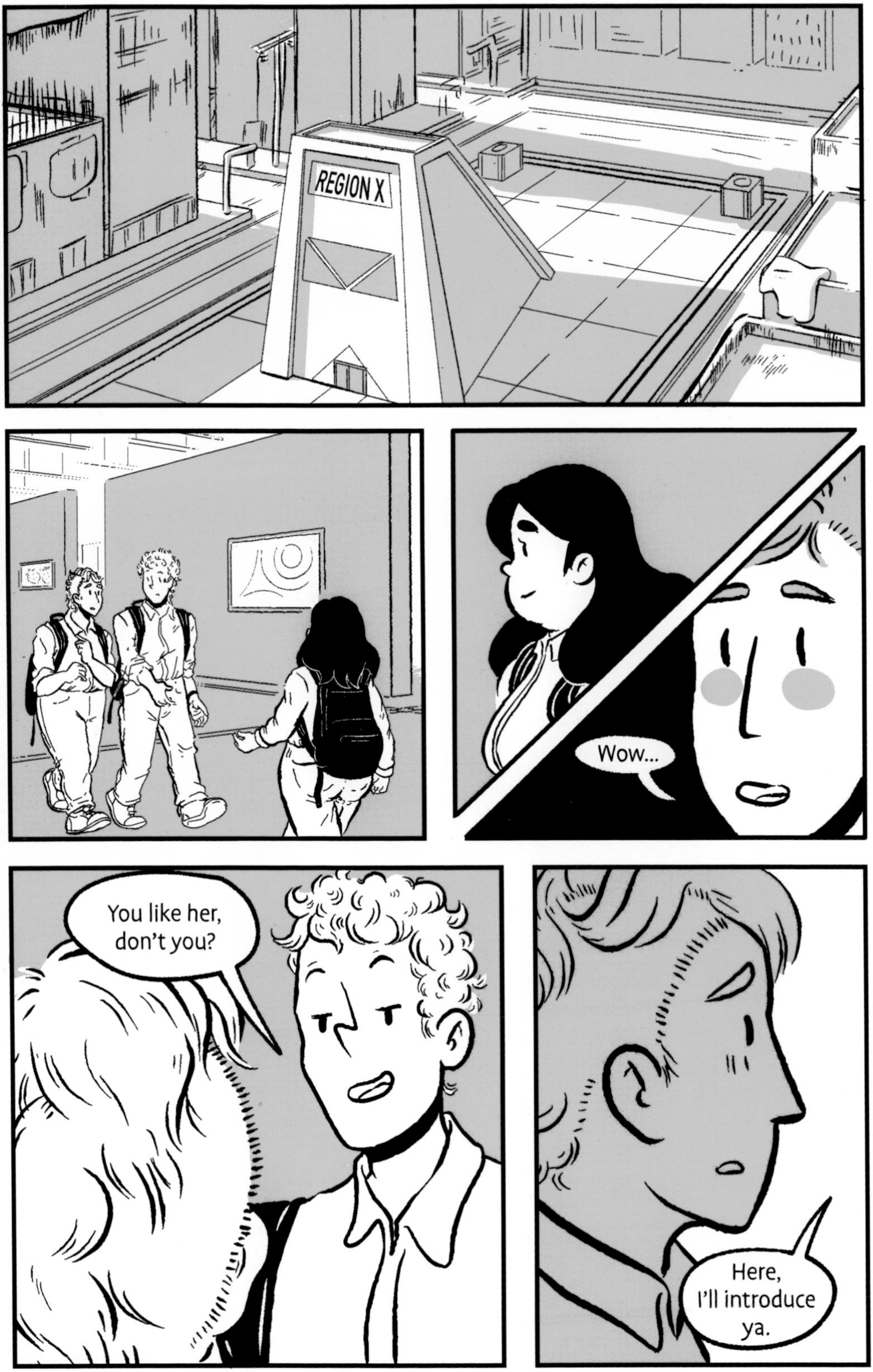
REGION X
Wow...
You like her, don't you?
Here, I'll introduce ya.

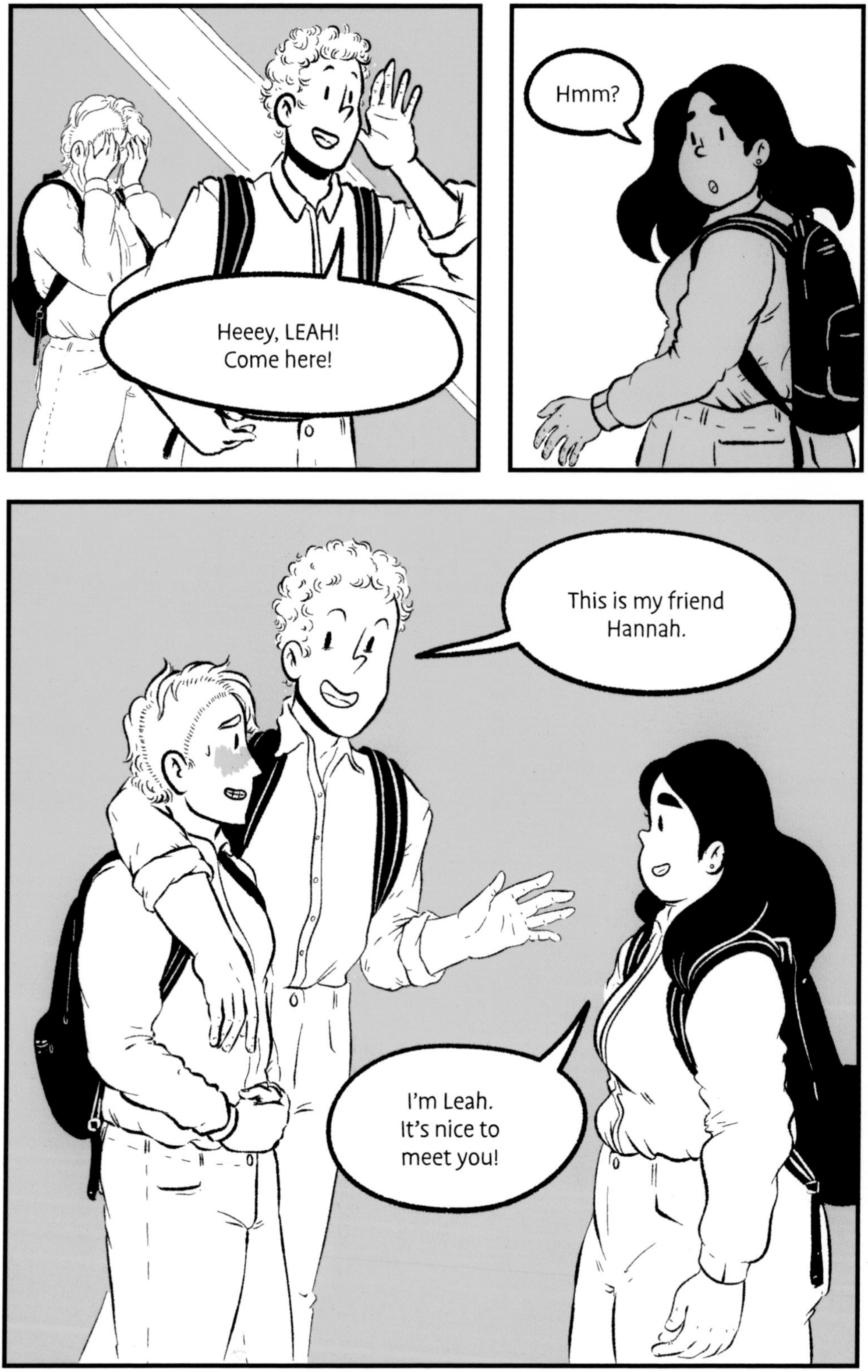
Heeey, LEAH! Come here!
Hmm?
This is my friend Hannah.
I'm Leah. It's nice to meet you!

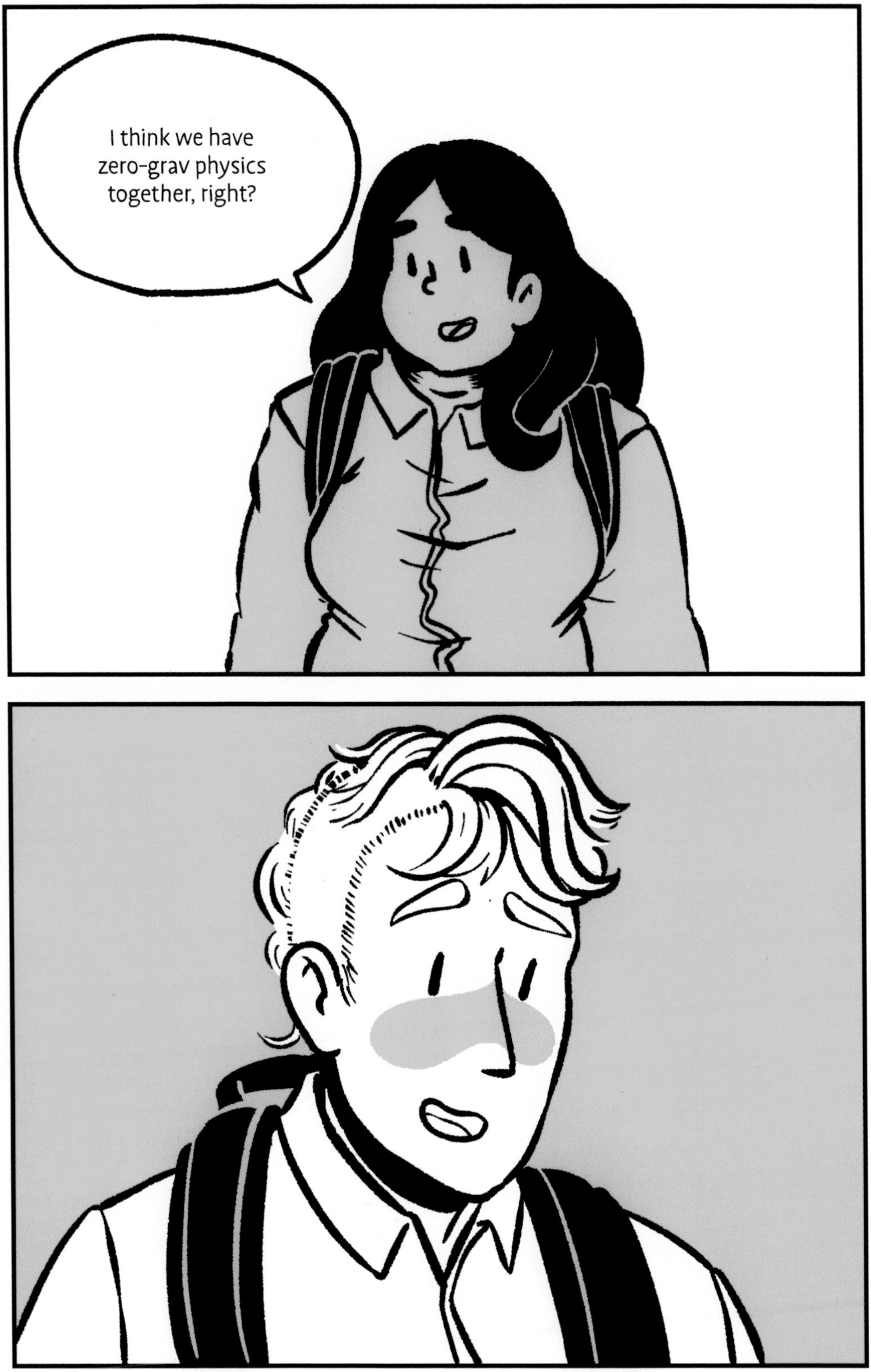
I think we have zero-grav physics together, right?

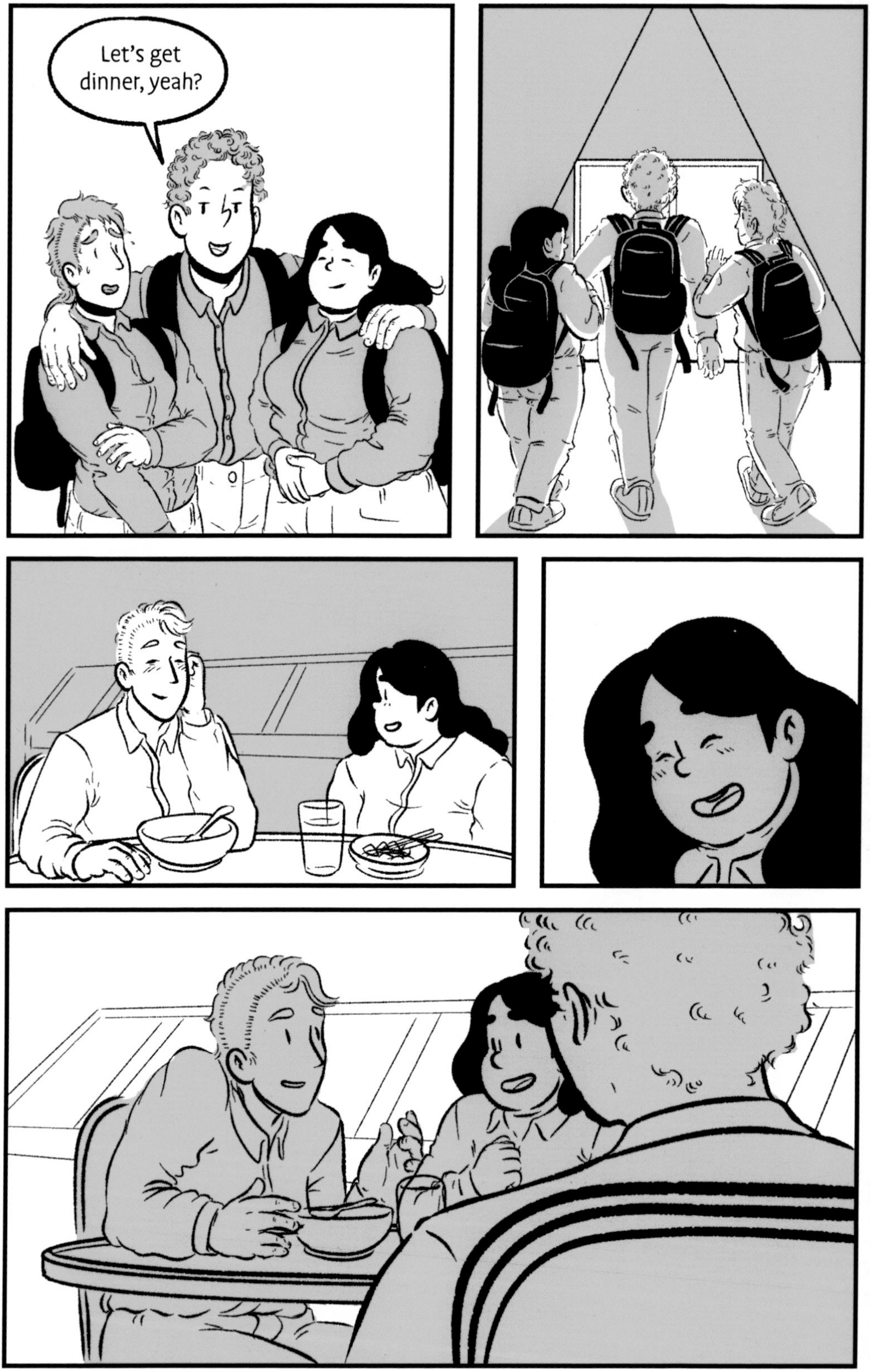
Let's get dinner, yeah?

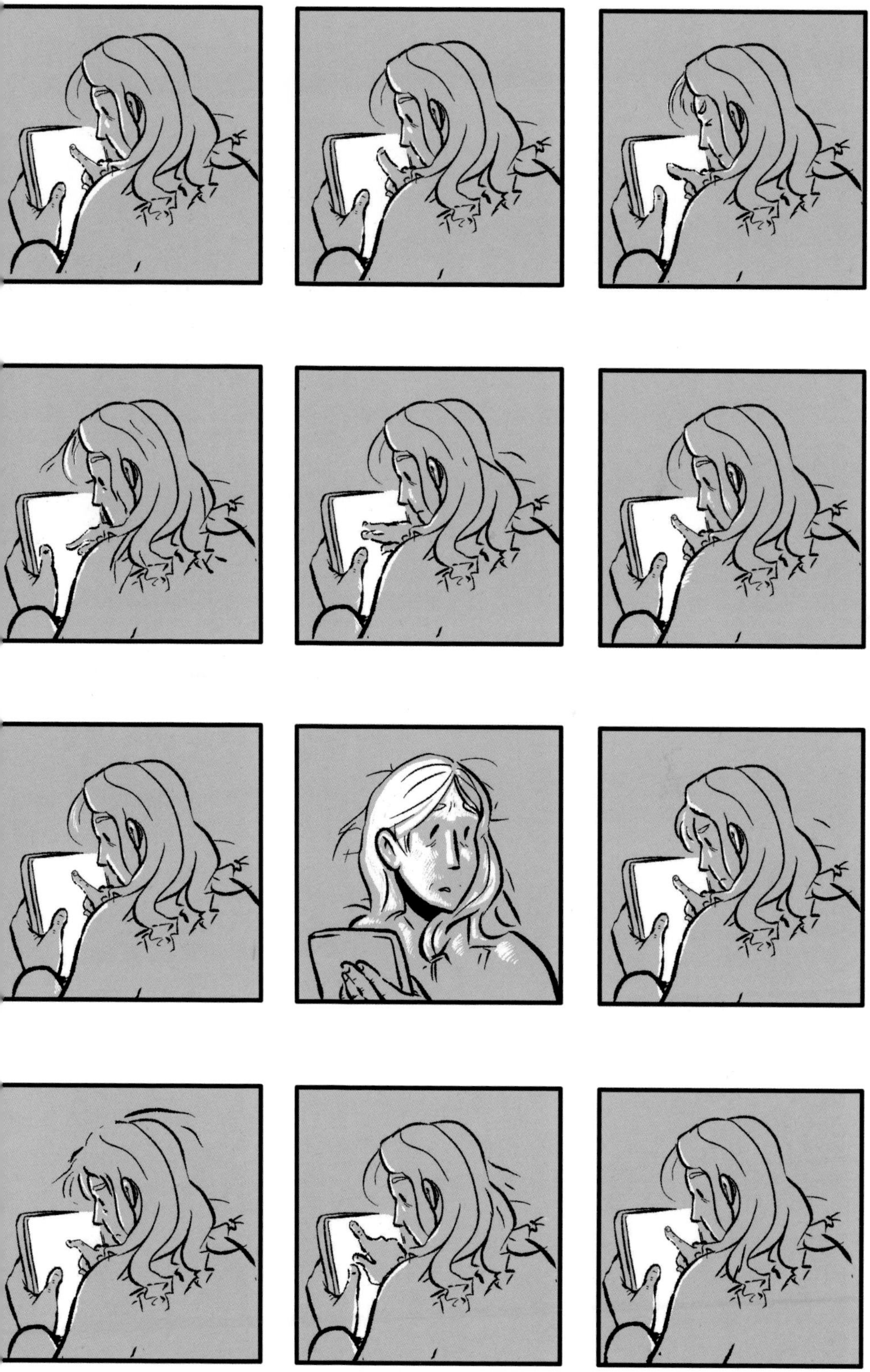

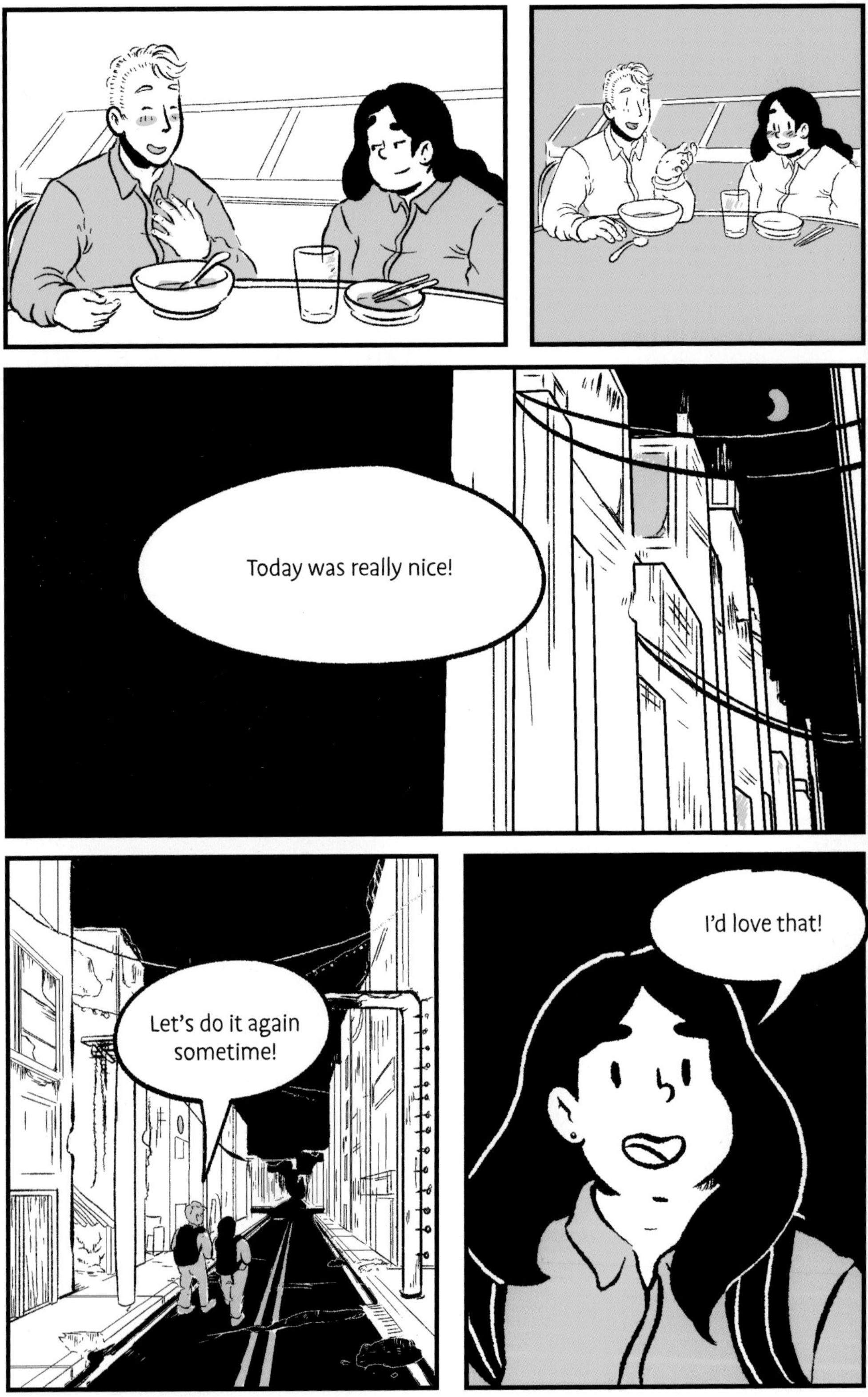
Today was really nice!
Let's do it again sometime!
I'd love that!

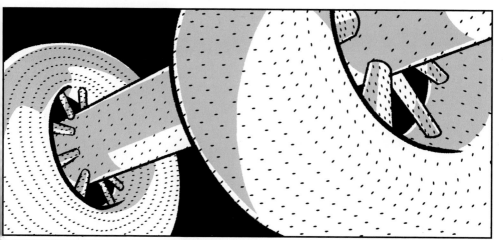

Come on.

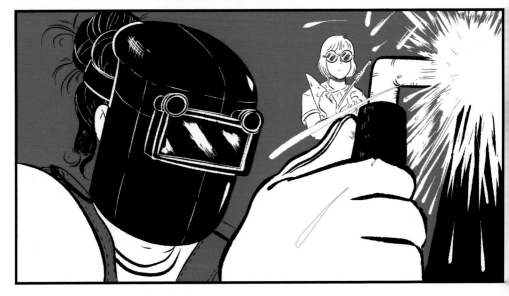

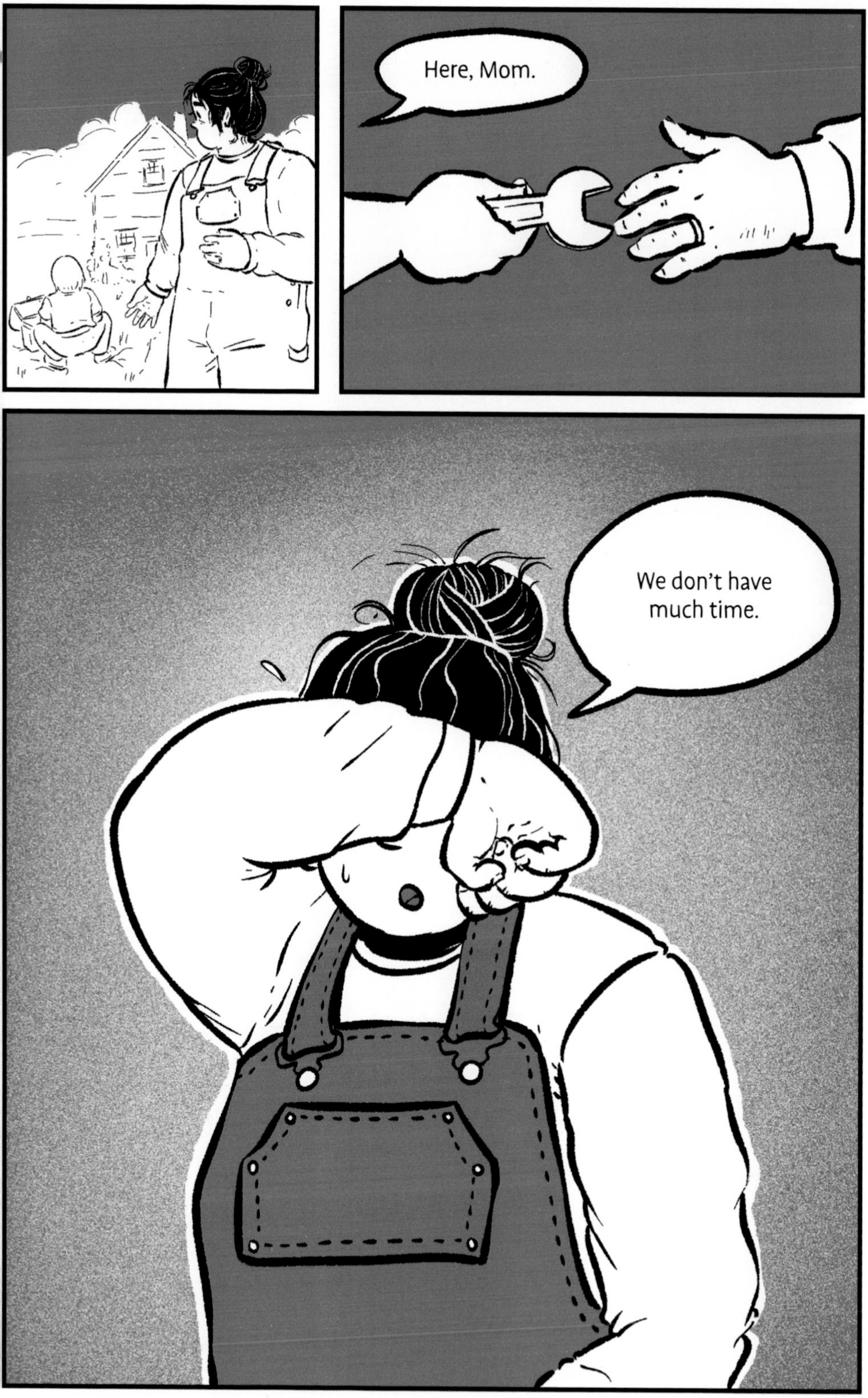
Here, Mom.
We don't have much time.

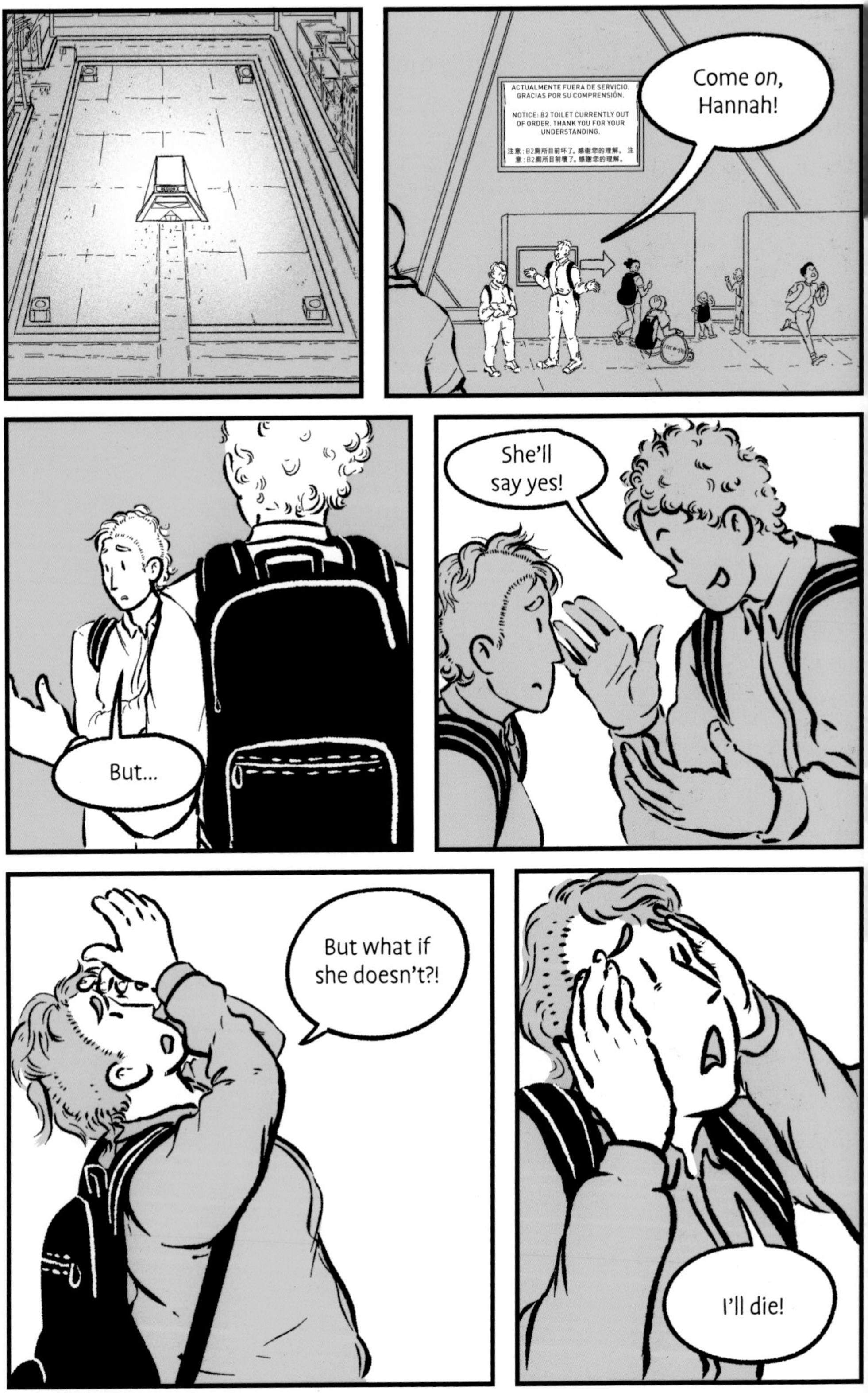
ACTUALMENTE FUERA DE SERVICIO. GRACIAS POR SU COMPRENSIÓN.
NOTICE: B2 TOILET CURRENTLY OUT OF ORDER. THANK YOU FOR YOUR UNDERSTANDING.
注意：B2厕所目前坏了。感谢您的理解。注意：B2廁所目前壞了。感謝您的理解。
Come *on*, Hannah!
But...
She'll say yes!
But what if she doesn't?!
I'll die!

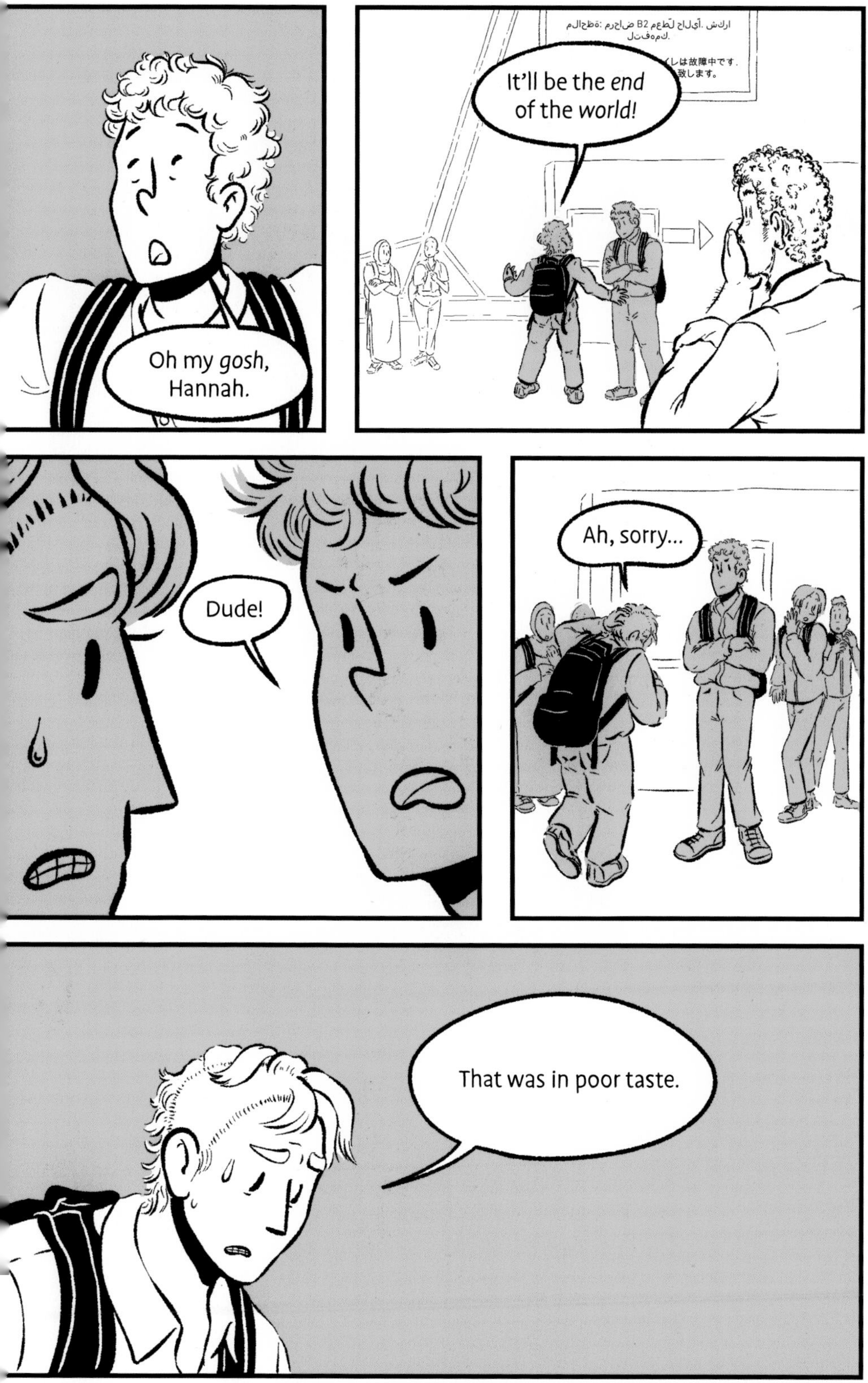
Oh my *gosh*, Hannah.
It'll be the *end* of the *world!*
Dude!
Ah, sorry...
That was in poor taste.

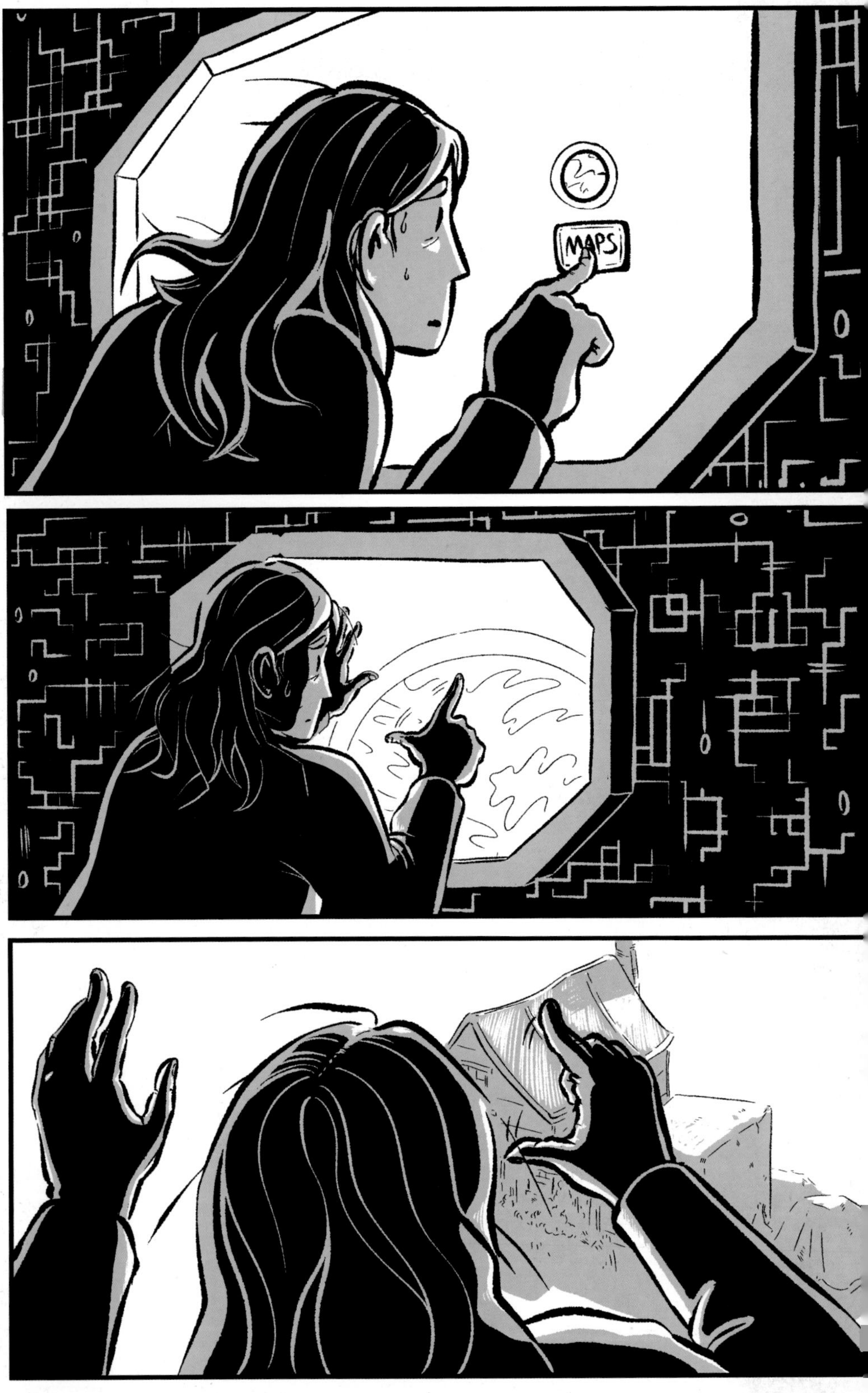
MAPS

They're still there.

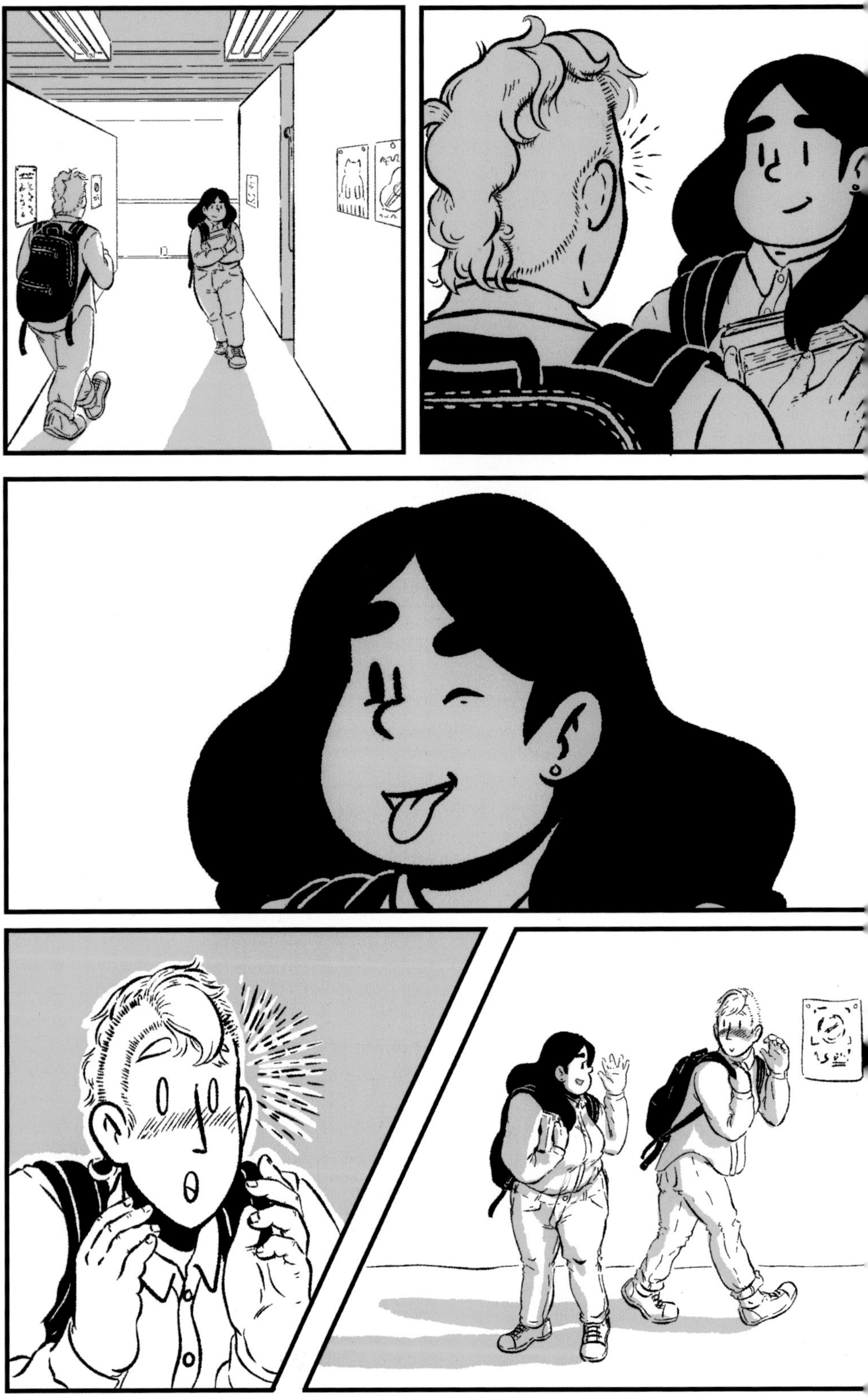

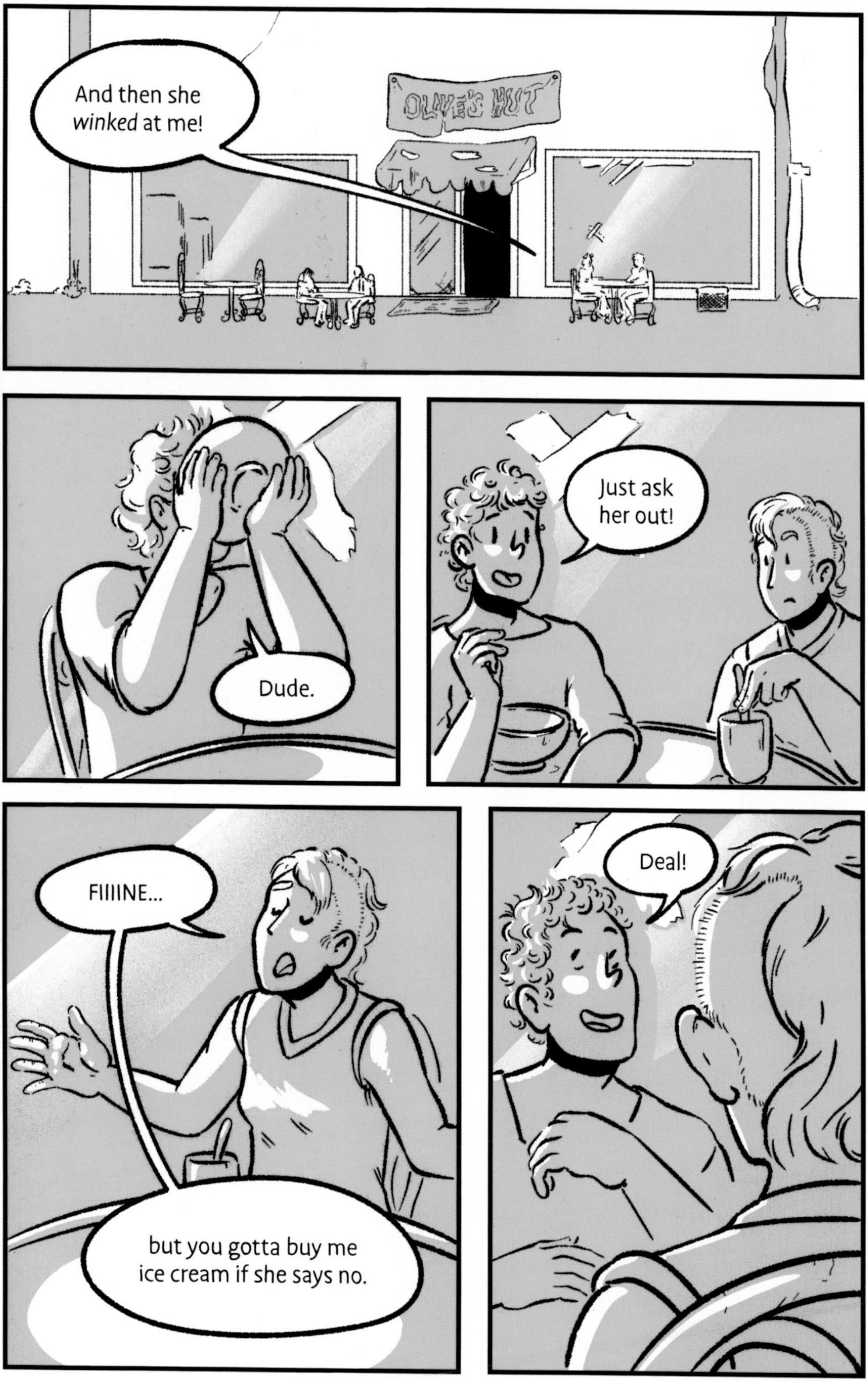
And then she *winked* at me!
OLIVE'S HUT
Dude.
Just ask her out!
FIIIINE...
but you gotta buy me ice cream if she says no.
Deal!

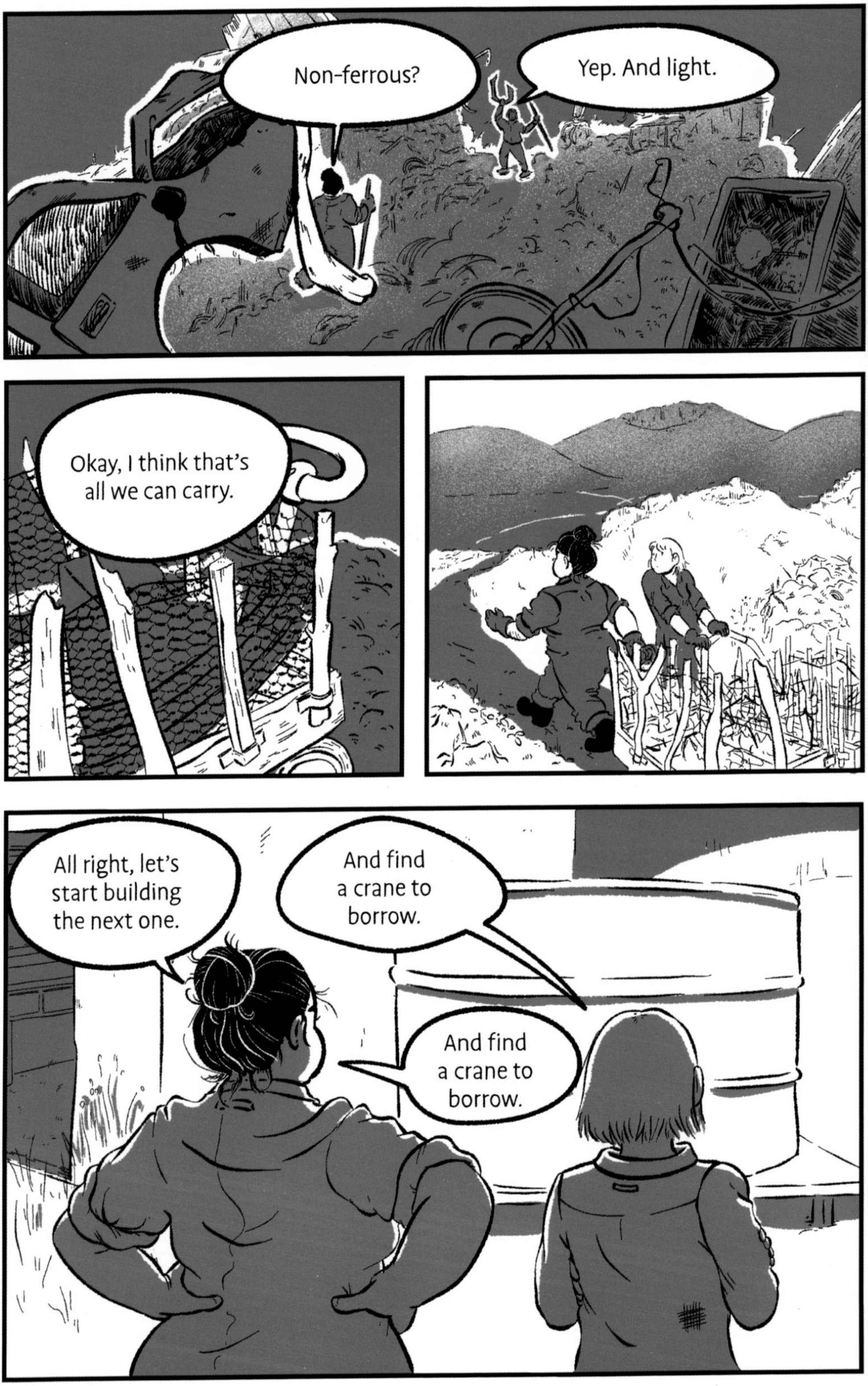
Non-ferrous?
Yep. And light.
Okay, I think that's all we can carry.
All right, let's start building the next one.
And find a crane to borrow.
And find a crane to borrow.

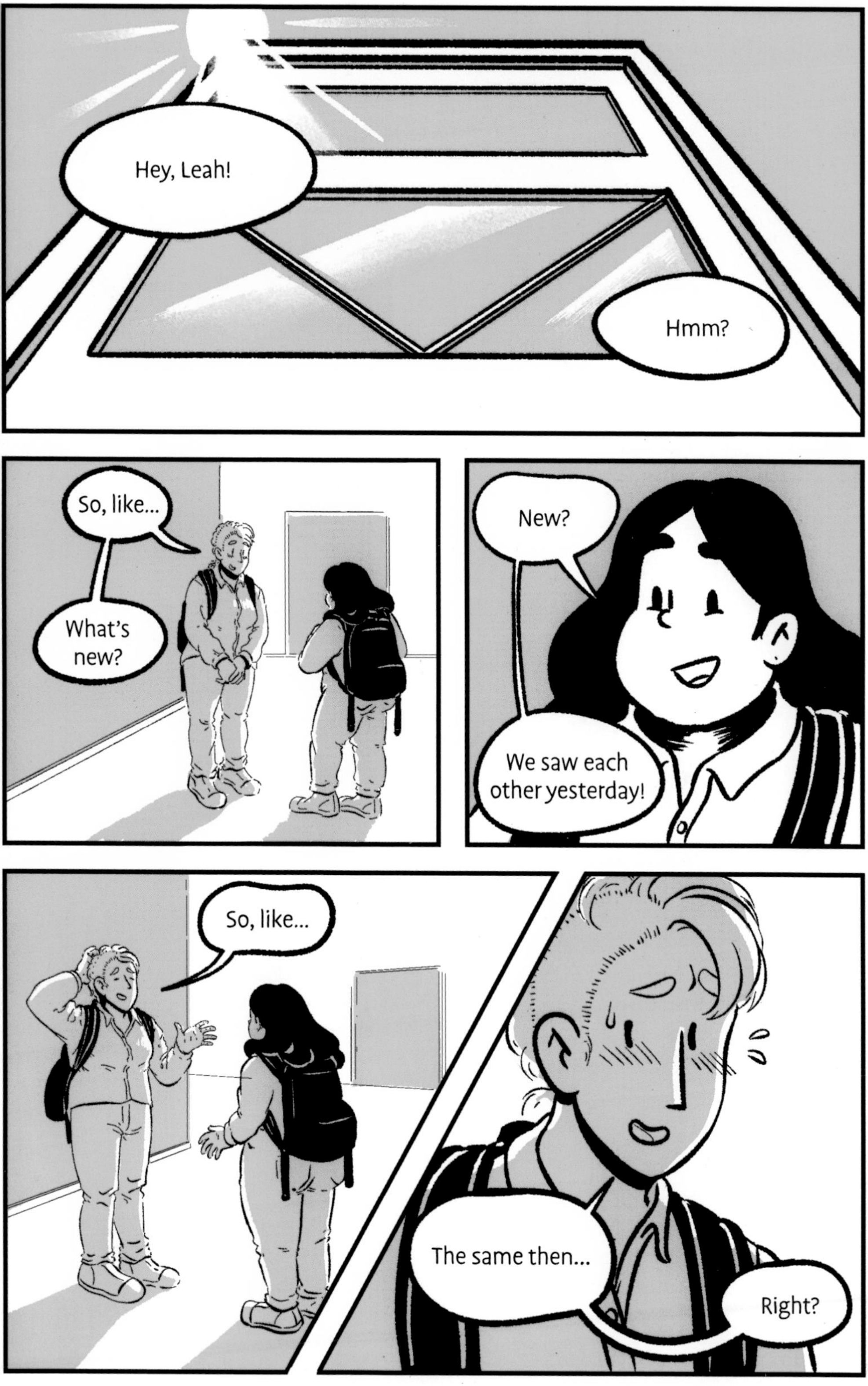
Hey, Leah!
Hmm?
So, like...
What's new?
New?
We saw each other yesterday!
So, like...
The same then...
Right?

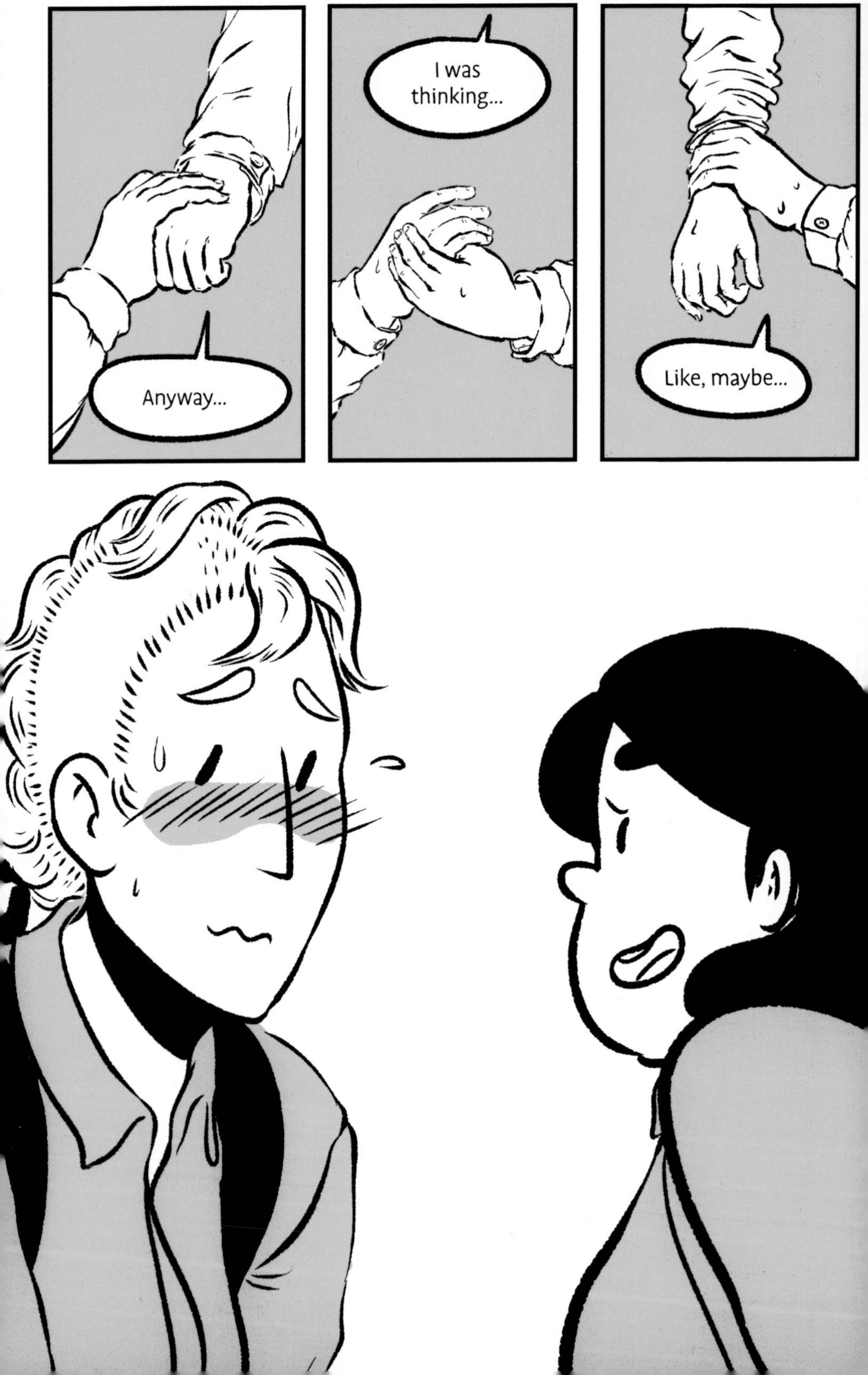
Anyway...
I was thinking...
Like, maybe...

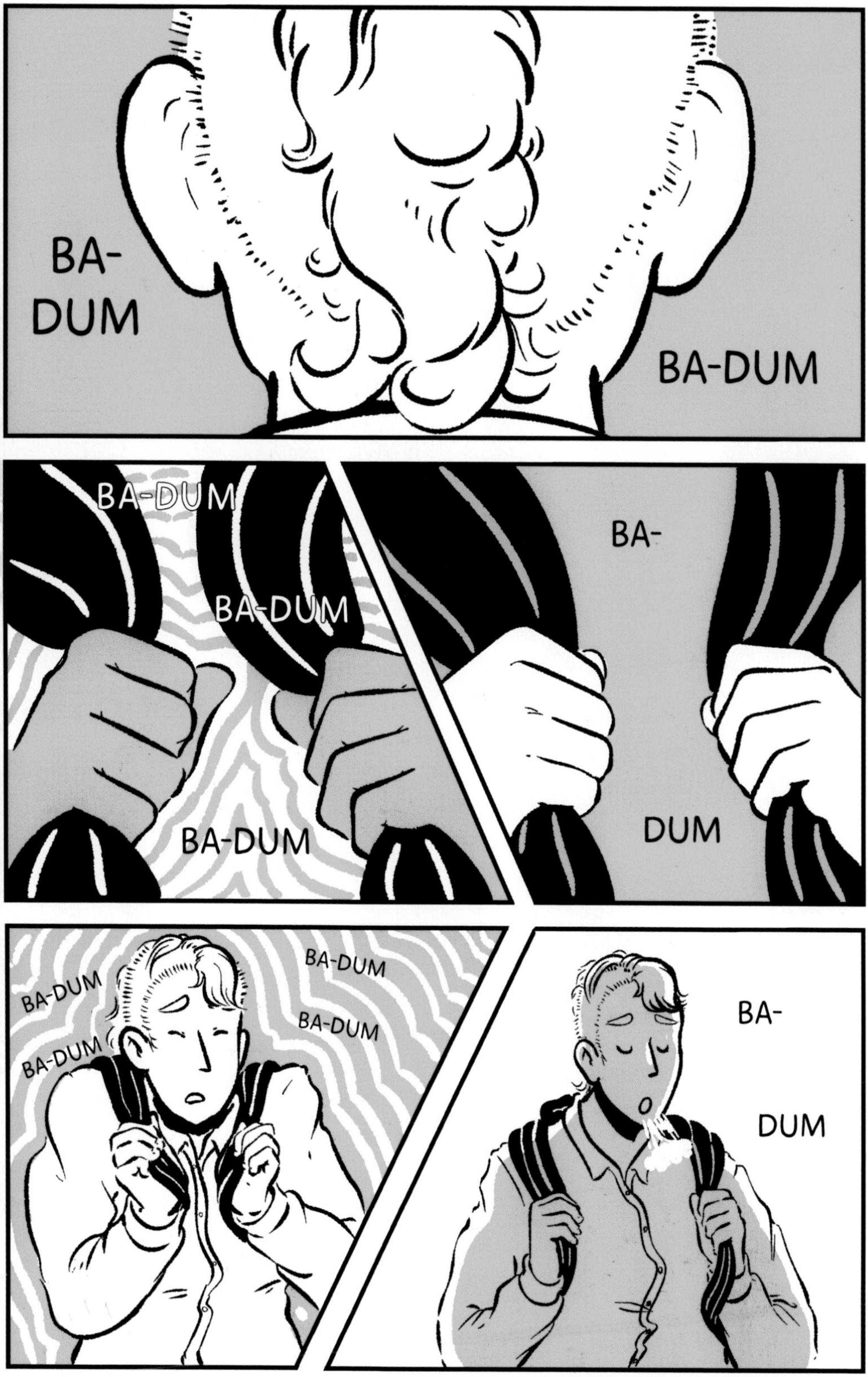
BA-
DUM
BA-DUM
BA-DUM
BA-DUM
BA-DUM
BA-
DUM
BA-DUM
BA-DUM
BA-DUM
BA-DUM
BA-
DUM

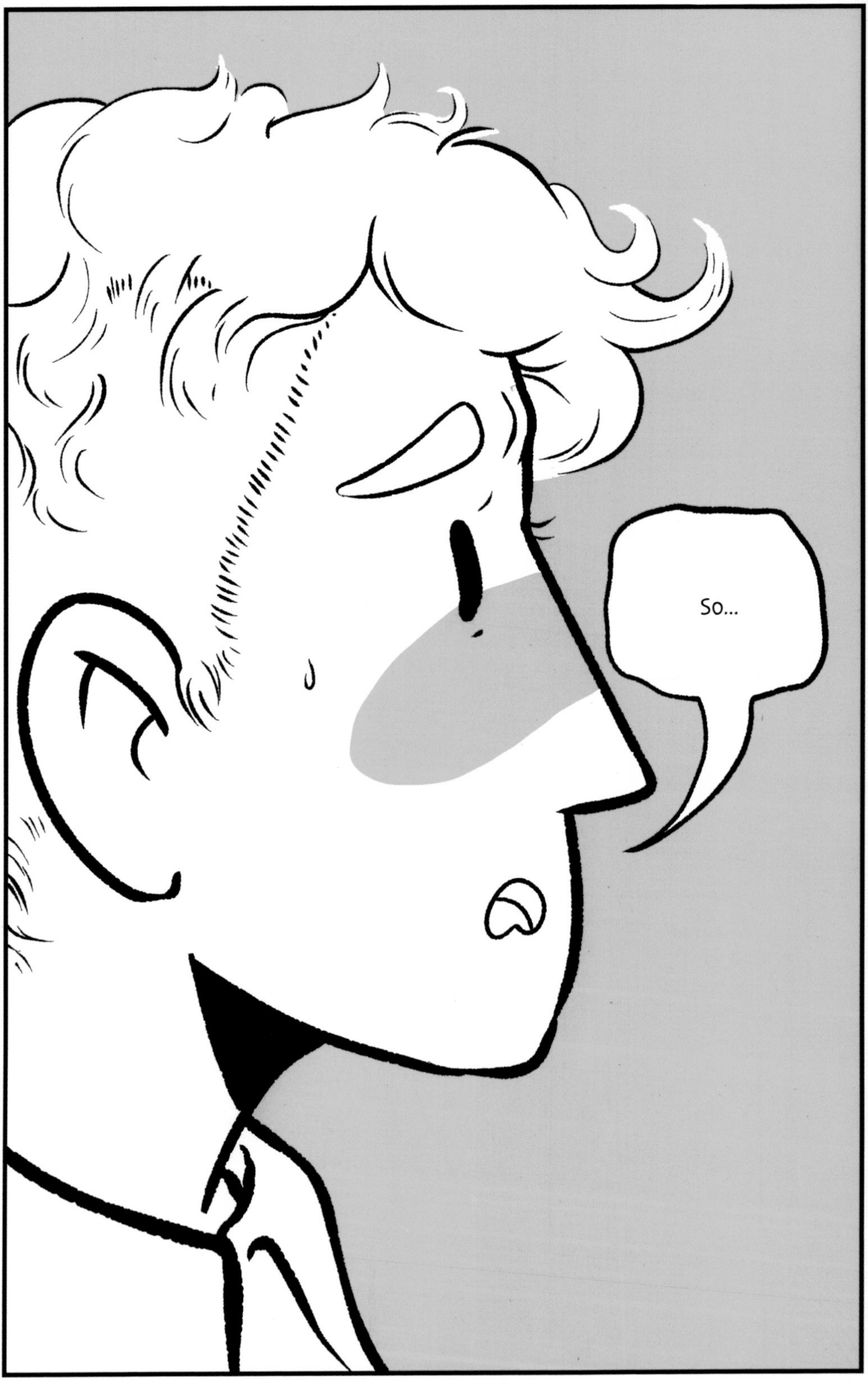
So...

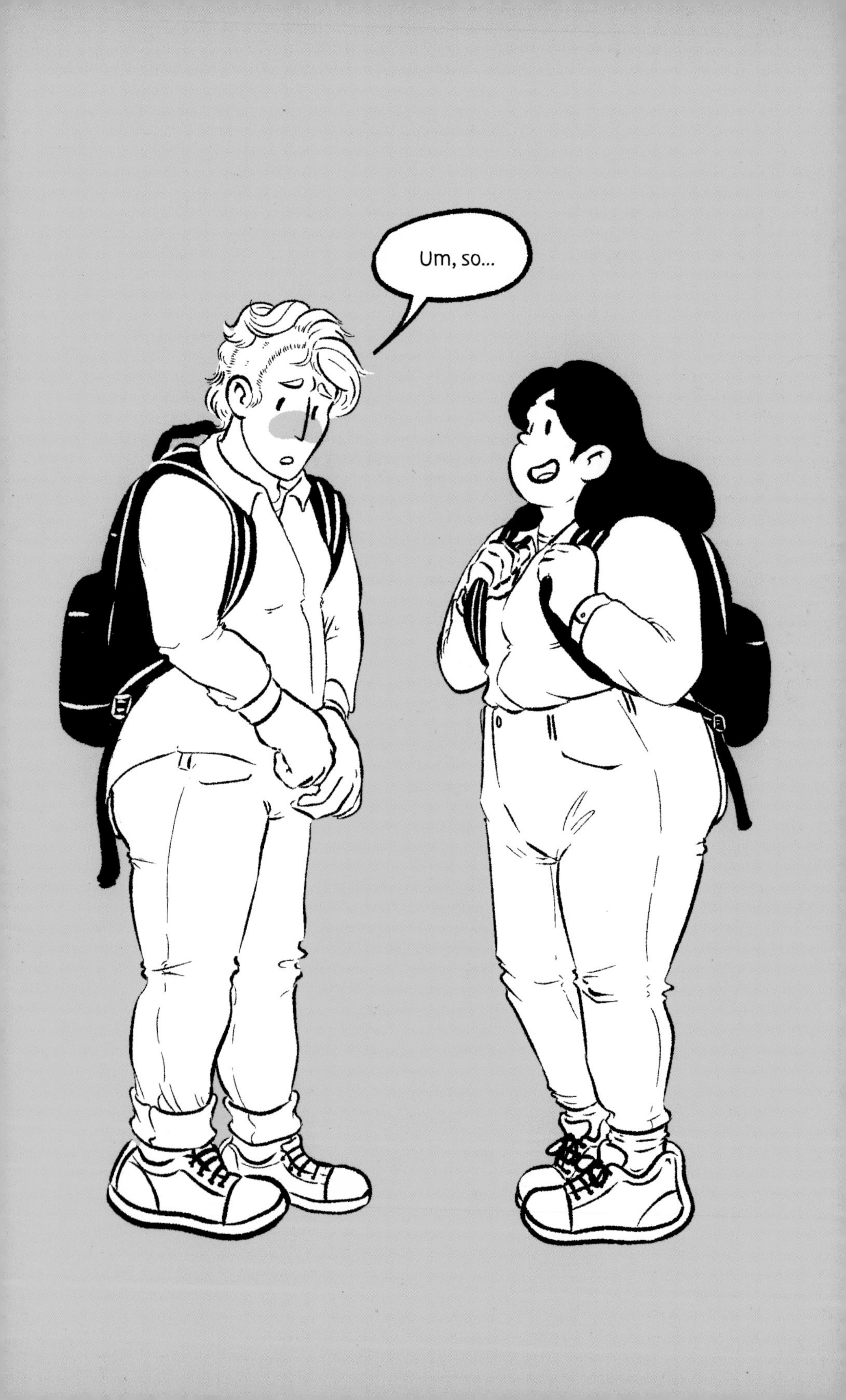
Um, so...

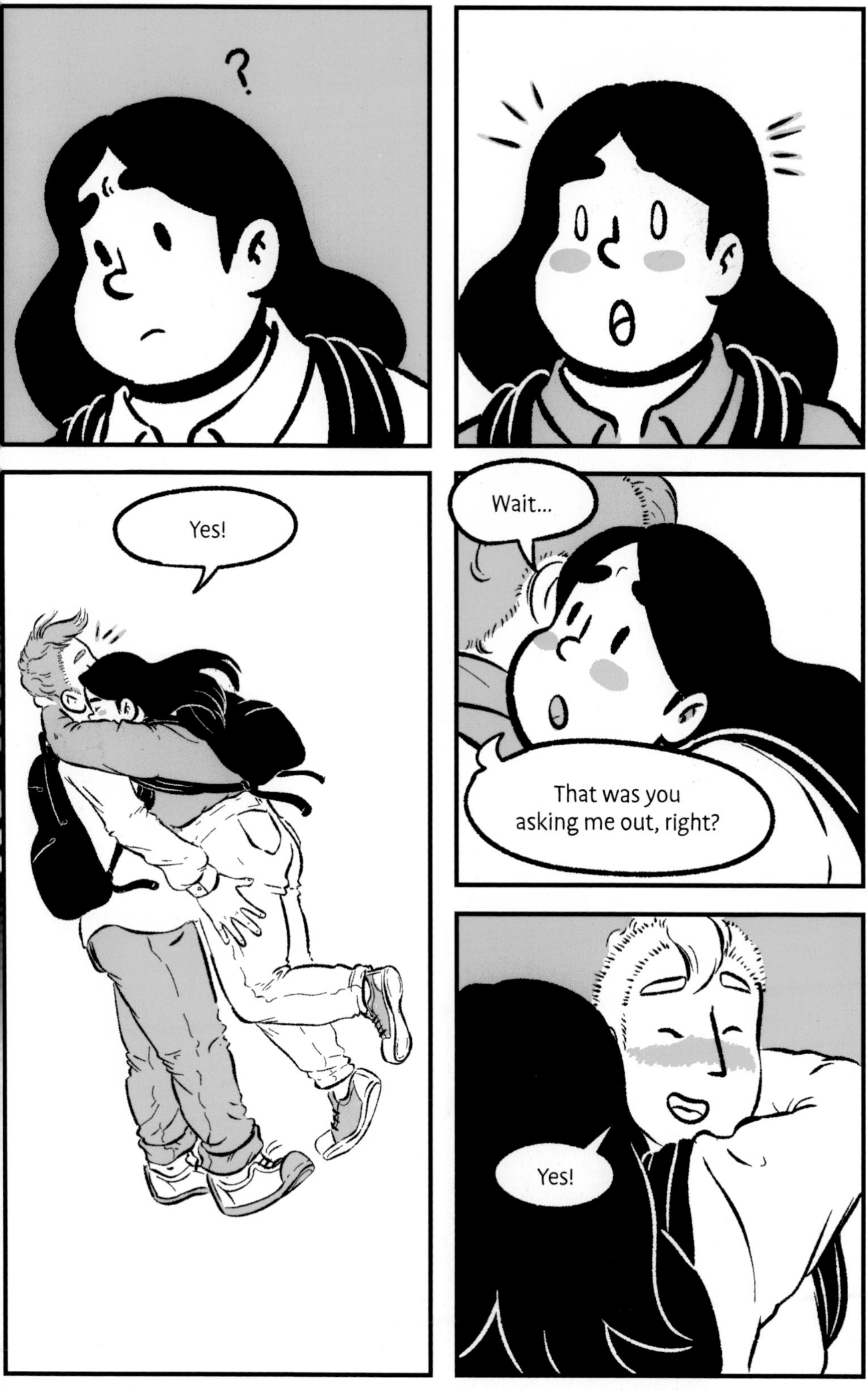
?
Yes!
Wait...
That was you asking me out, right?
Yes!

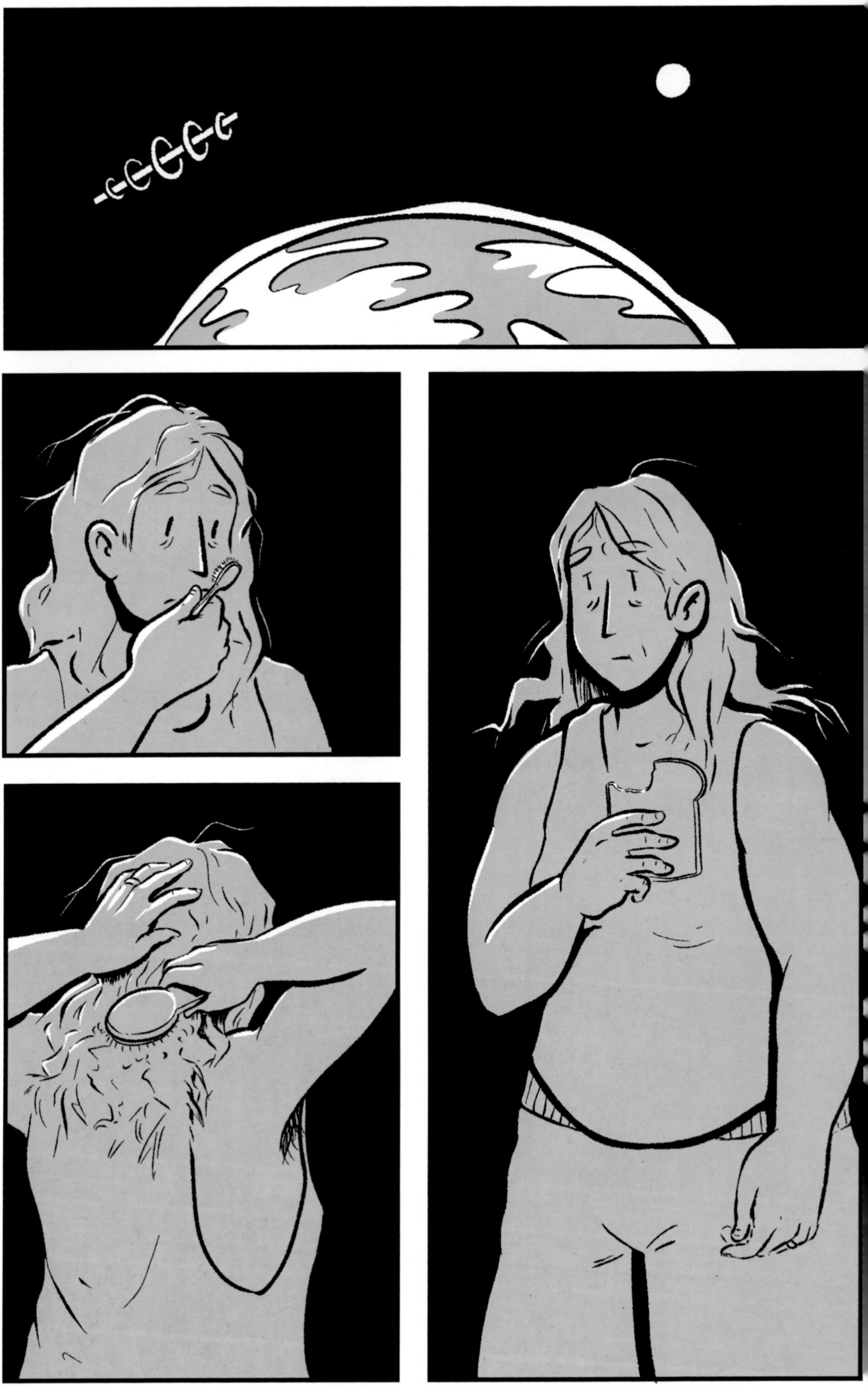

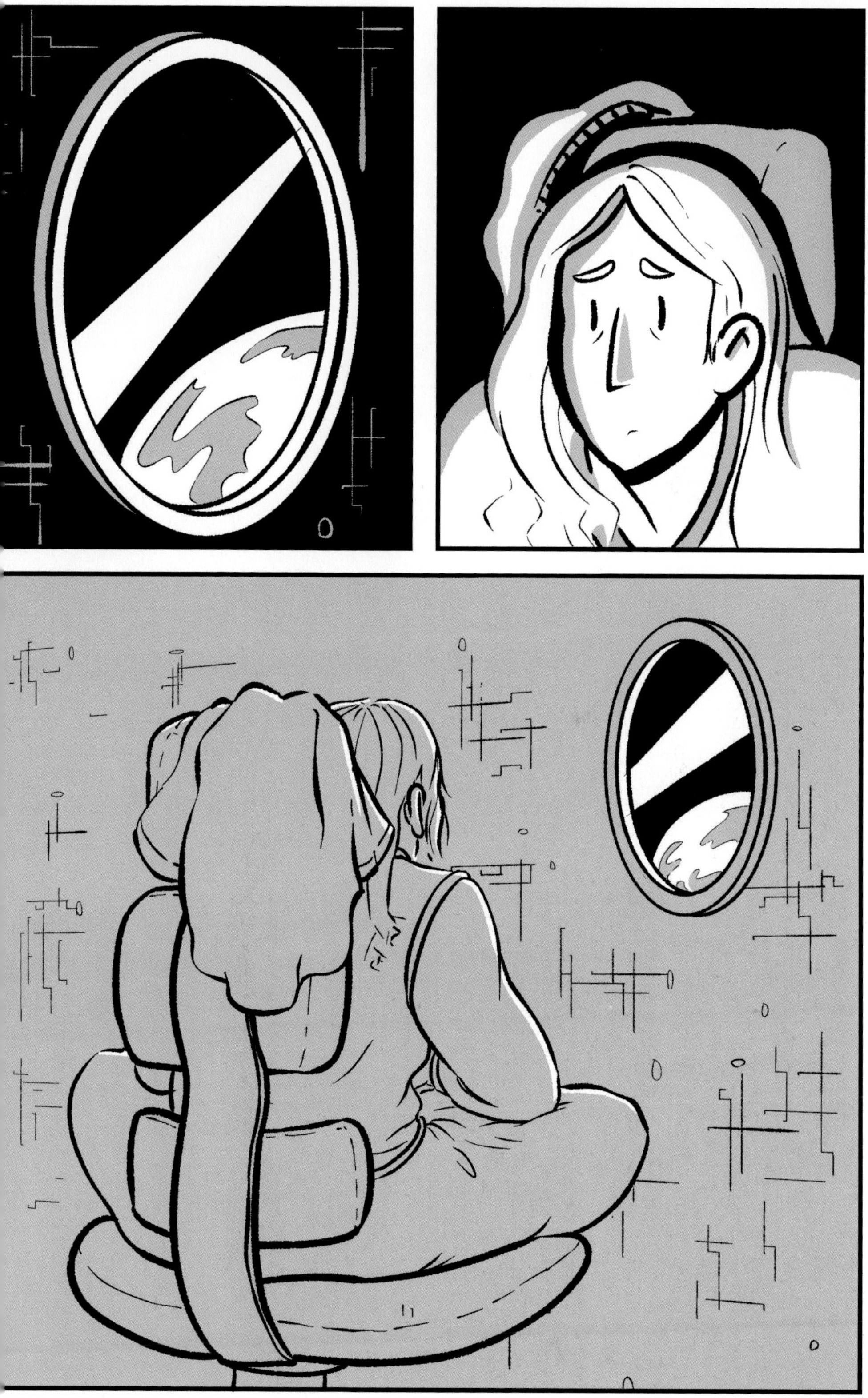

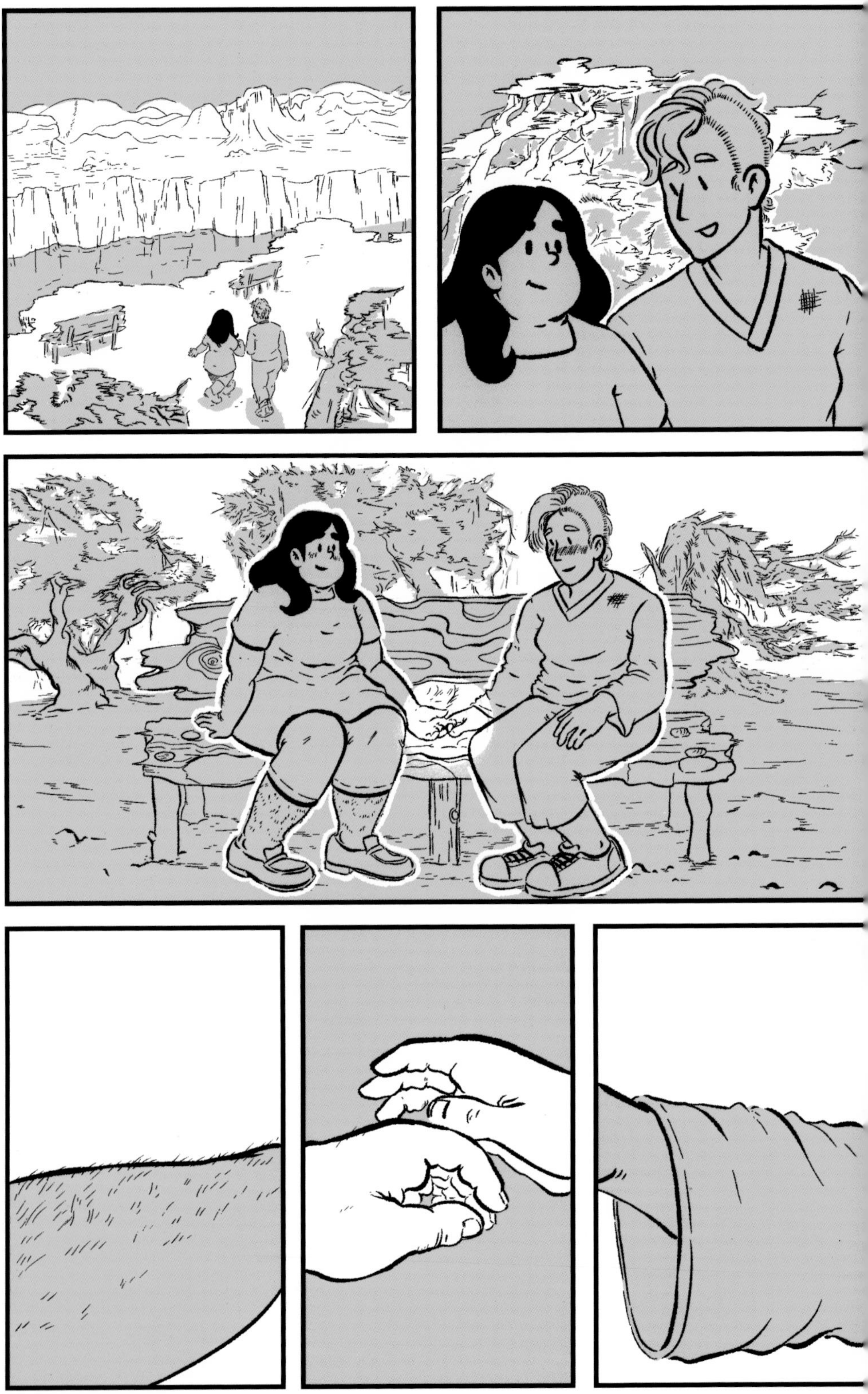

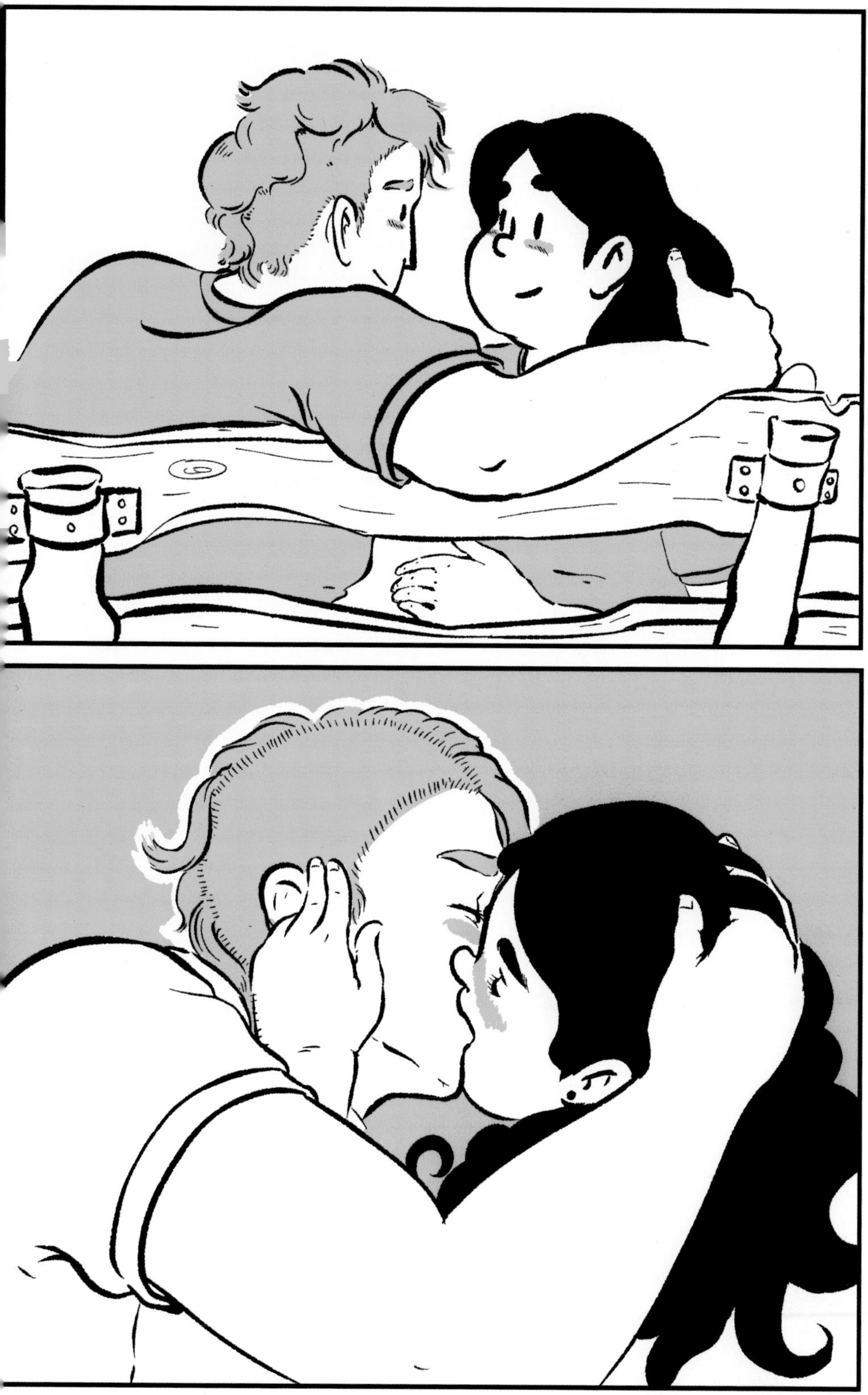

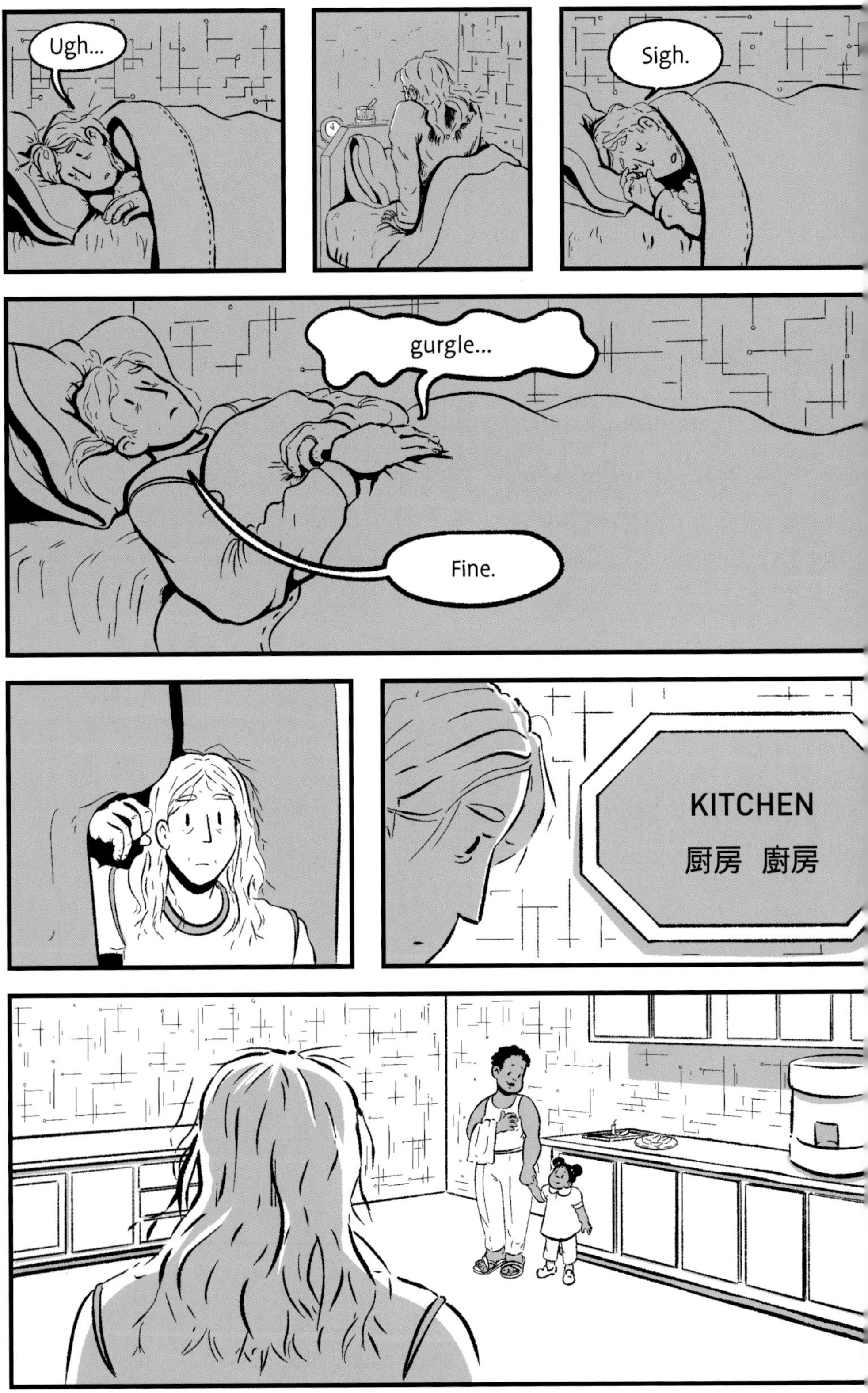

Ugh...
Sigh.
gurgle...
Fine.
KITCHEN
厨房 廚房

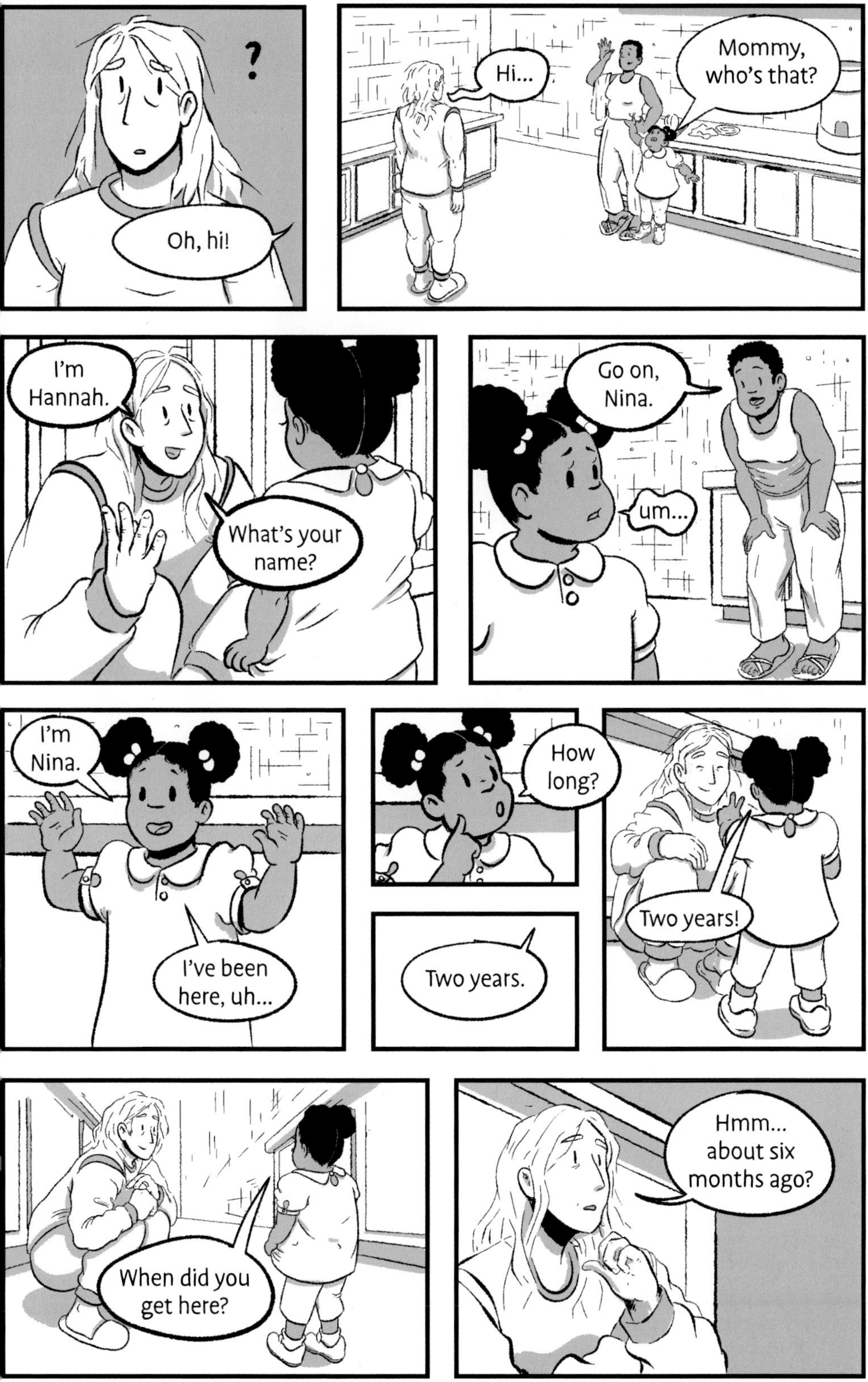
?
Oh, hi!
Hi...
Mommy, who's that?
I'm Hannah.
What's your name?
Go on, Nina.
um...
I'm Nina.
I've been here, uh...
How long?
Two years.
Two years!
When did you get here?
Hmm... about six months ago?

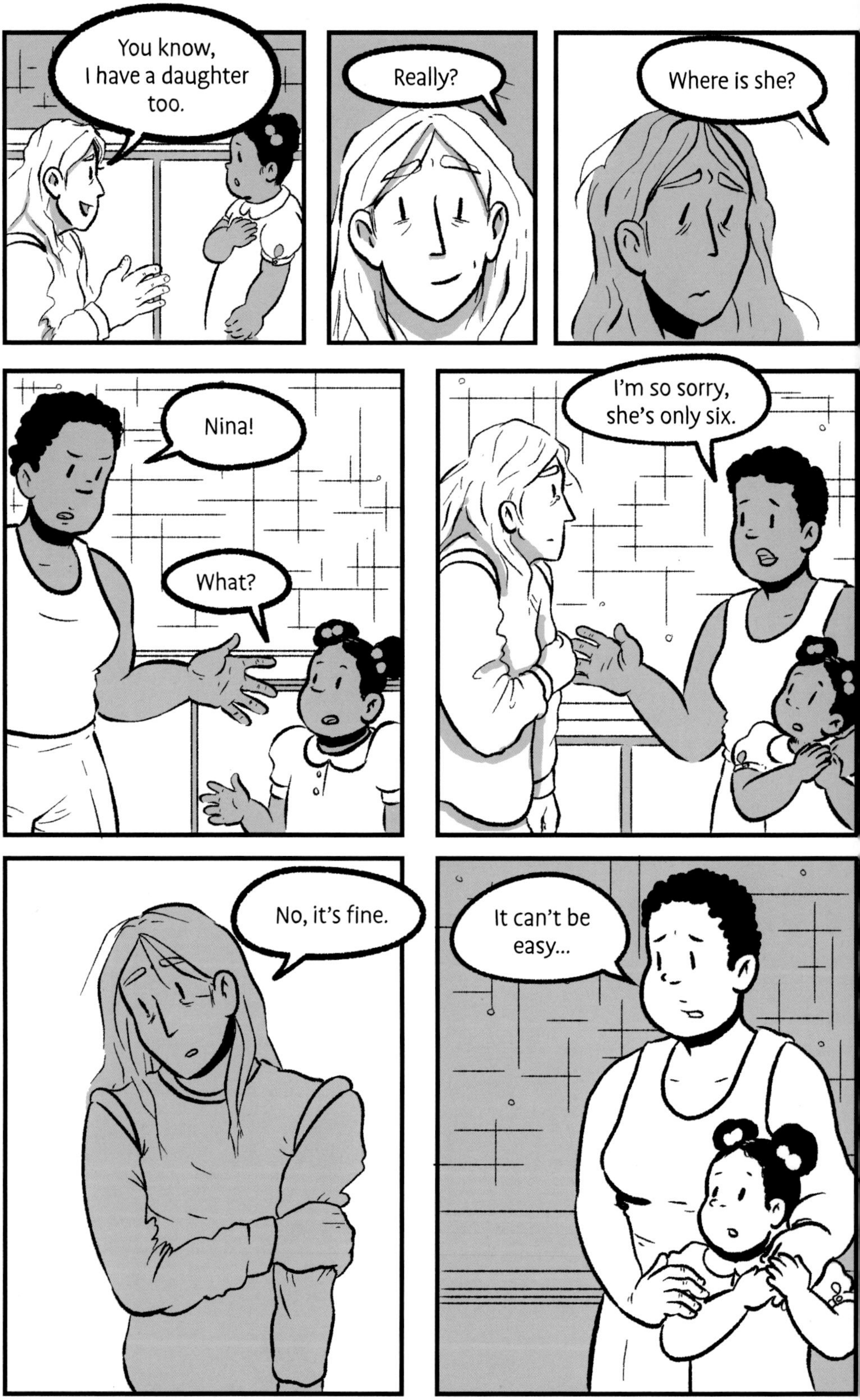
You know, I have a daughter too.
Really?
Where is she?
Nina!
What?
I'm so sorry, she's only six.
No, it's fine.
It can't be easy...

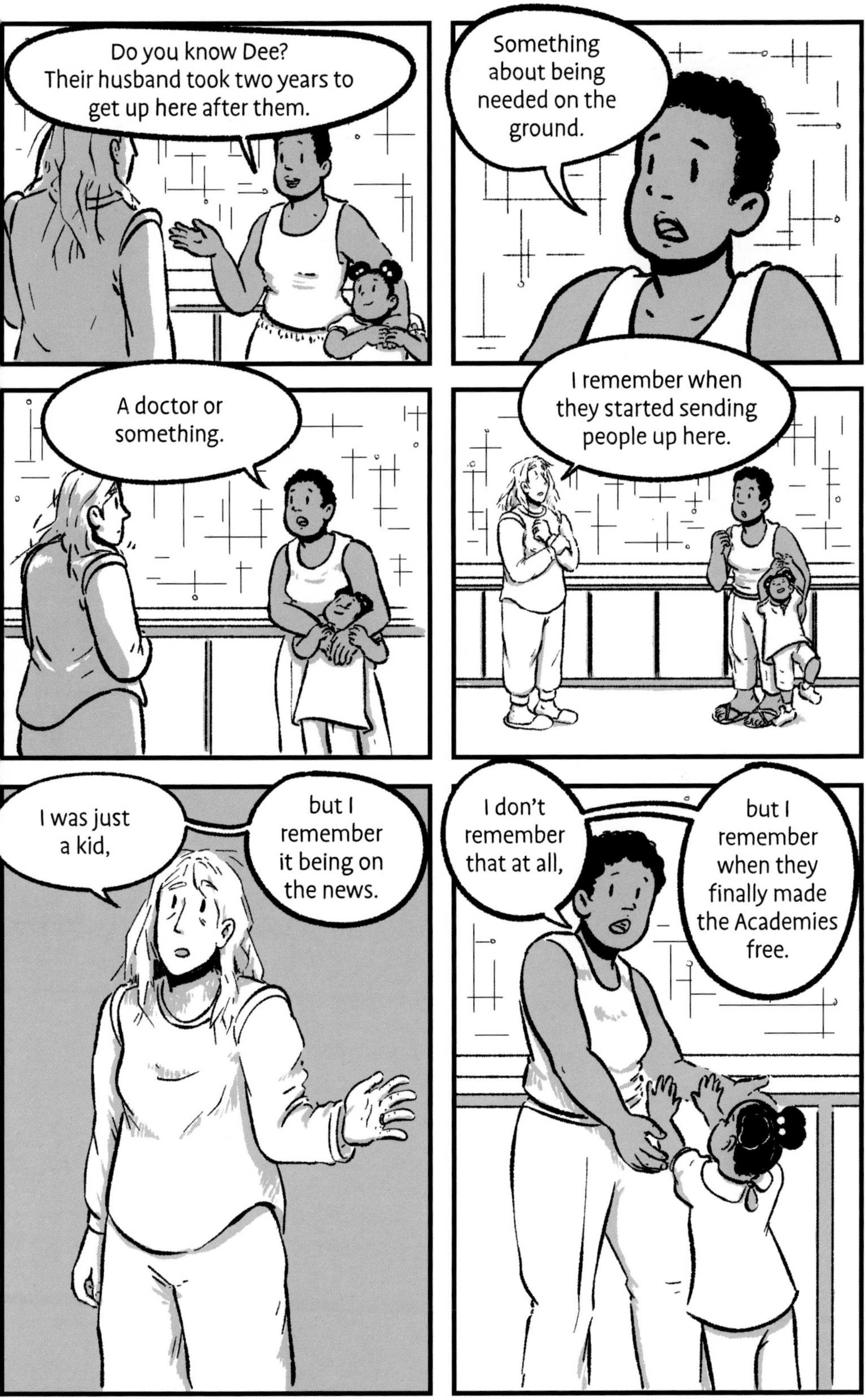

Do you know Dee? Their husband took two years to get up here after them.
Something about being needed on the ground.
A doctor or something.
I remember when they started sending people up here.
I was just a kid,
but I remember it being on the news.
I don't remember that at all,
but I remember when they finally made the Academies free.

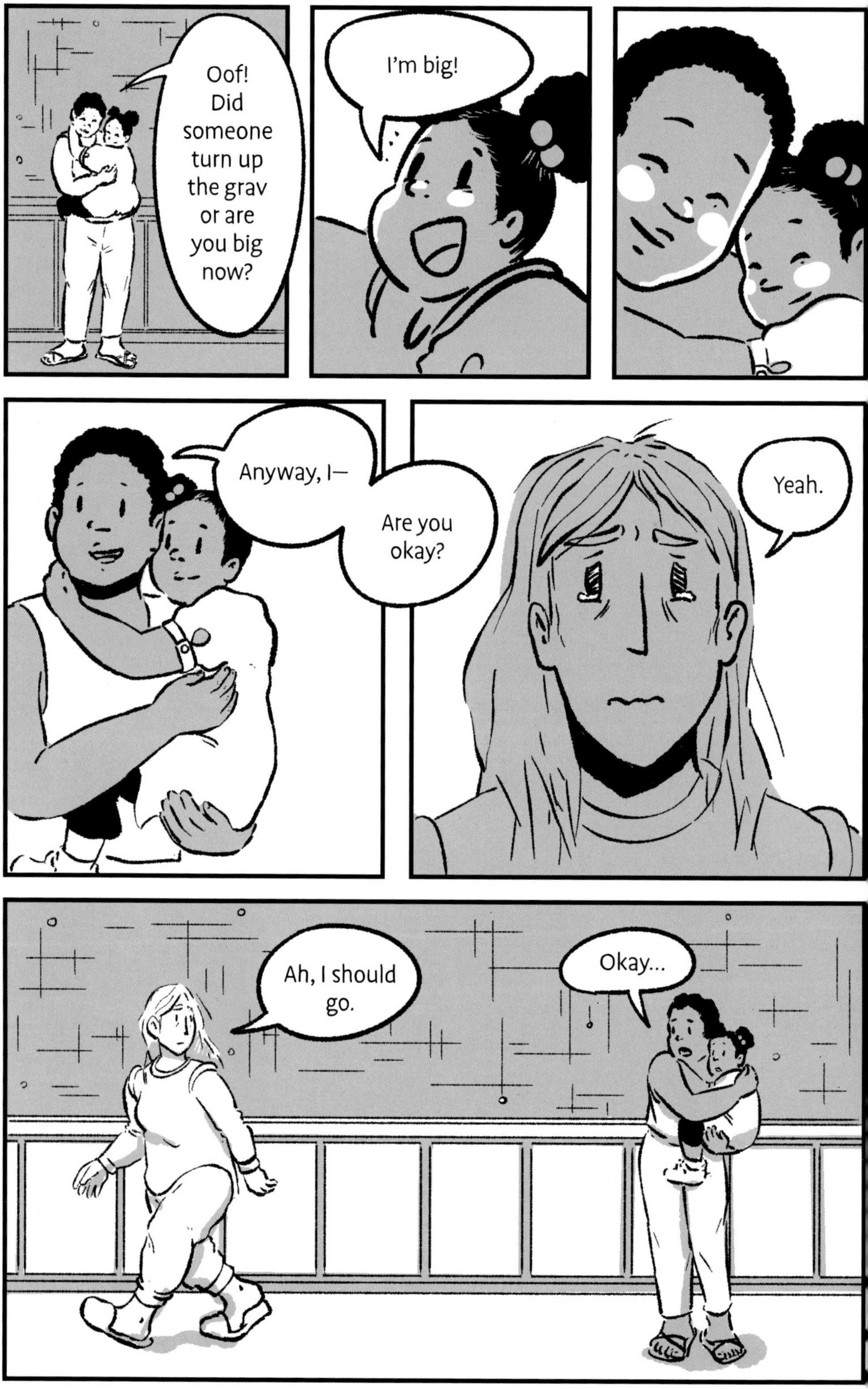
Oof! Did someone turn up the grav or are you big now?
I'm big!
Anyway, I—
Are you okay?
Yeah.
Ah, I should go.
Okay...

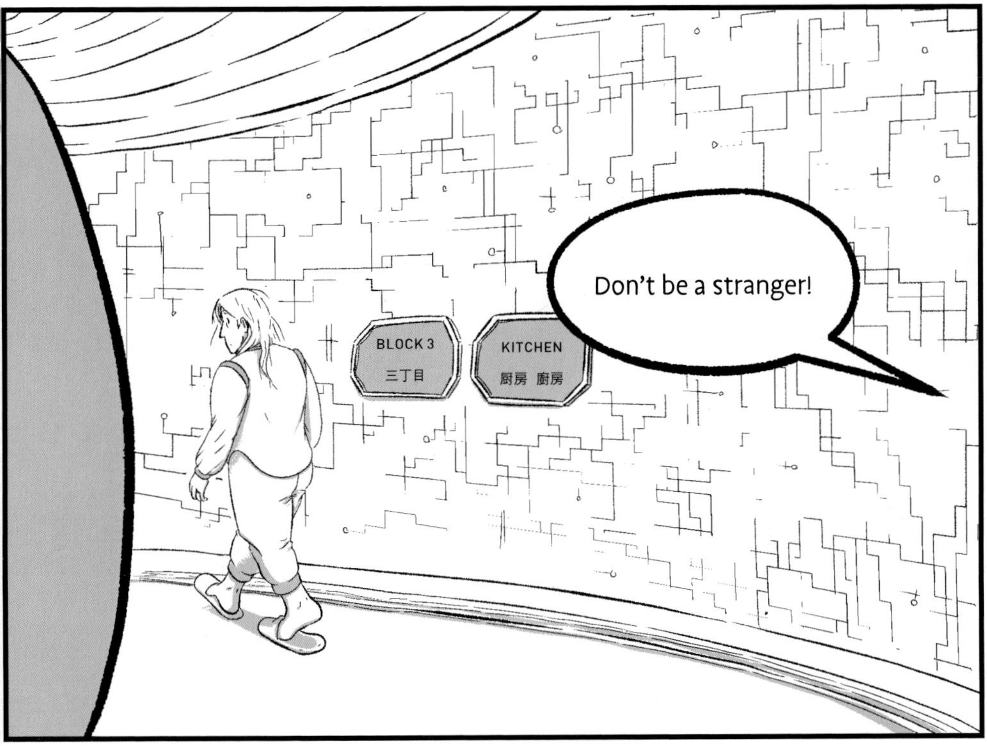
BLOCK 3
三丁目
KITCHEN
厨房 厨房
Don’t be a stranger!

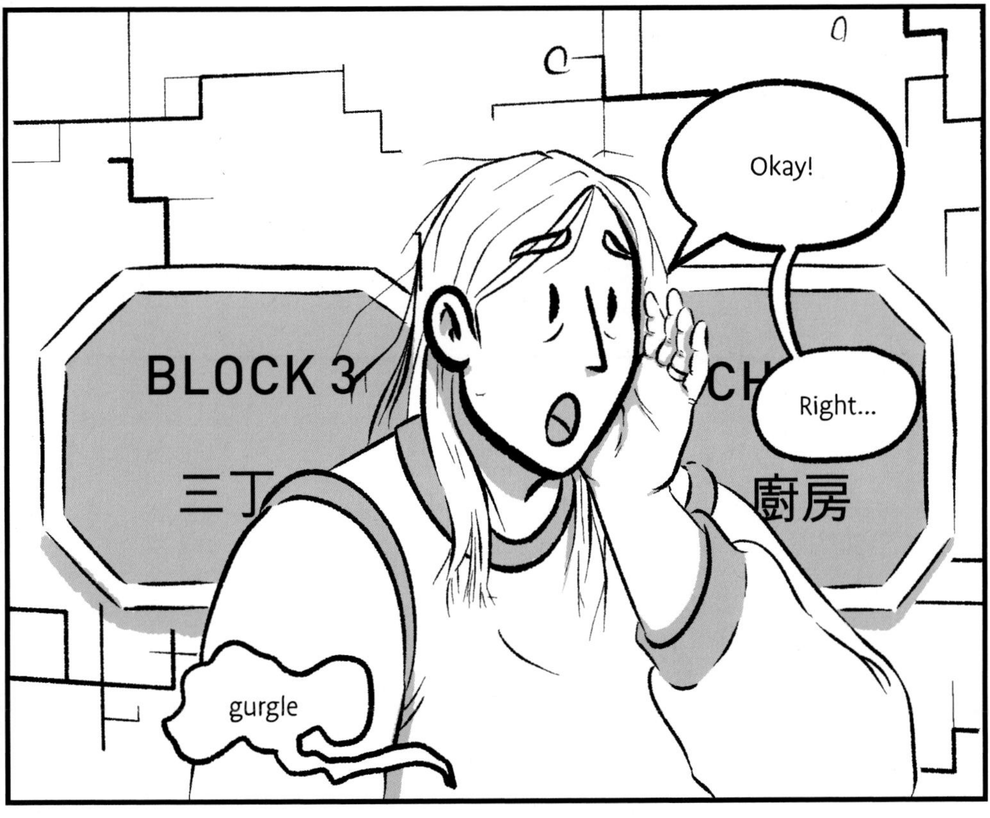
BLOCK 3
三丁
厨房
Okay!
Right...
gurgle

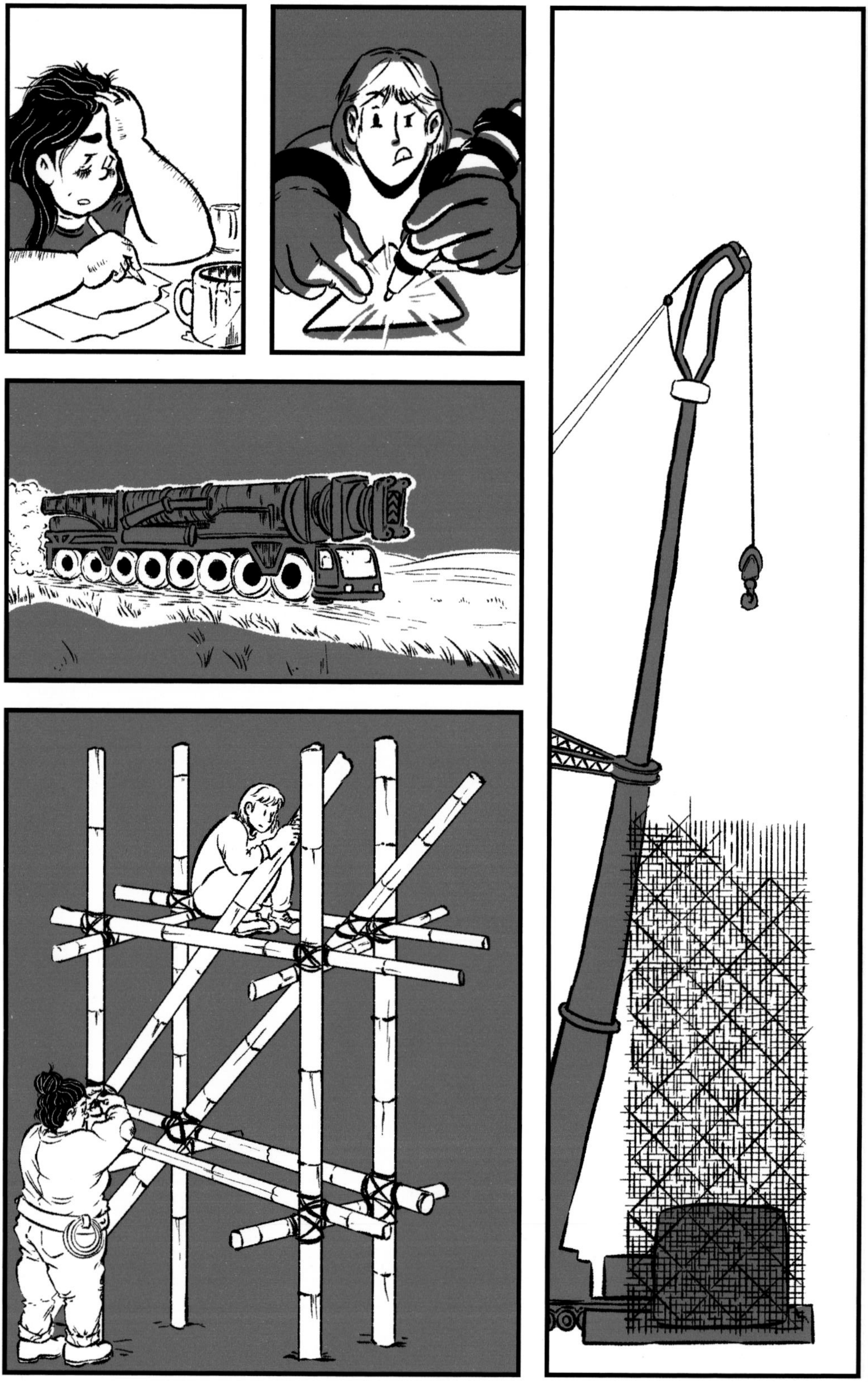

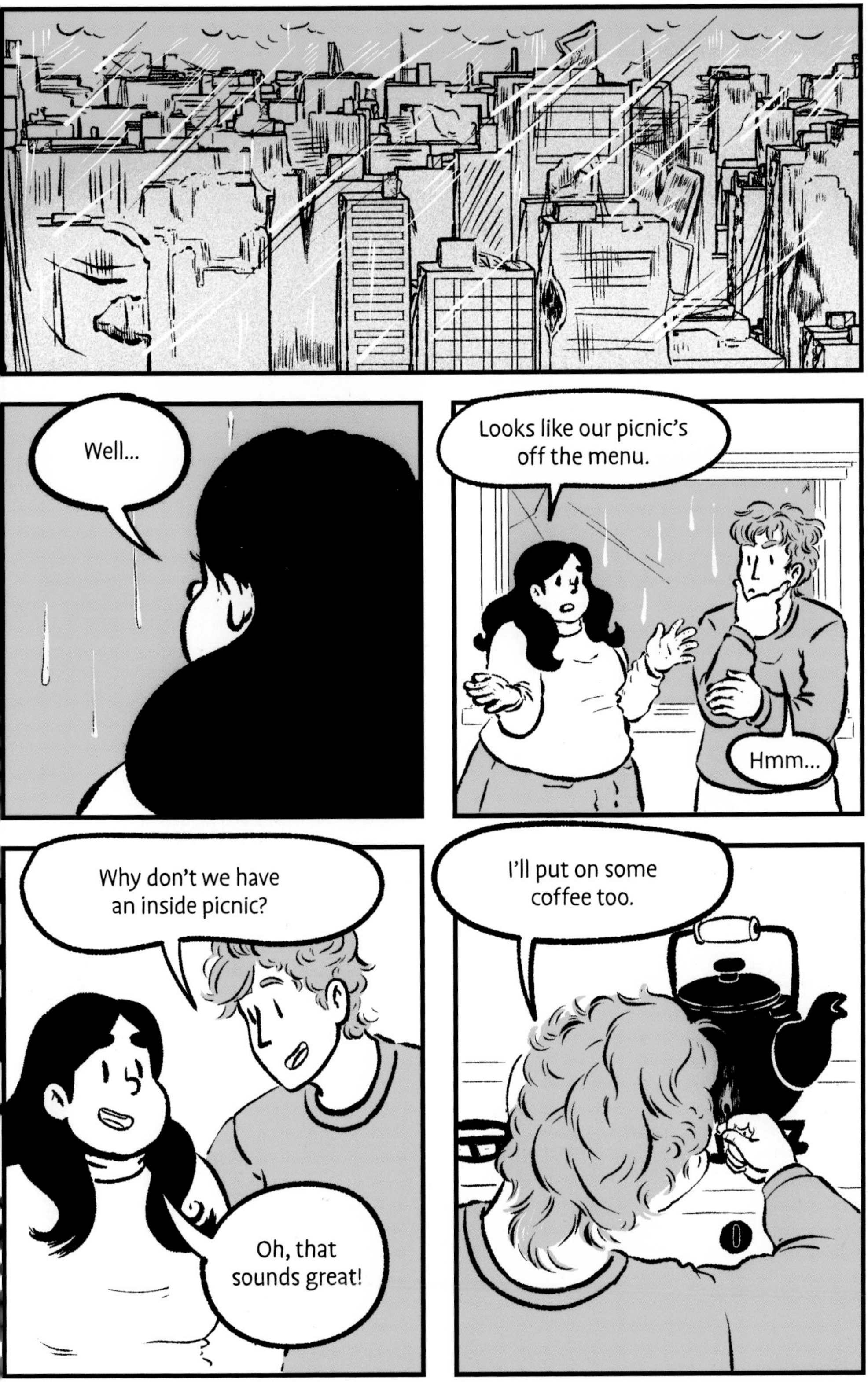
Well...
Looks like our picnic's off the menu.
Hmm...
Why don't we have an inside picnic?
Oh, that sounds great!
I'll put on some coffee too.

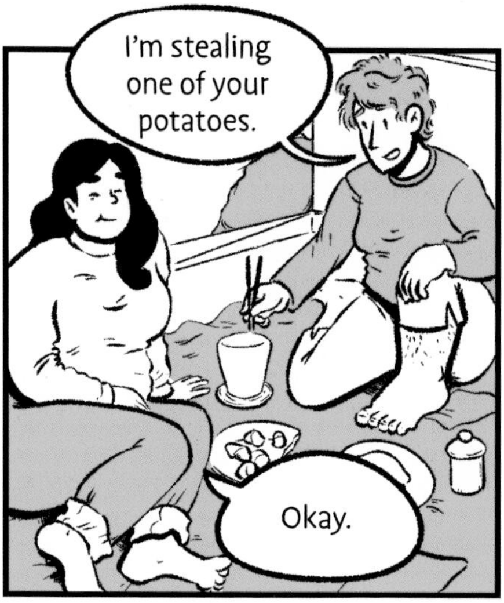
I'm stealing one of your potatoes.
Okay.

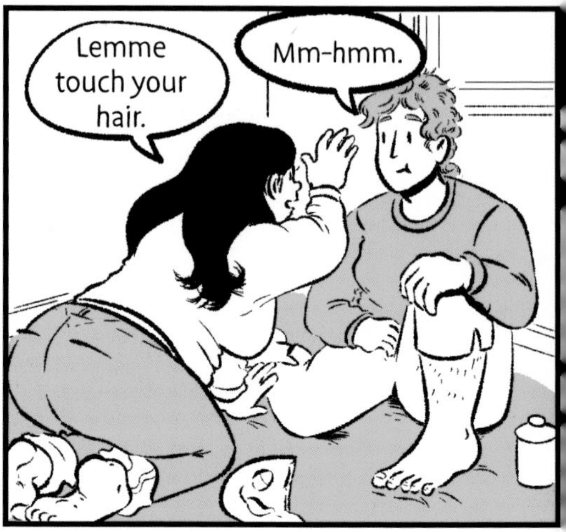
Lemme touch your hair.
Mm-hmm.

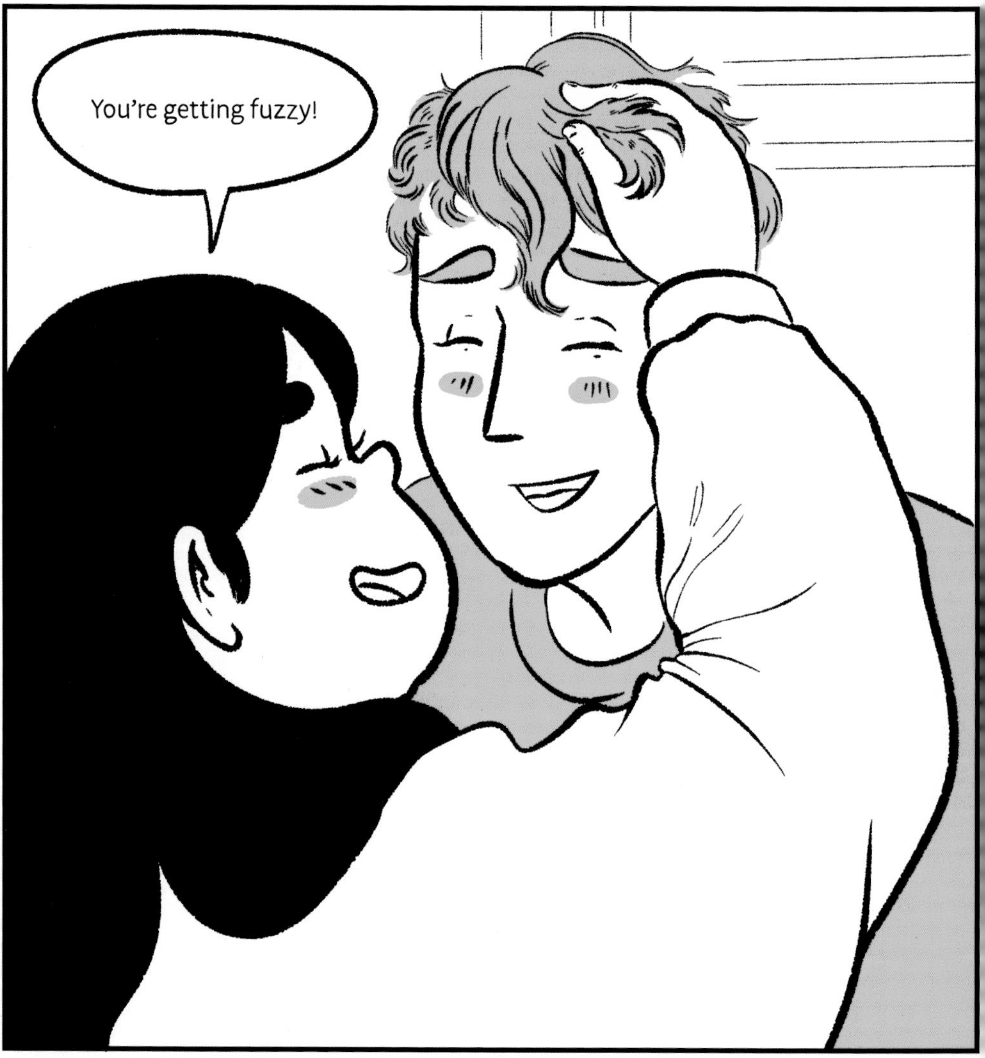
You're getting fuzzy!

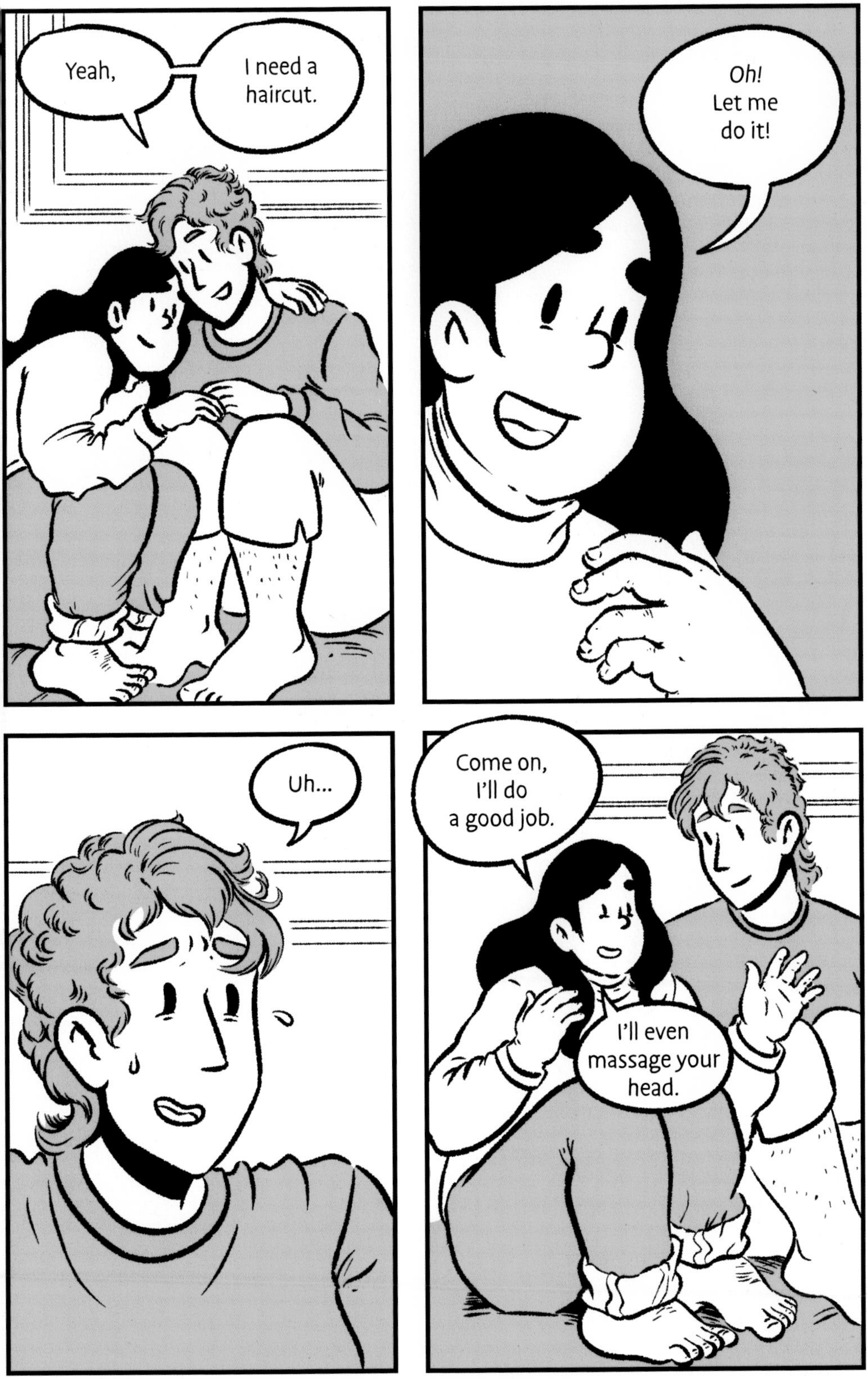
Yeah,
I need a haircut.
Oh! Let me do it!
Uh...
Come on, I'll do a good job.
I'll even massage your head.

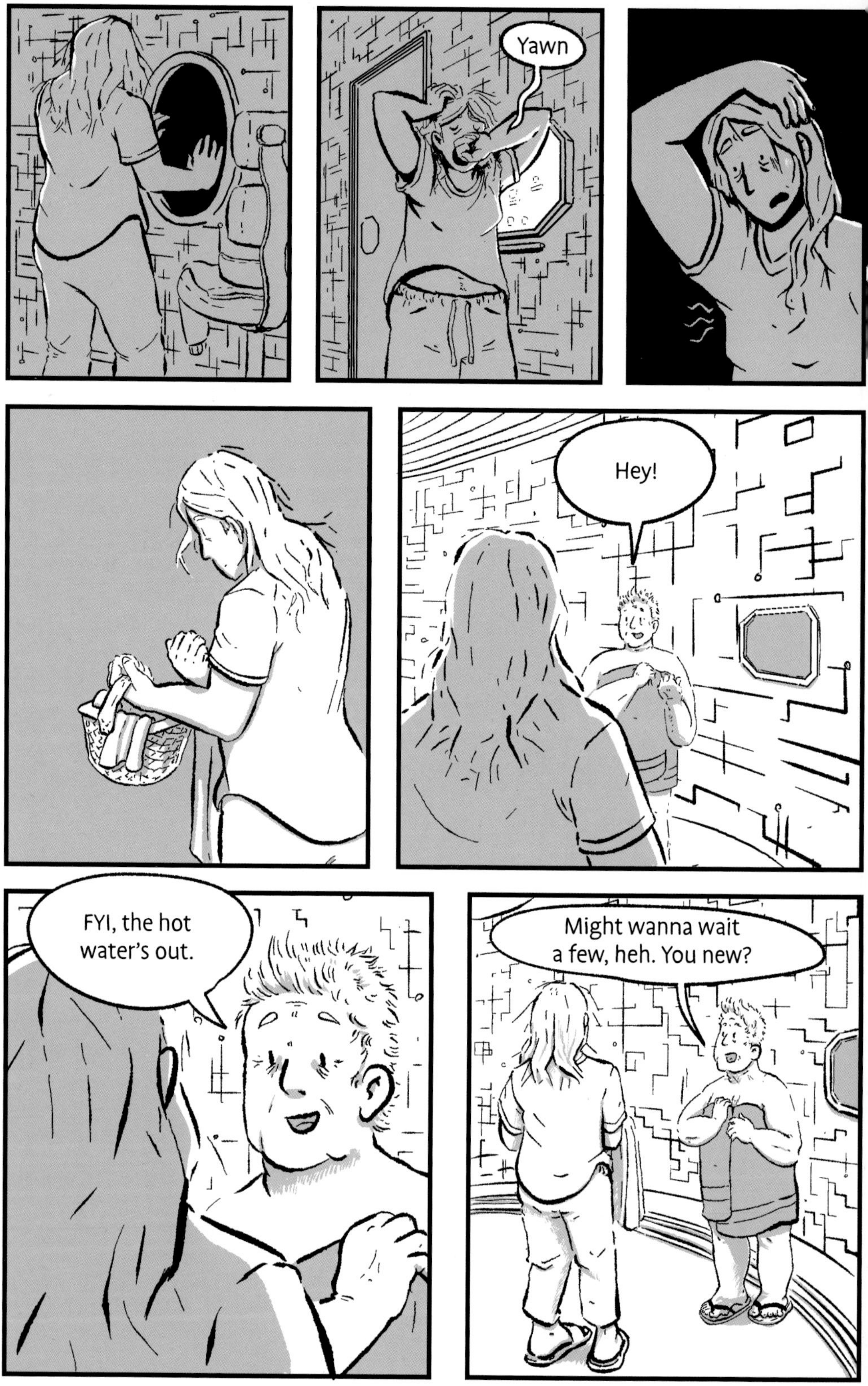
Yawn
Hey!
FYI, the hot water's out.
Might wanna wait a few, heh. You new?

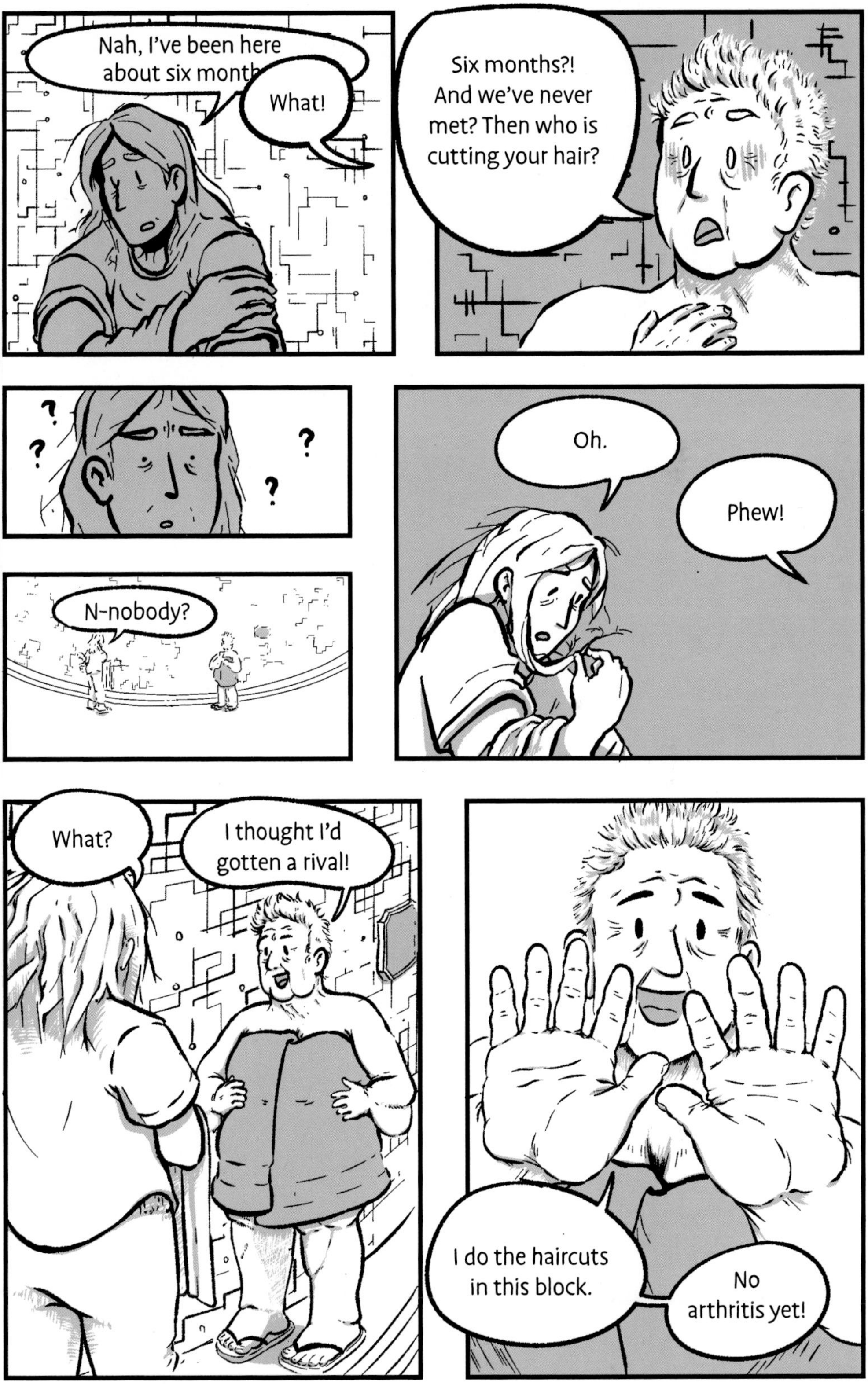
Nah, I've been here about six month
What!
Six months?! And we've never met? Then who is cutting your hair?
?
?
?
?
Oh.
Phew!
N-nobody?
What?
I thought I'd gotten a rival!
I do the haircuts in this block.
No arthritis yet!

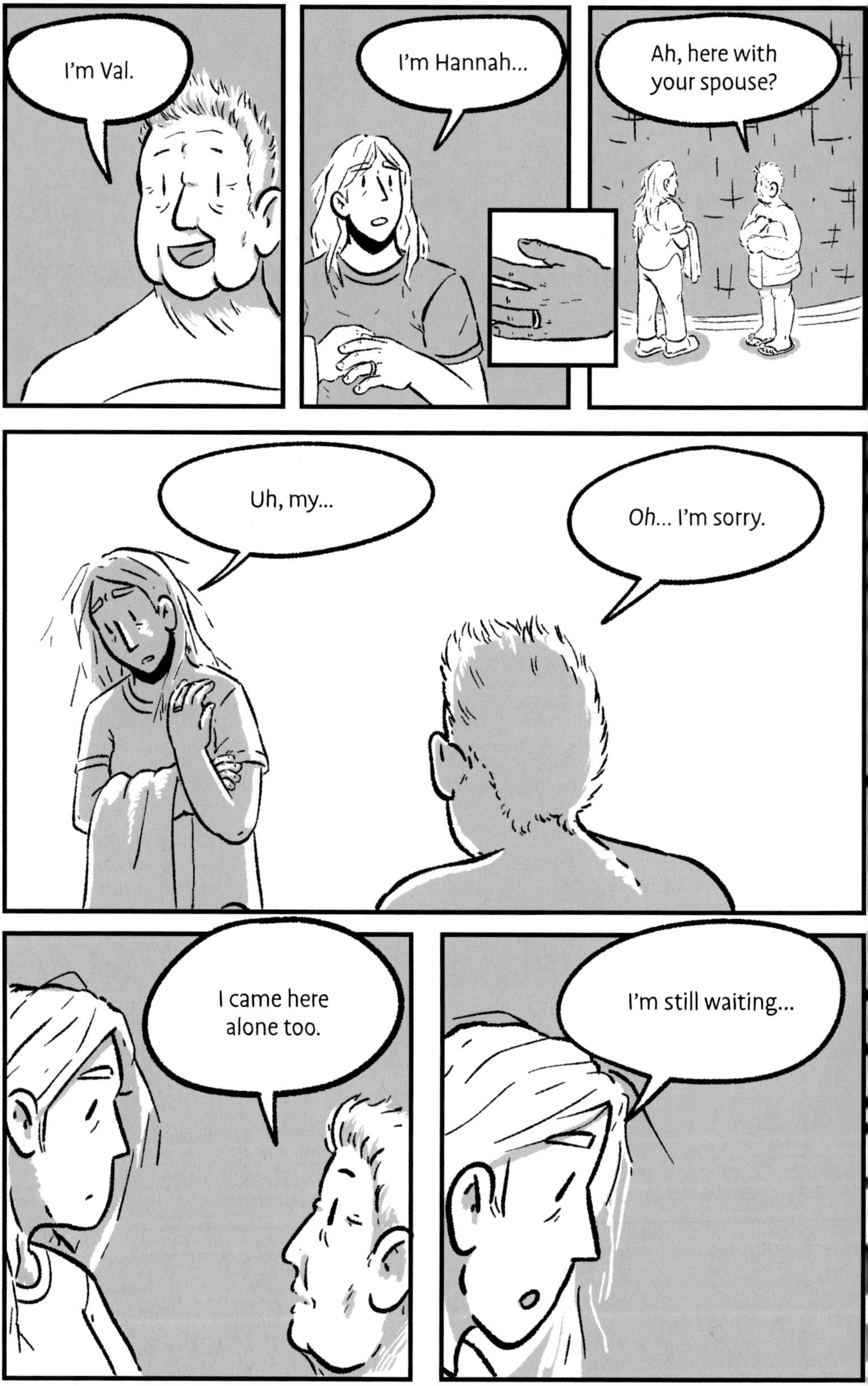
I'm Val.
I'm Hannah...
Ah, here with your spouse?
Uh, my...
Oh... I'm sorry.
I came here alone too.
I'm still waiting...

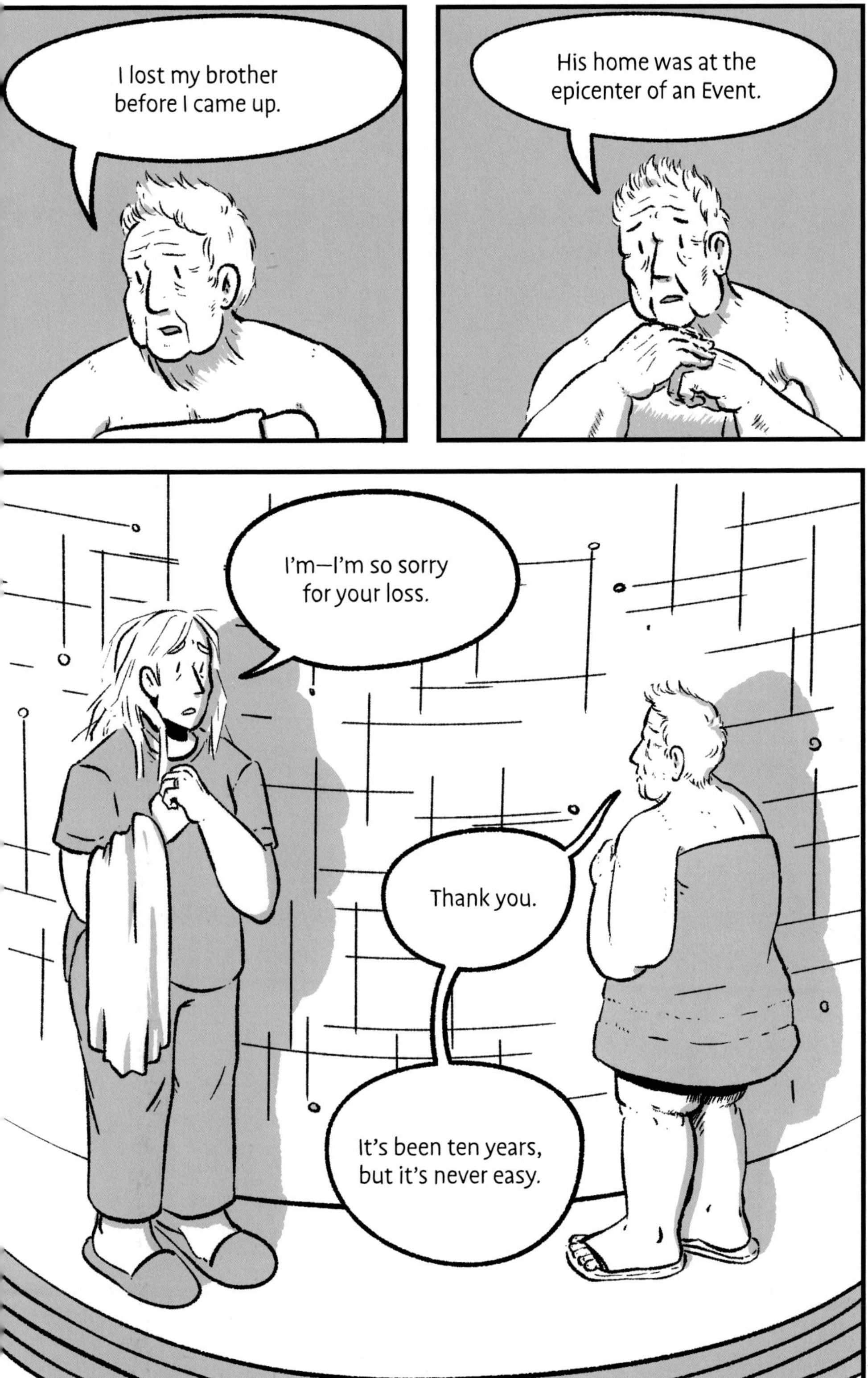
I lost my brother before I came up.
His home was at the epicenter of an Event.
I'm—I'm so sorry for your loss.
Thank you.
It's been ten years, but it's never easy.

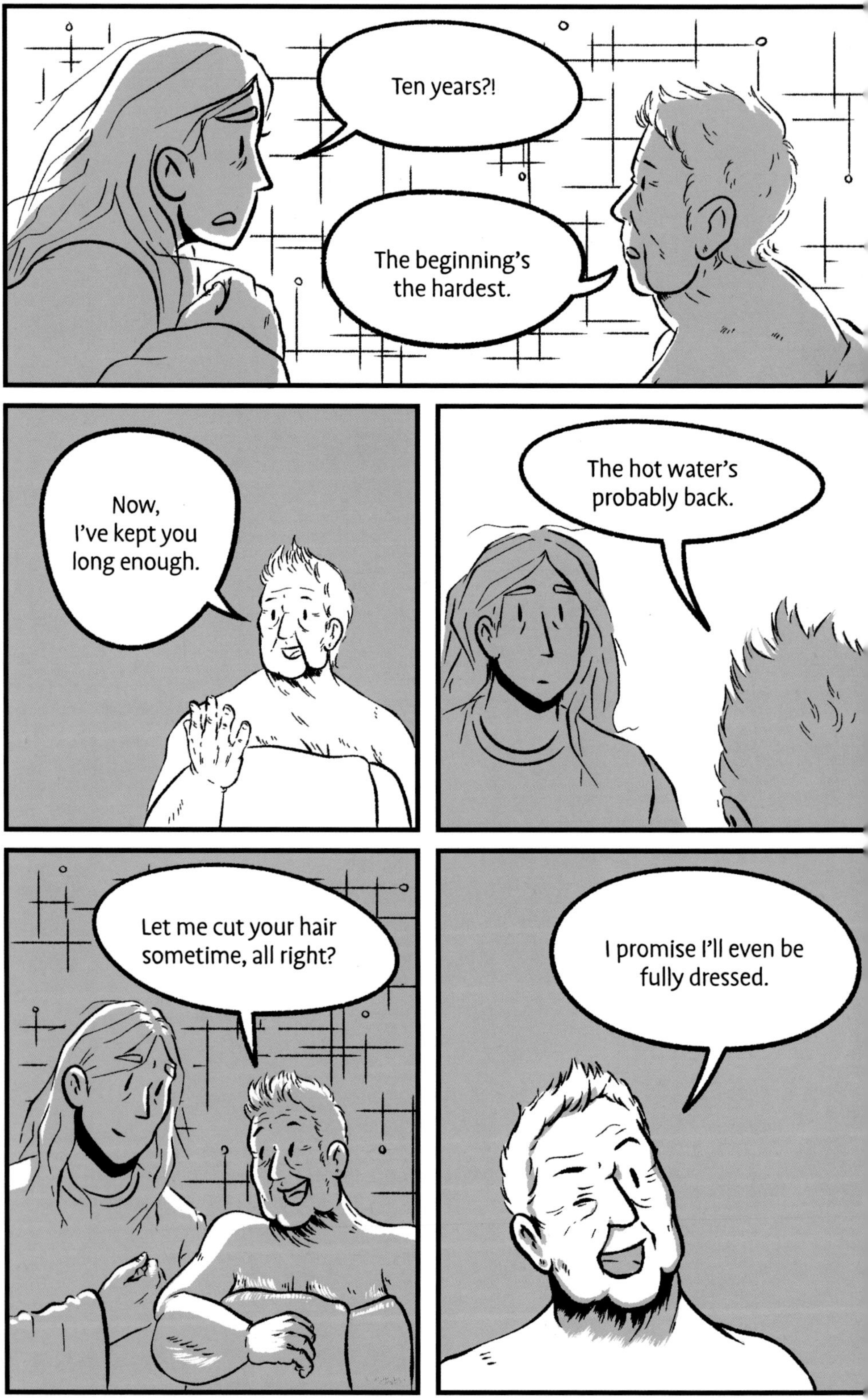
Ten years?!
The beginning's the hardest.
Now, I've kept you long enough.
The hot water's probably back.
Let me cut your hair sometime, all right?
I promise I'll even be fully dressed.

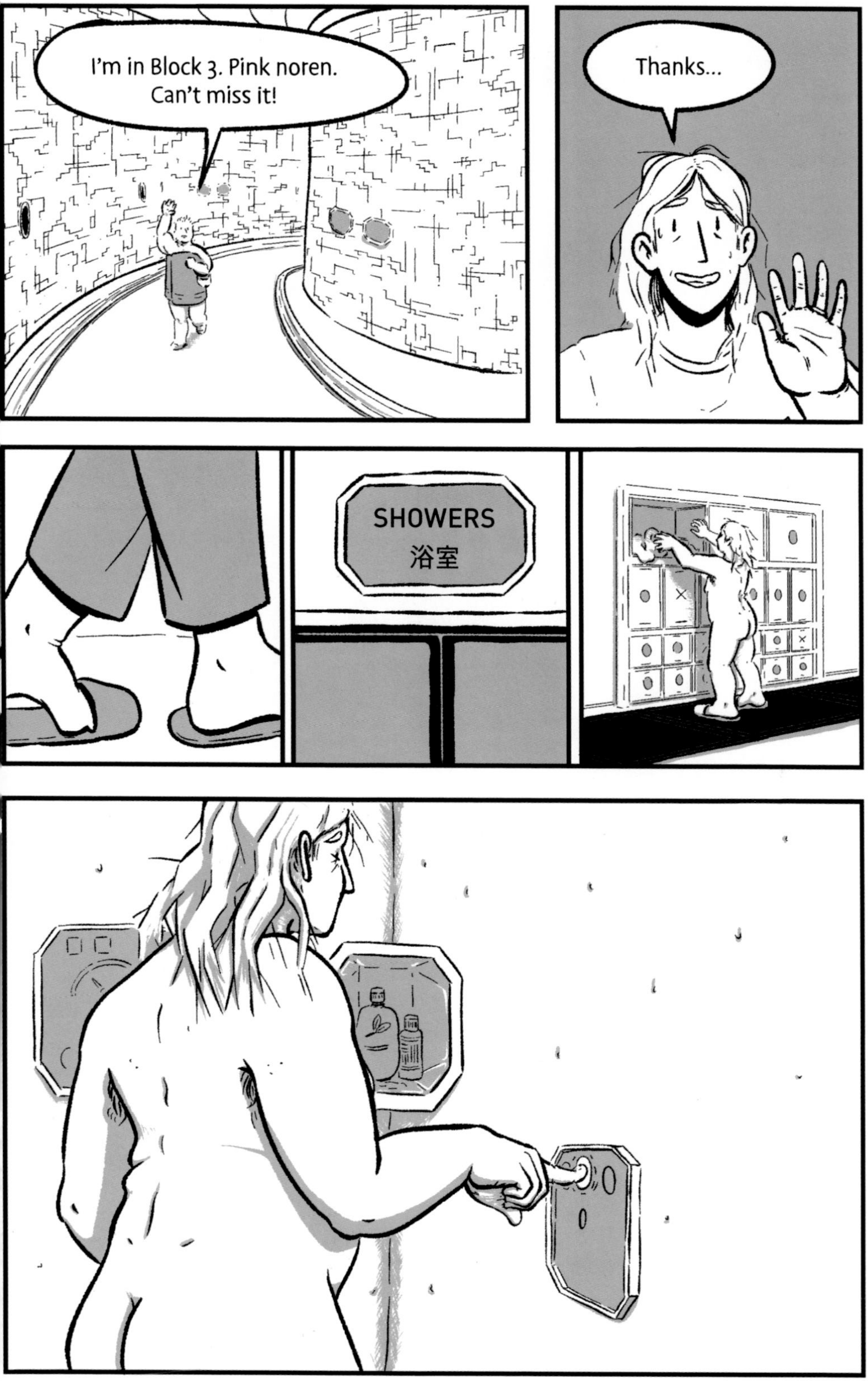
I'm in Block 3. Pink noren.
Can't miss it!
Thanks...
SHOWERS
浴室

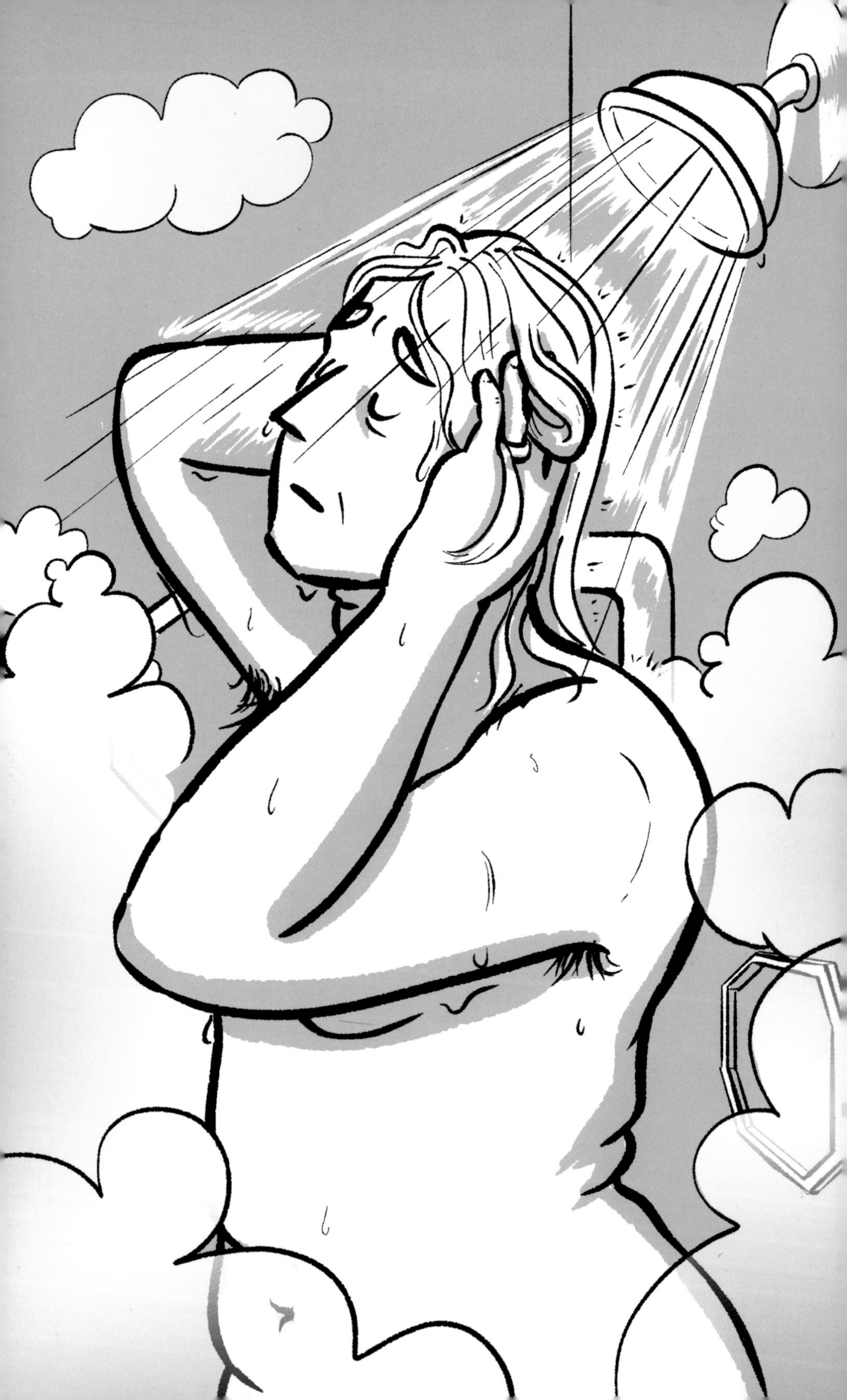

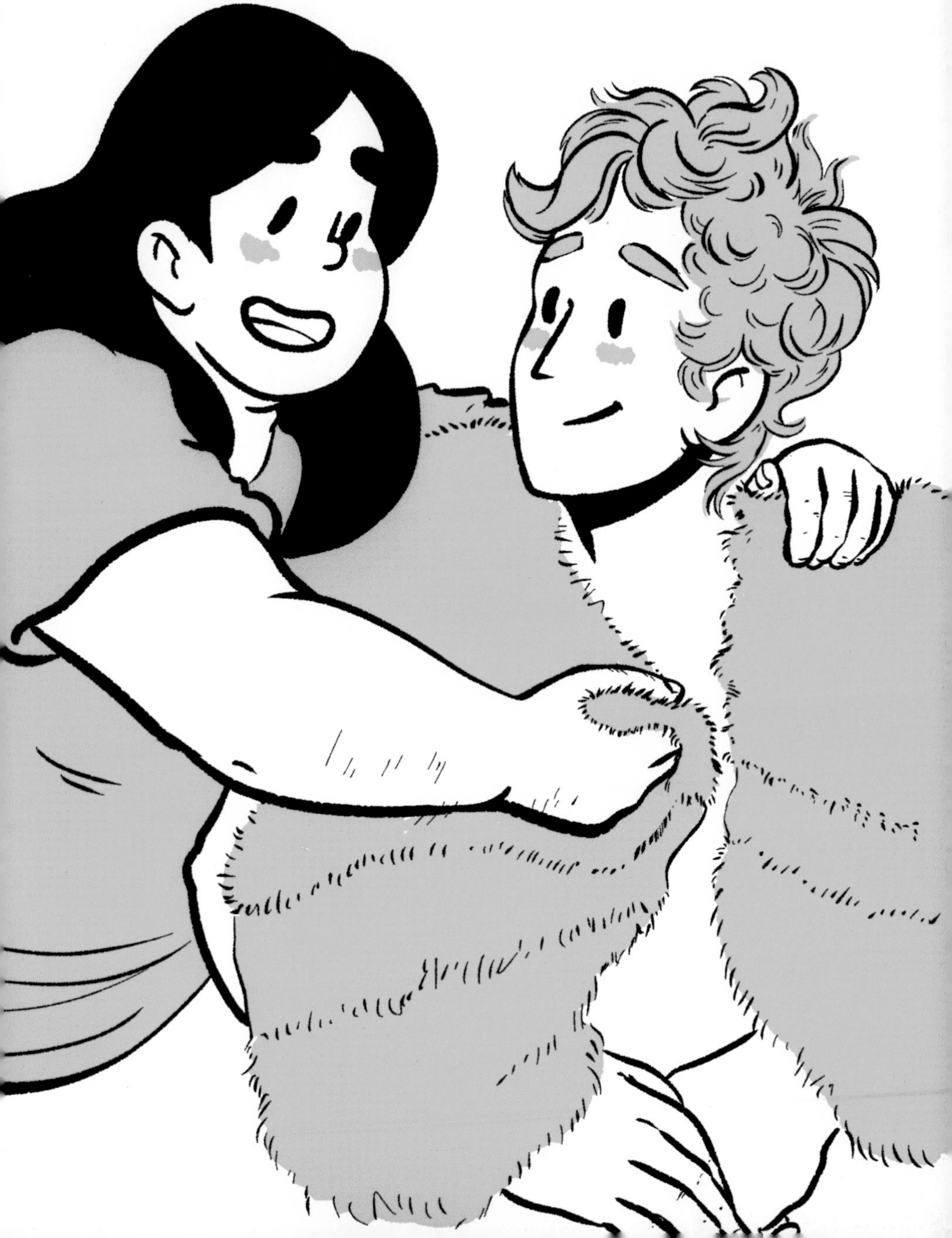

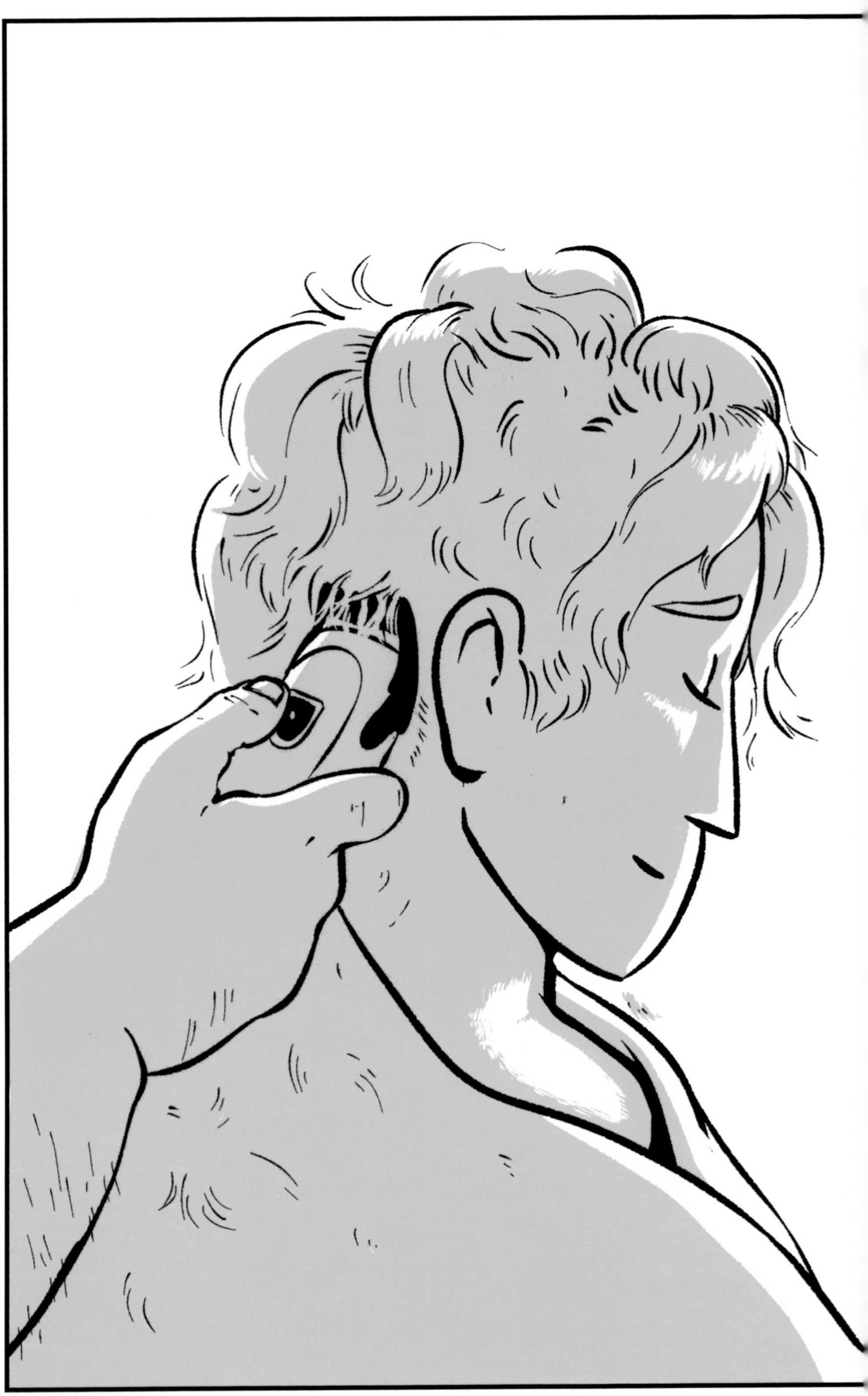

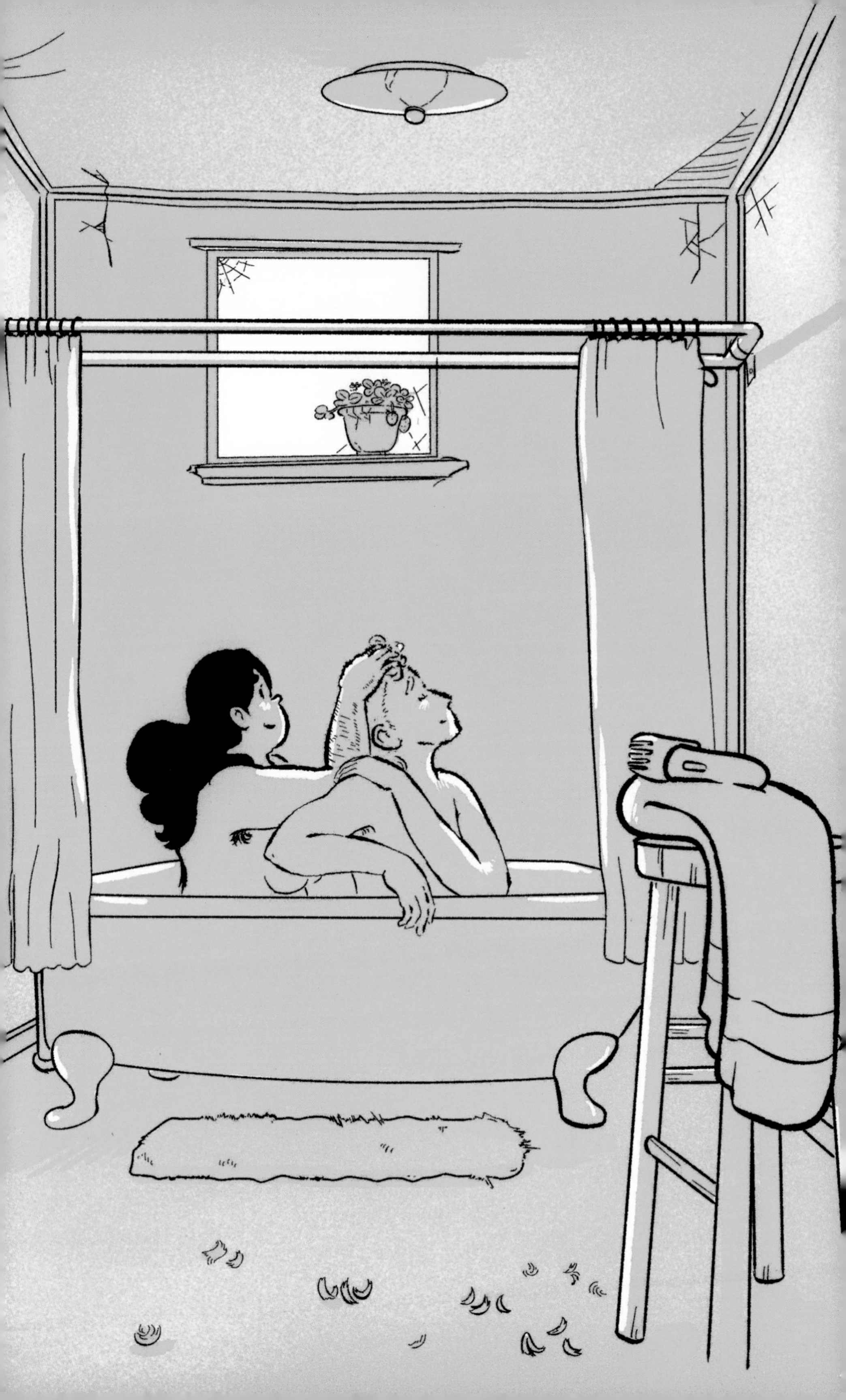

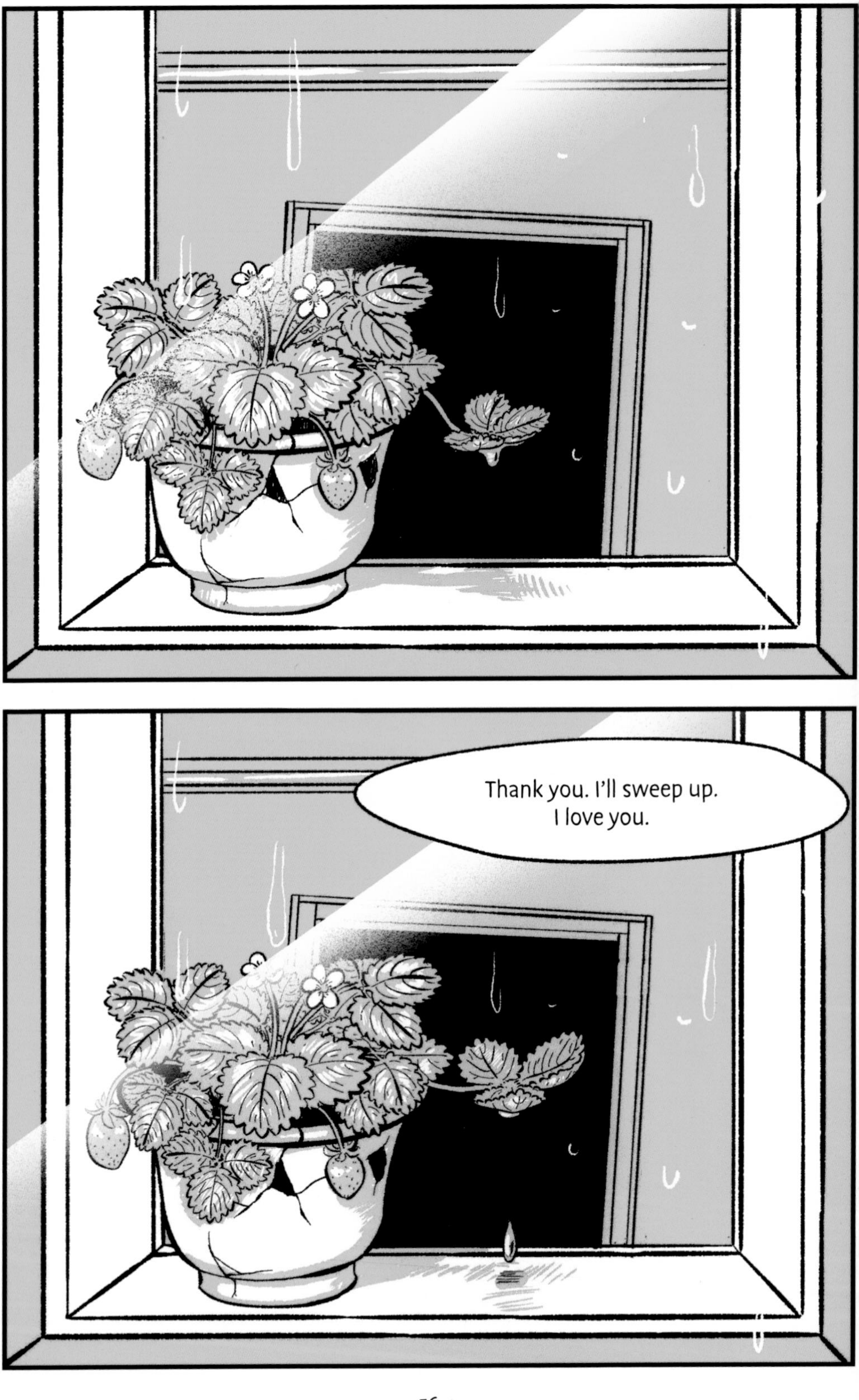
Thank you. I'll sweep up.
I love you.

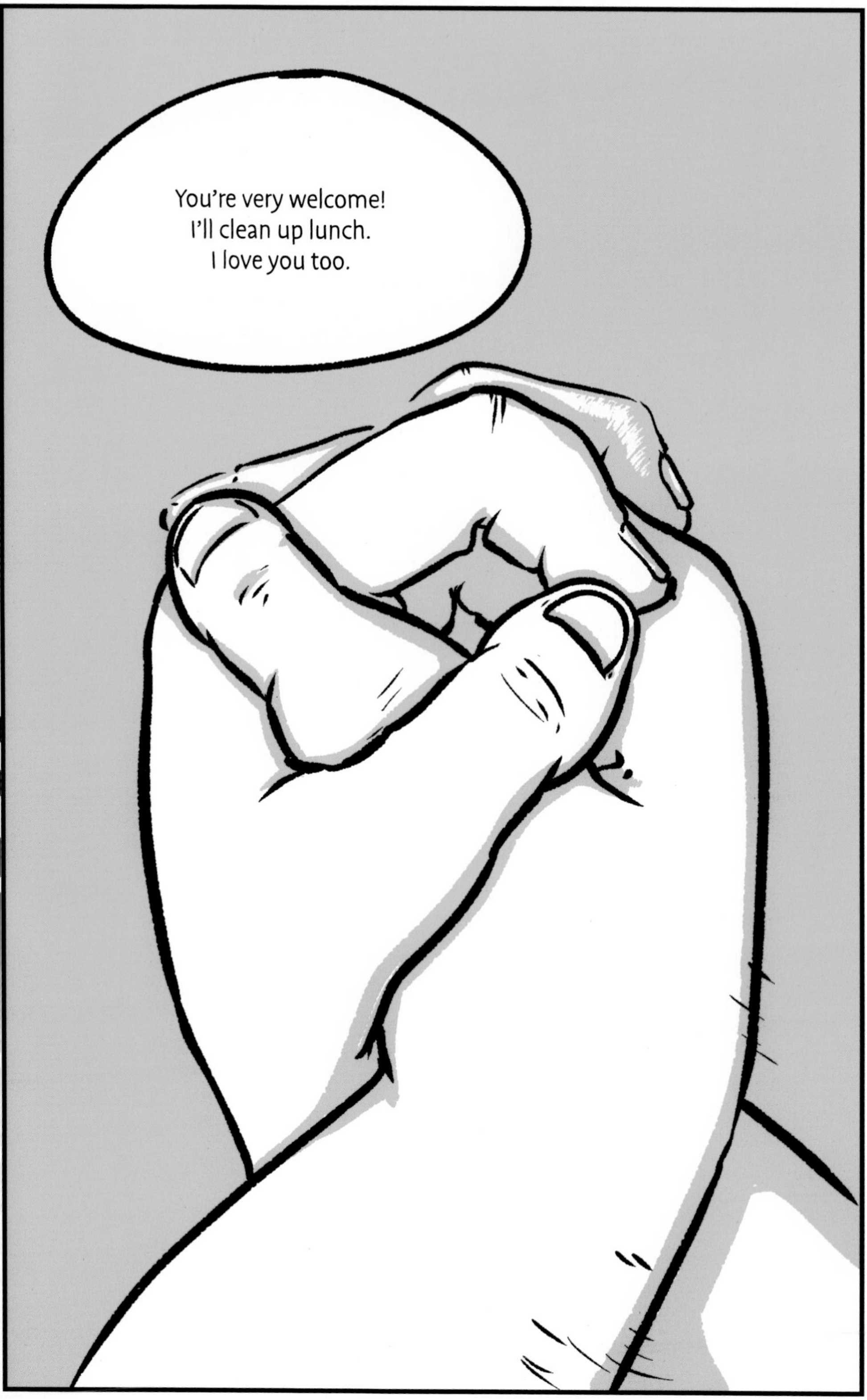
You're very welcome!
I'll clean up lunch.
I love you too.

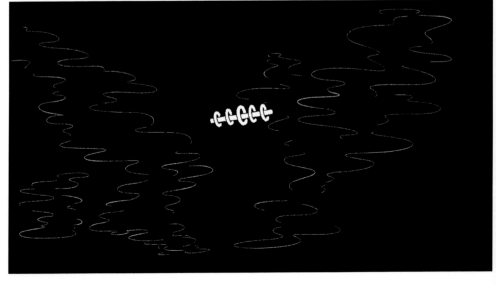

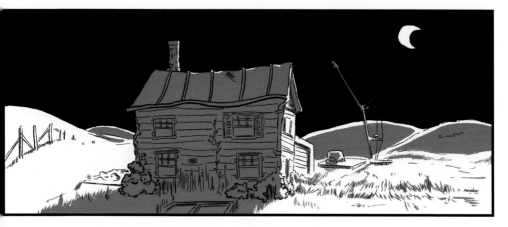

Hey, Mom.

We've been working nonstop. Let's take a break.

There's no time.

Can't we just wait to be called up again?

sigh

I have something to show you.

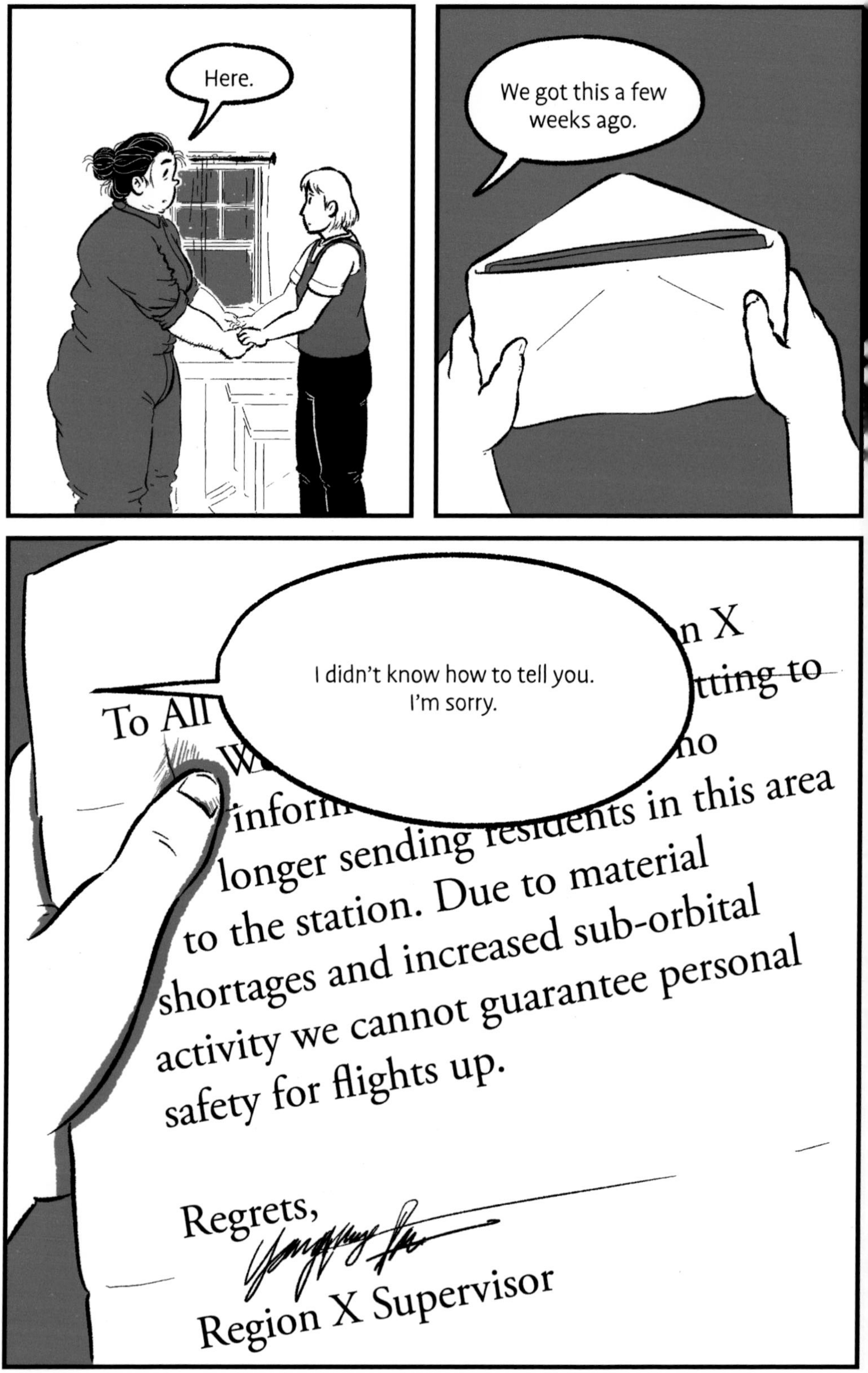
Here.
We got this a few weeks ago.
I didn't know how to tell you. I'm sorry.
longer sending residents in this area
to the station. Due to material
shortages and increased sub-orbital
activity we cannot guarantee personal
safety for flights up.
Regrets,
Region X Supervisor

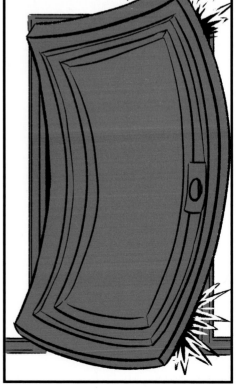

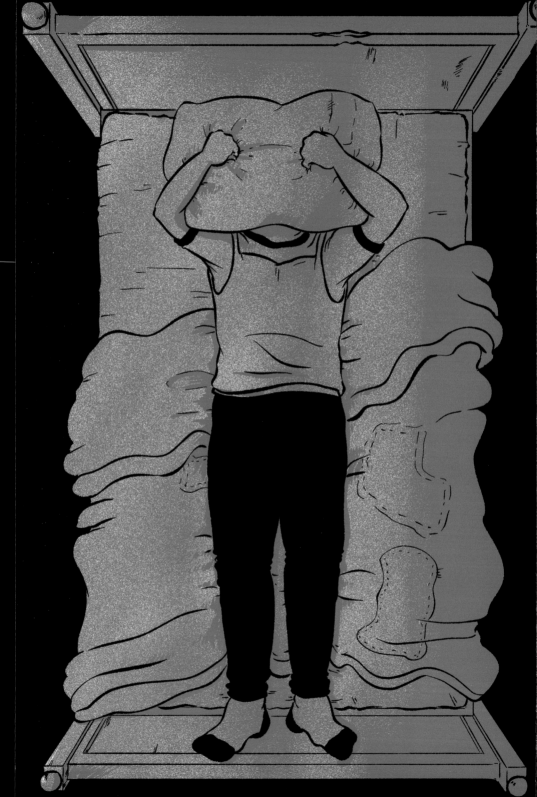

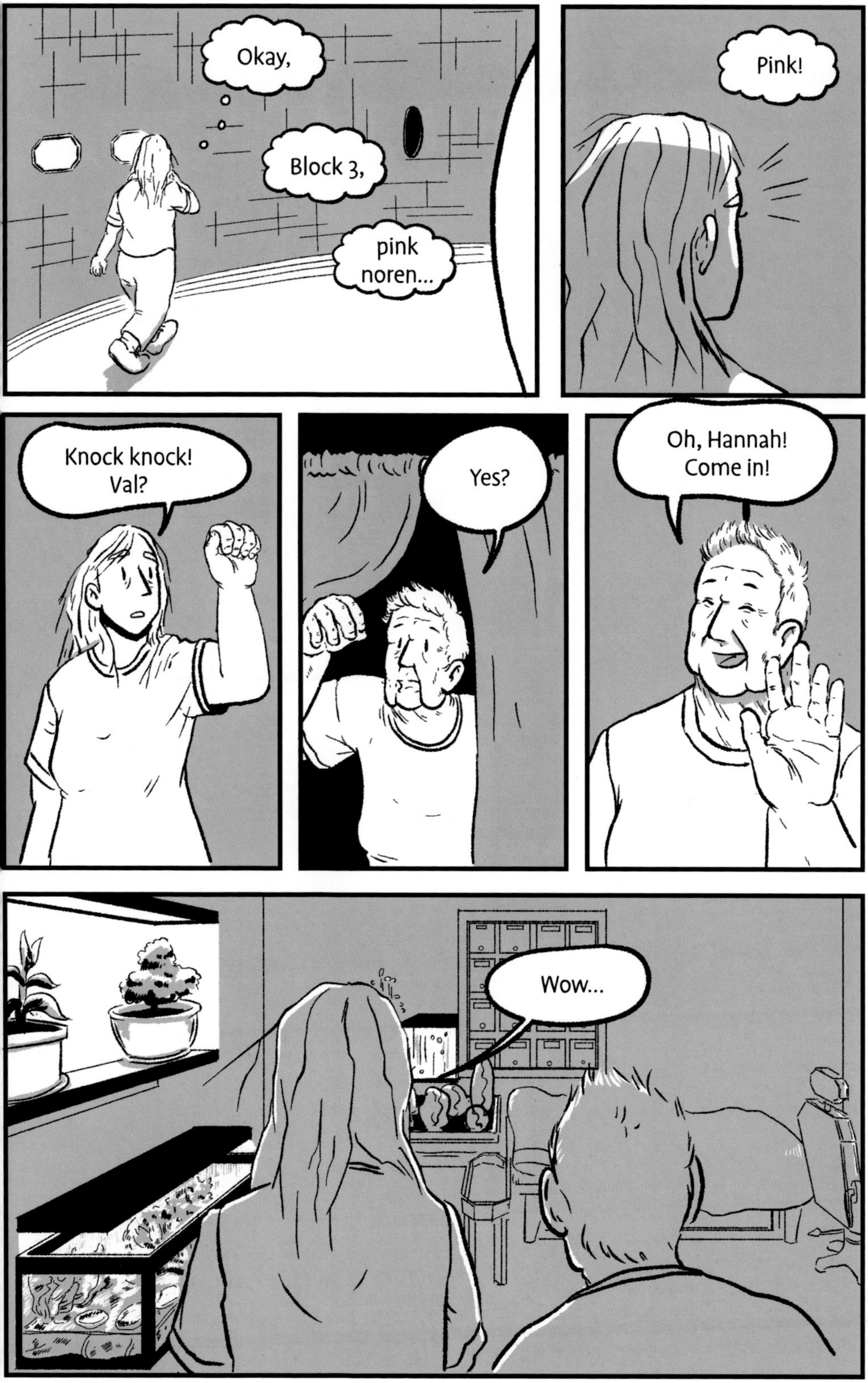
Okay,
Block 3,
pink noren...
Pink!
Knock knock! Val?
Yes?
Oh, Hannah! Come in!
Wow...

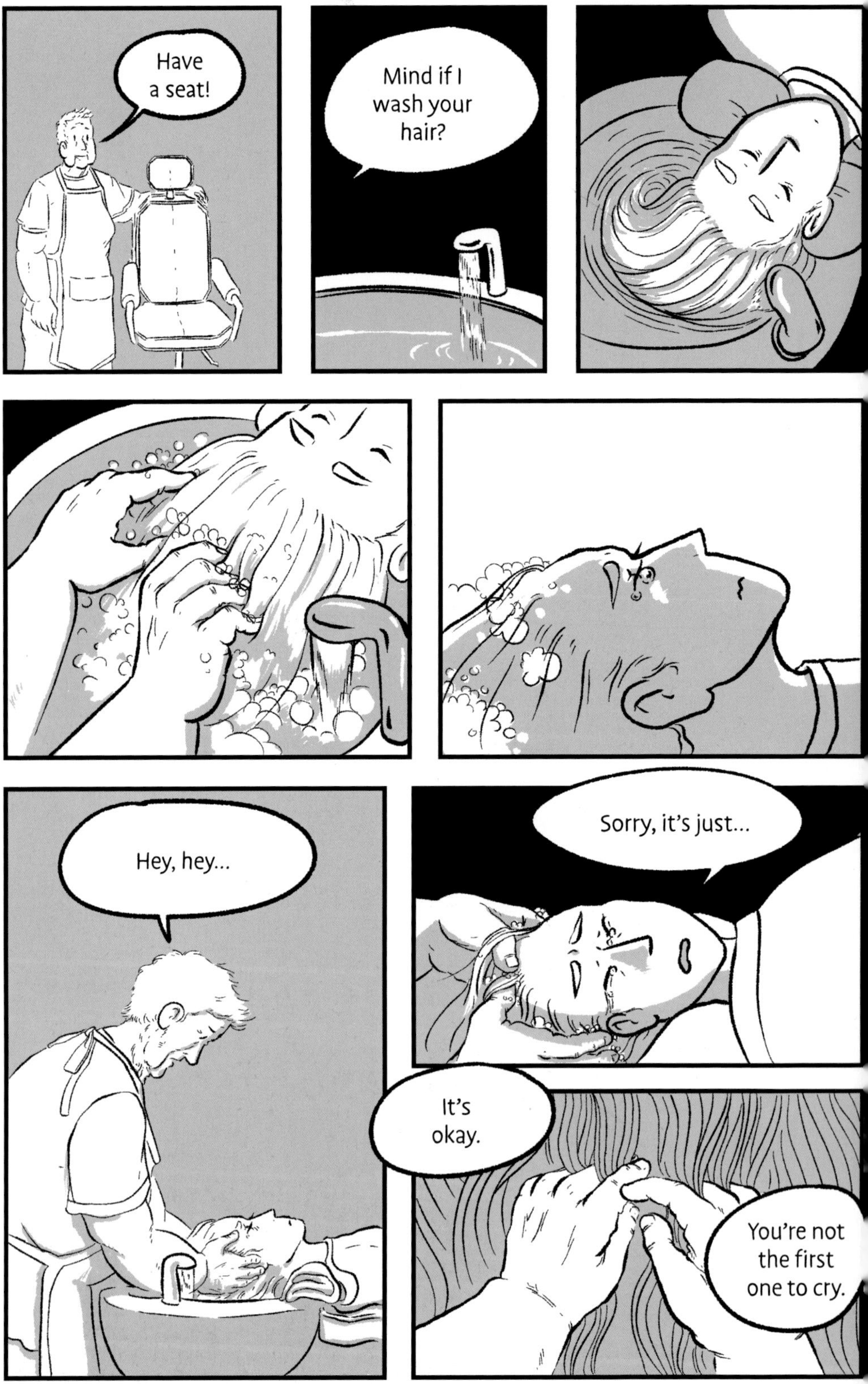
Have a seat!
Mind if I wash your hair?
Hey, hey...
Sorry, it's just...
It's okay.
You're not the first one to cry.

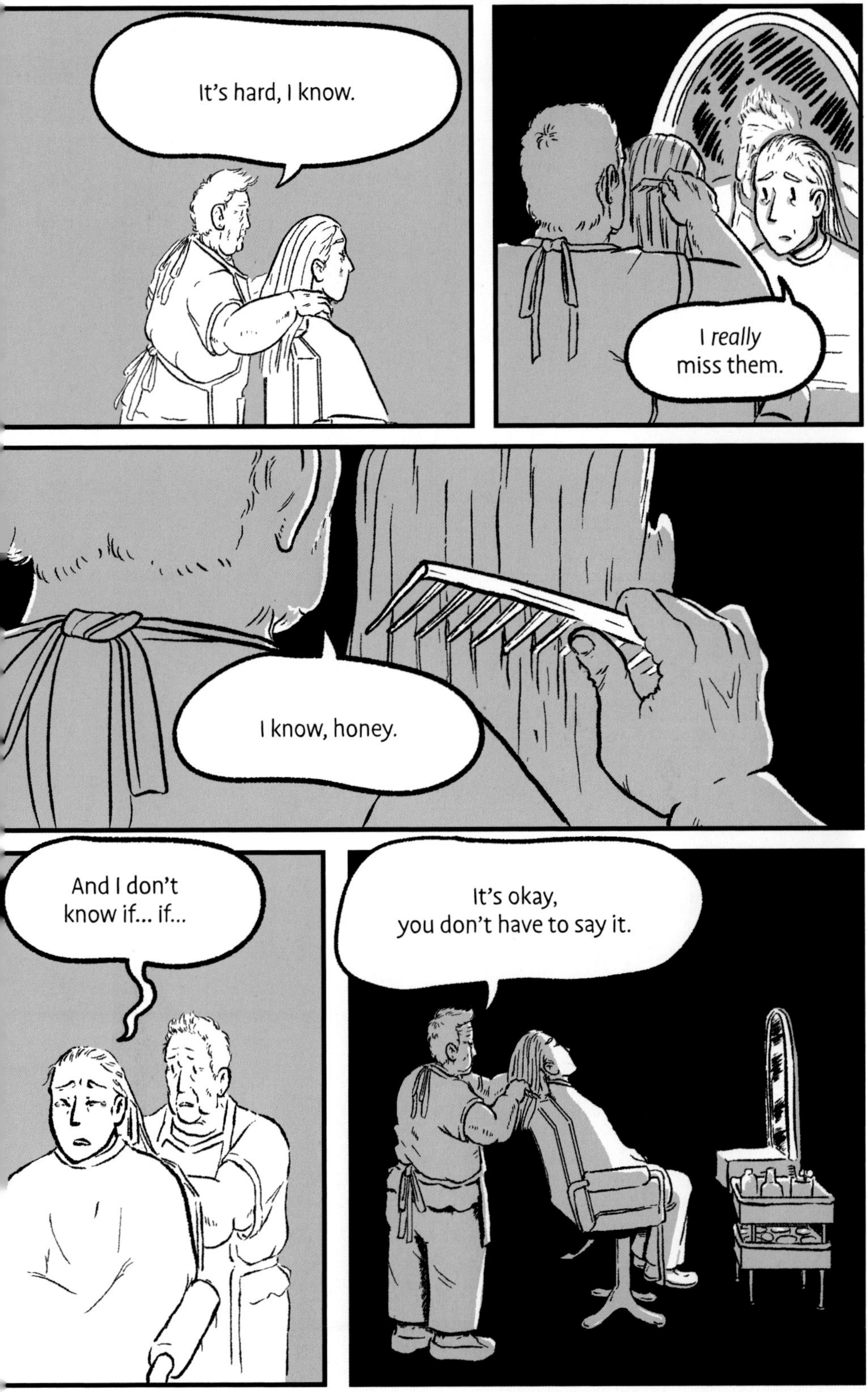
It's hard, I know.
I *really* miss them.
I know, honey.
And I don't know if... if...
It's okay, you don't have to say it.

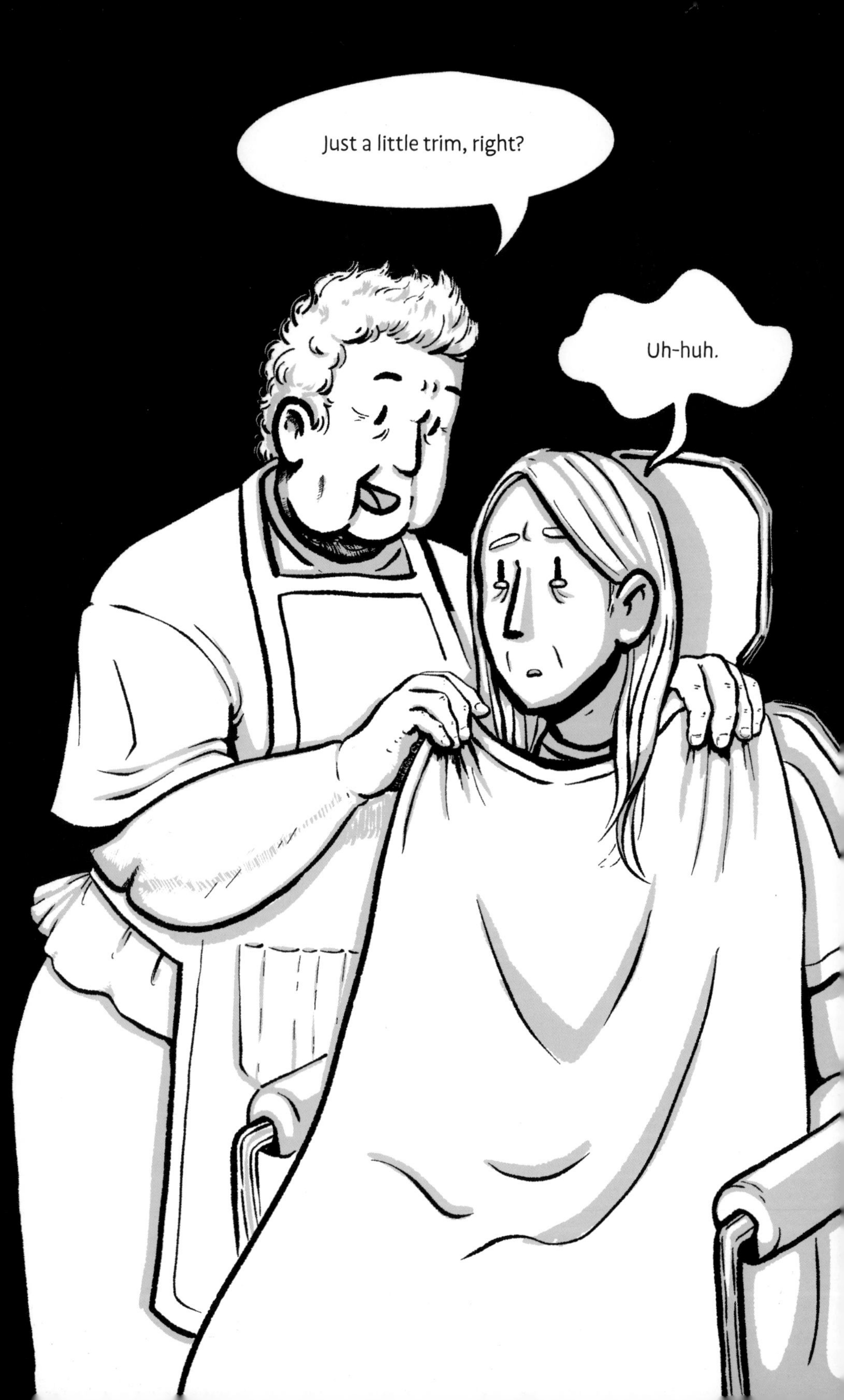
Just a little trim, right?
Uh-huh.

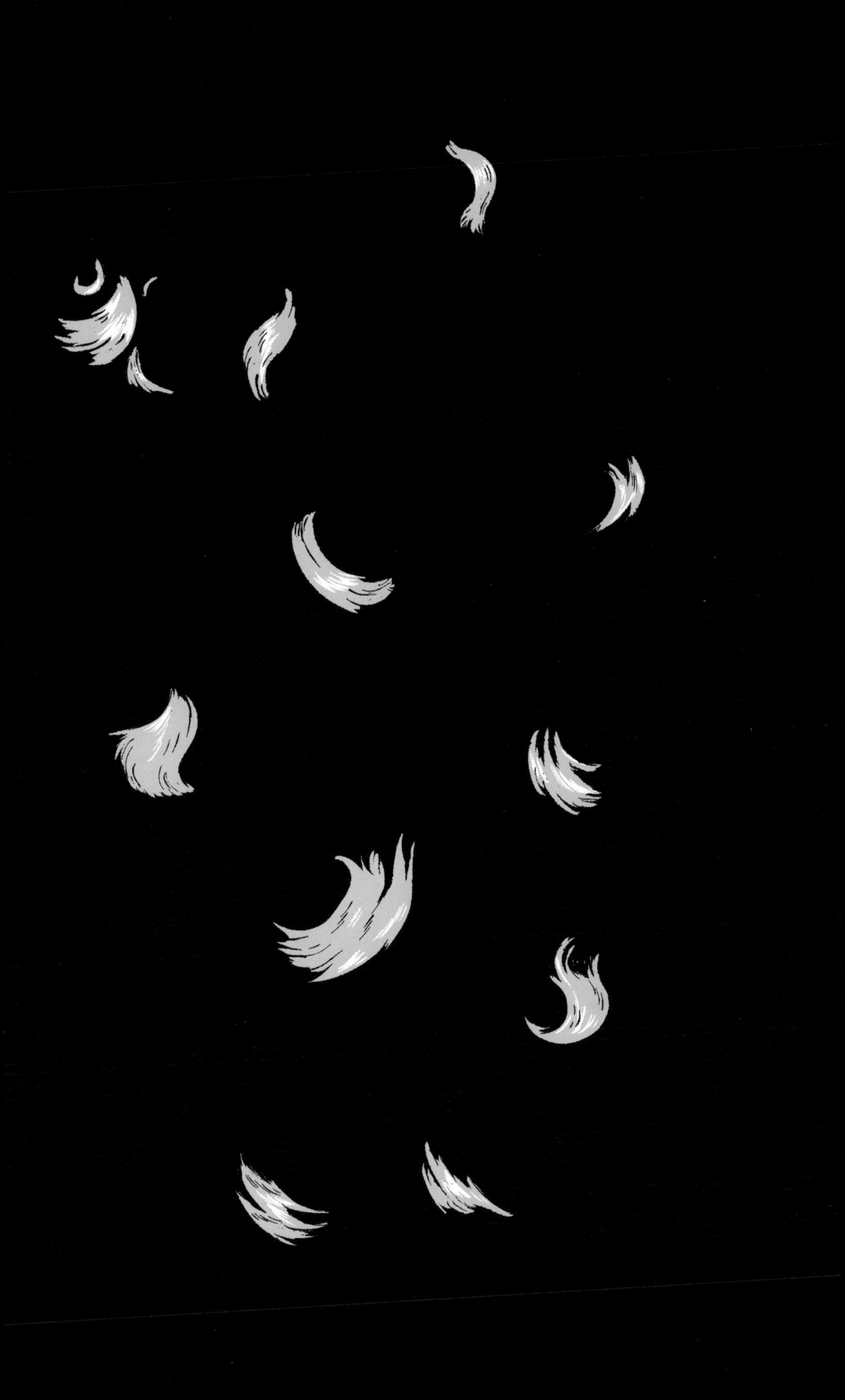

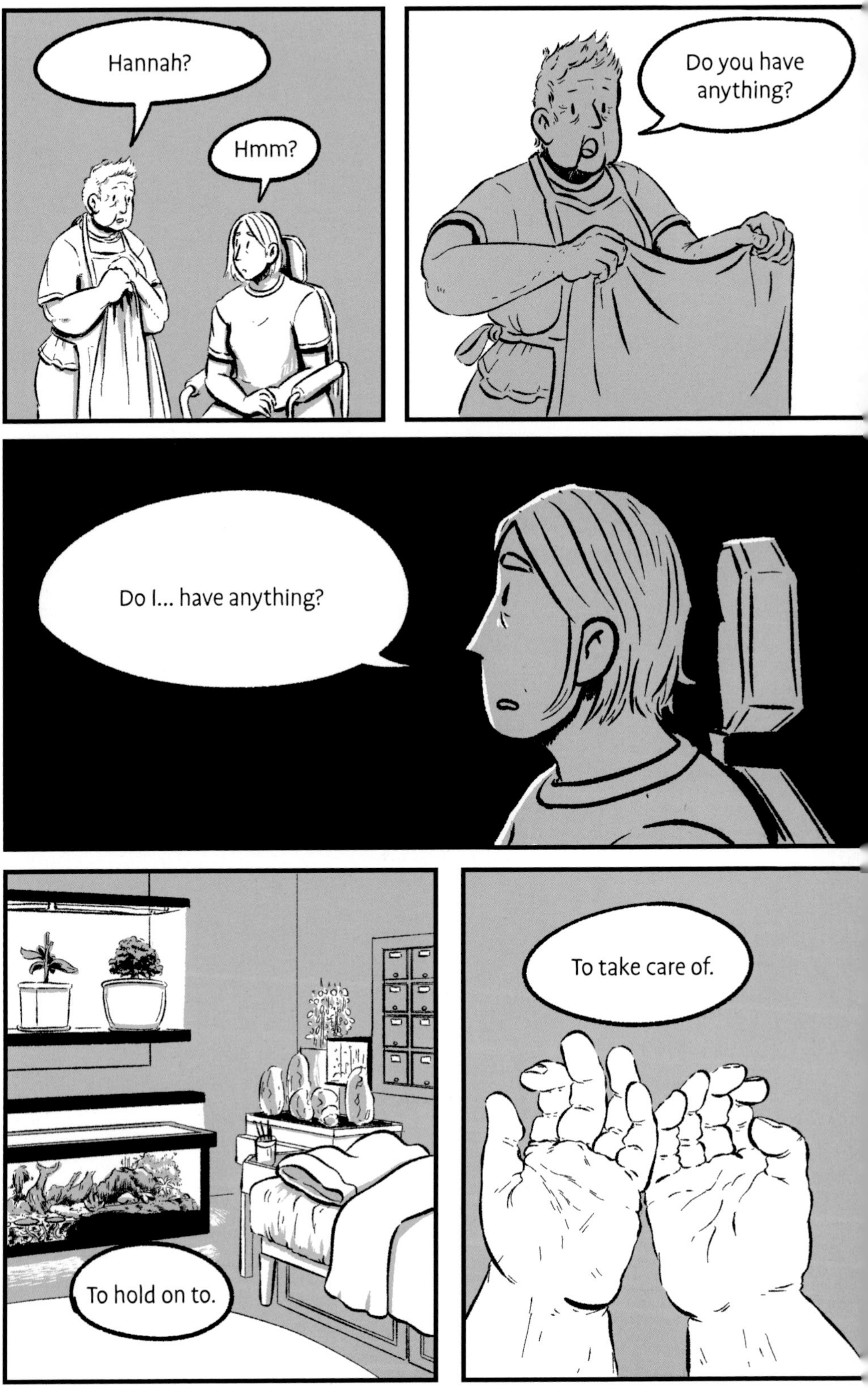
Hannah?
Hmm?
Do you have anything?
Do I... have anything?
To hold on to.
To take care of.

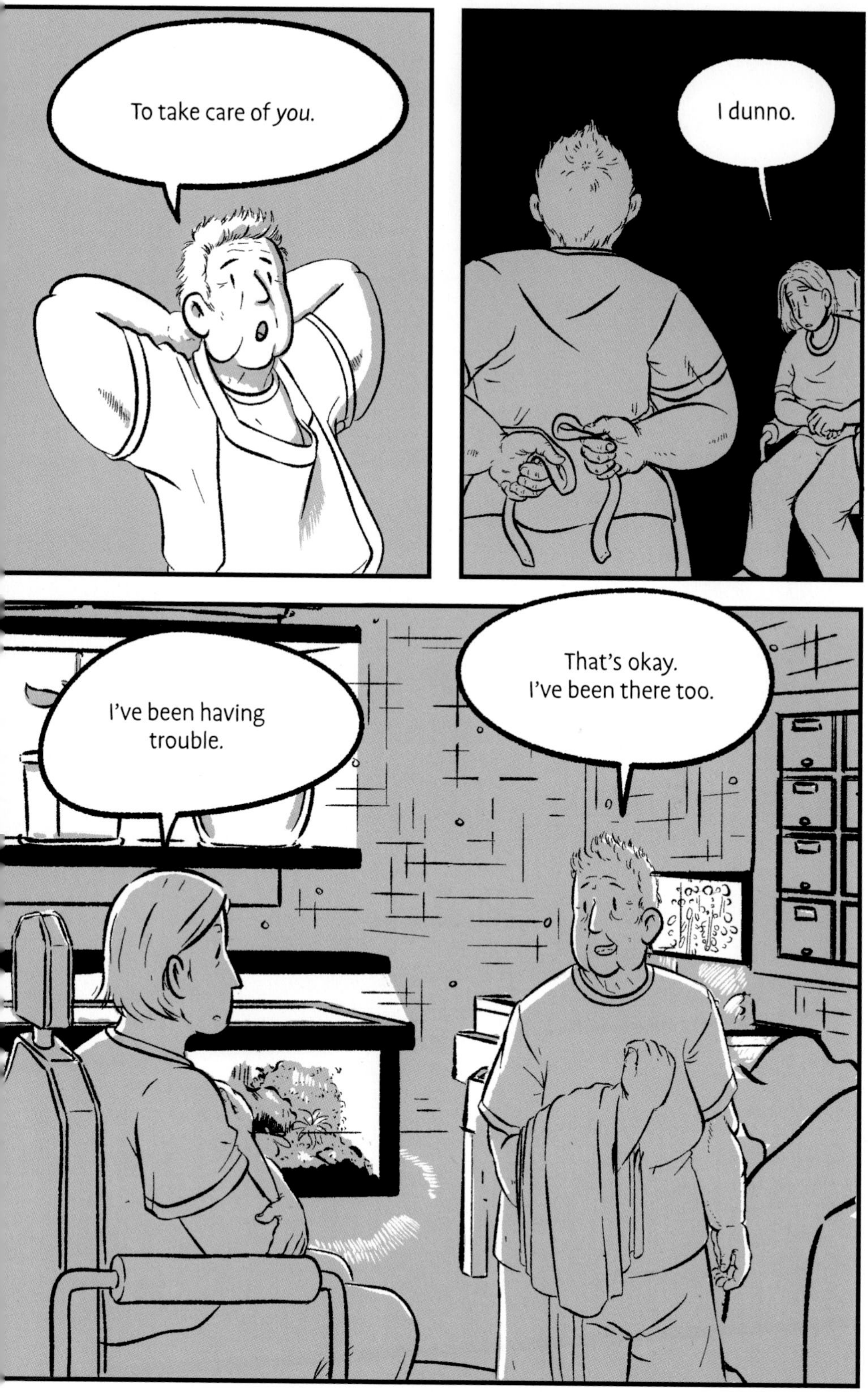
To take care of *you*.
I dunno.
I've been having trouble.
That's okay. I've been there too.

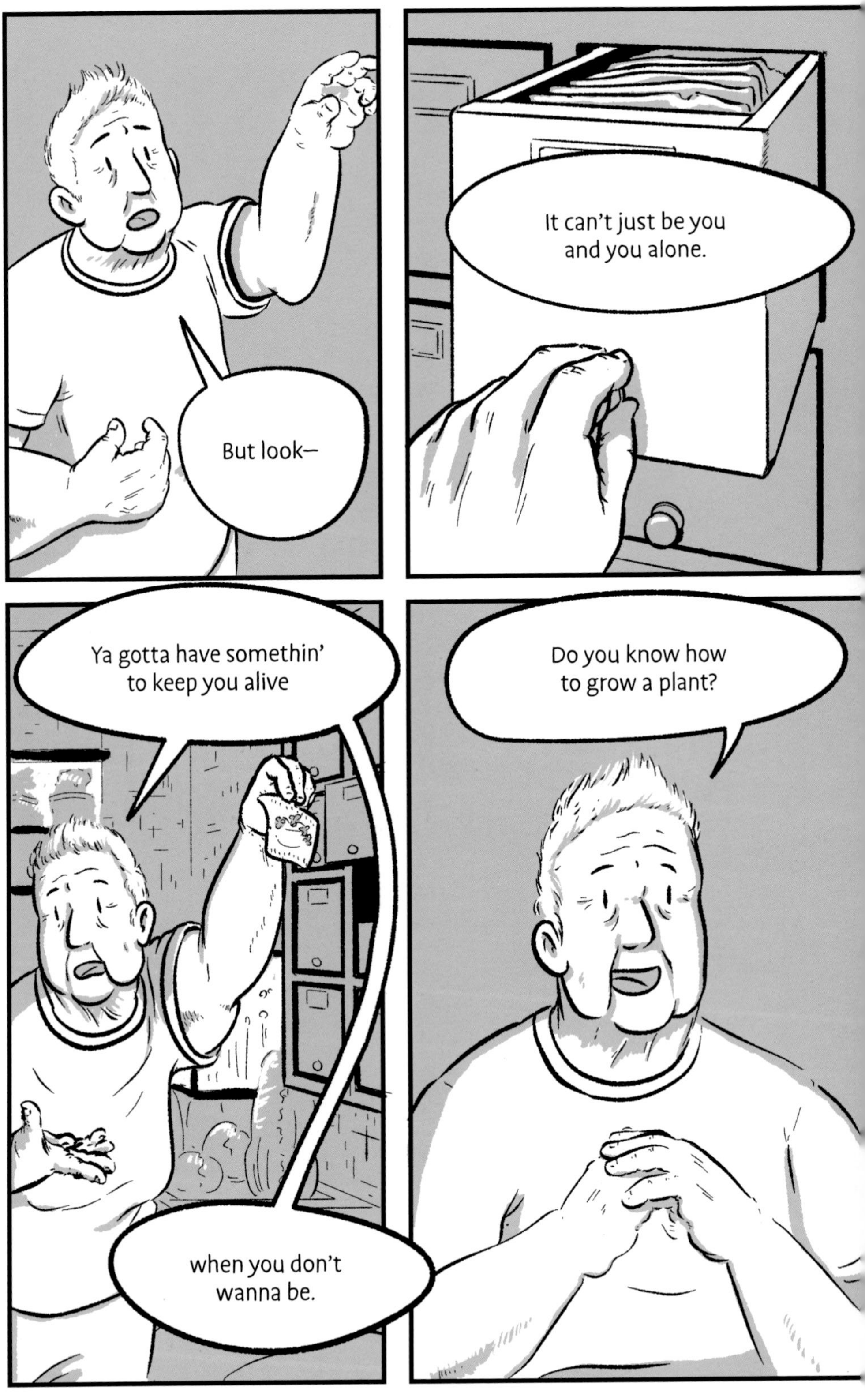
But look–
It can't just be you and you alone.
Ya gotta have somethin' to keep you alive
when you don't wanna be.
Do you know how to grow a plant?

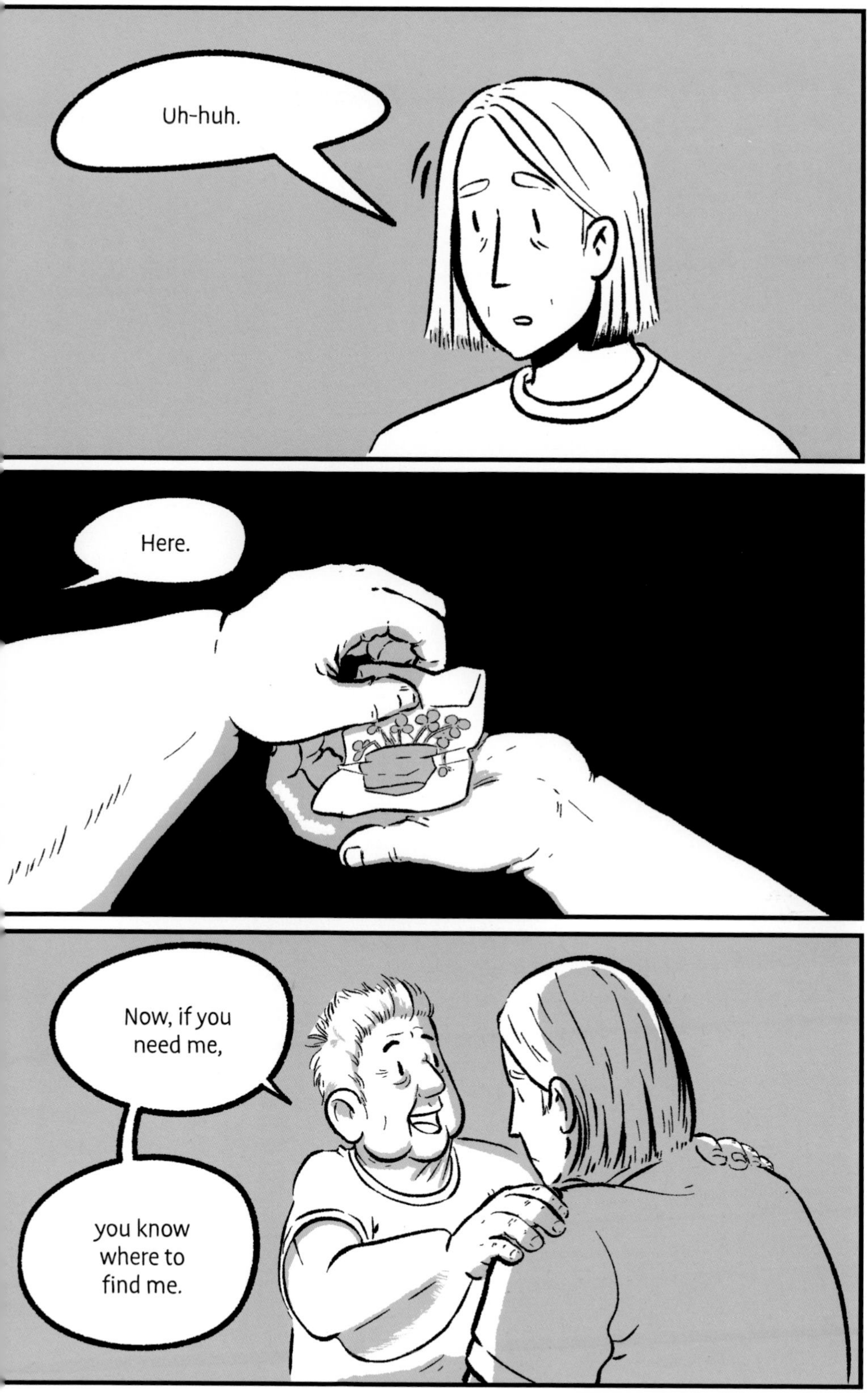
Uh-huh.
Here.
Now, if you need me,
you know where to find me.

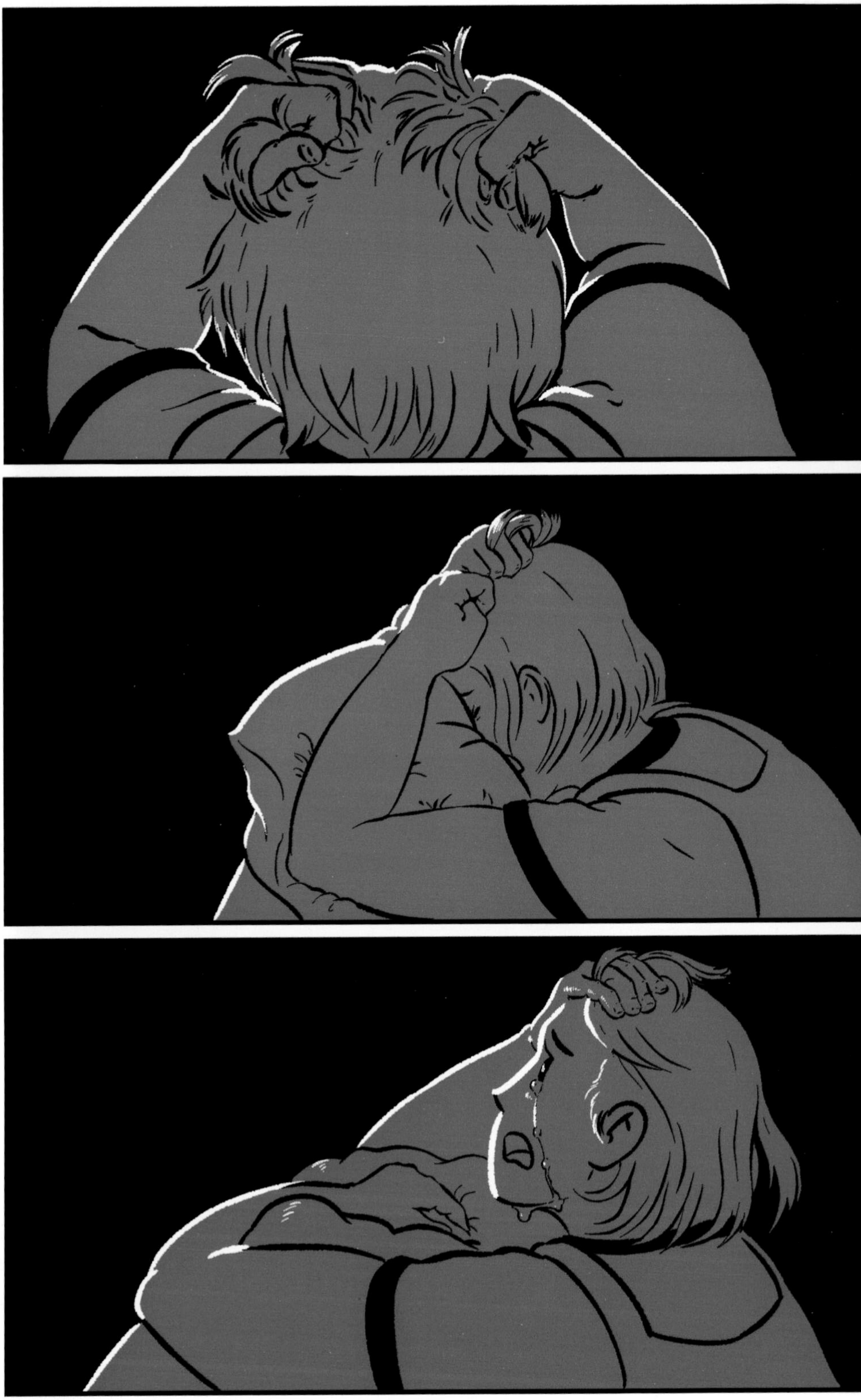

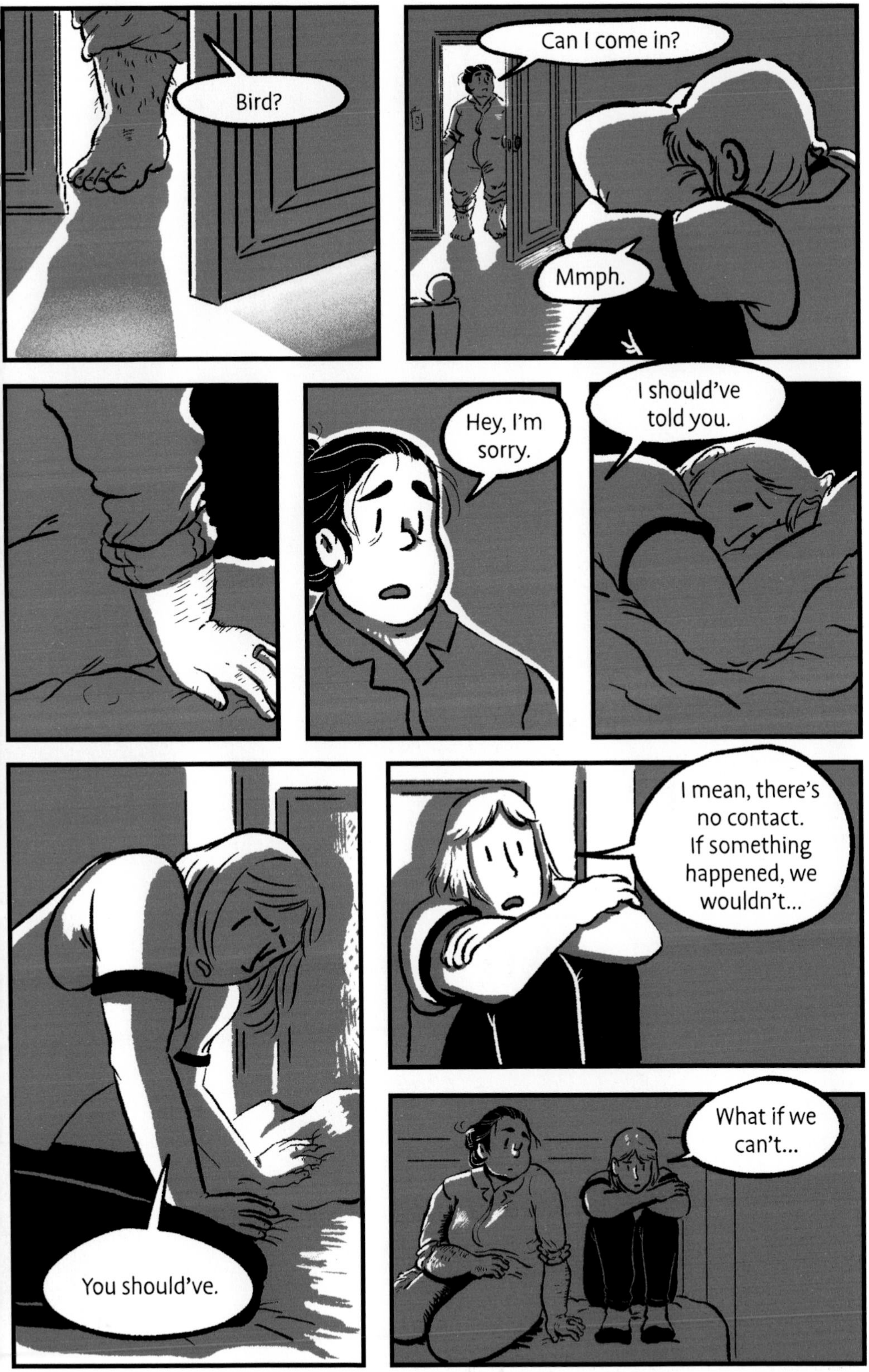
Bird?
Can I come in?
Mmph.
Hey, I'm sorry.
I should've told you.
You should've.
I mean, there's no contact. If something happened, we wouldn't...
What if we can't...

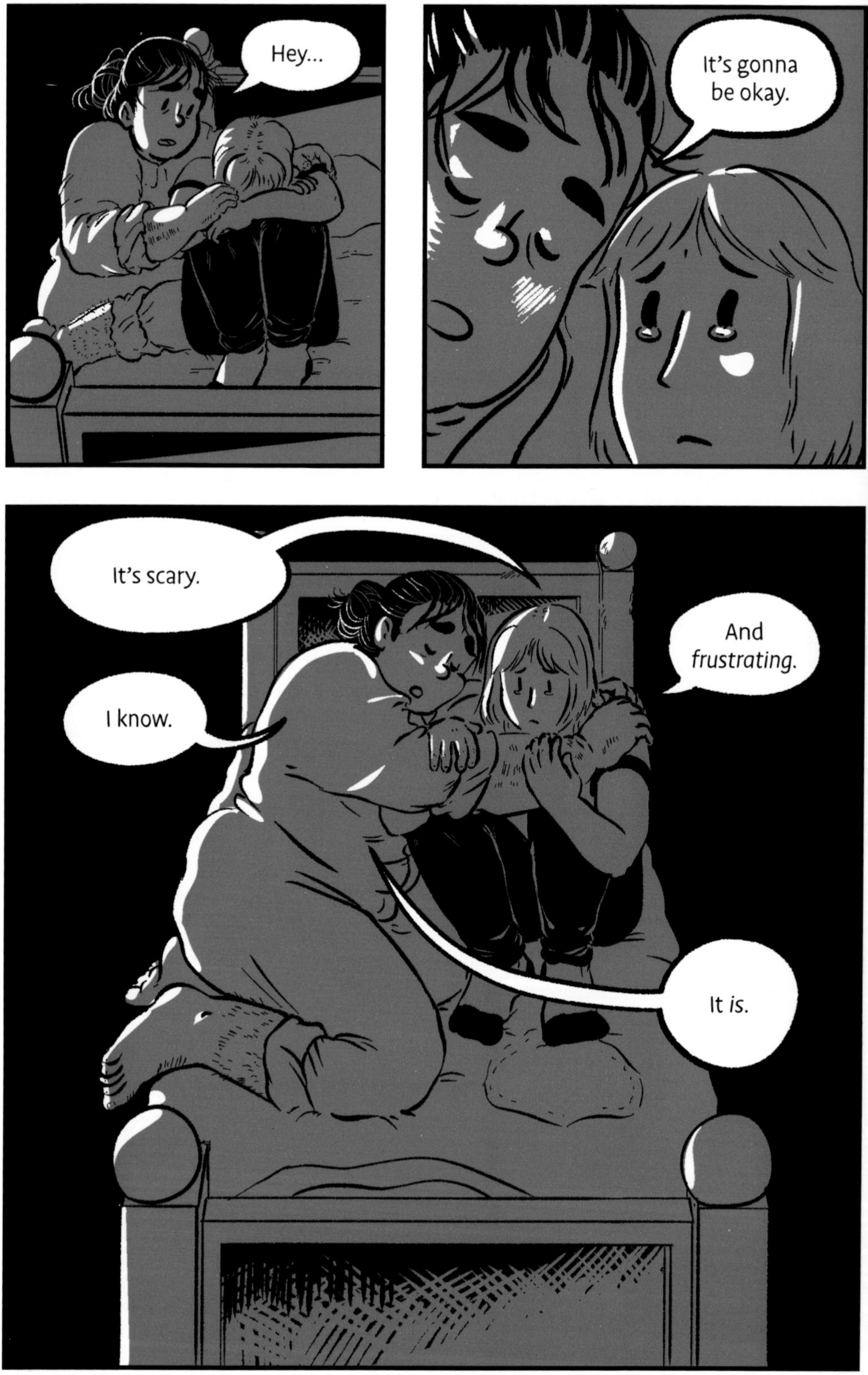
Hey...
It's gonna be okay.
It's scary.
And *frustrating*.
I know.
It *is*.

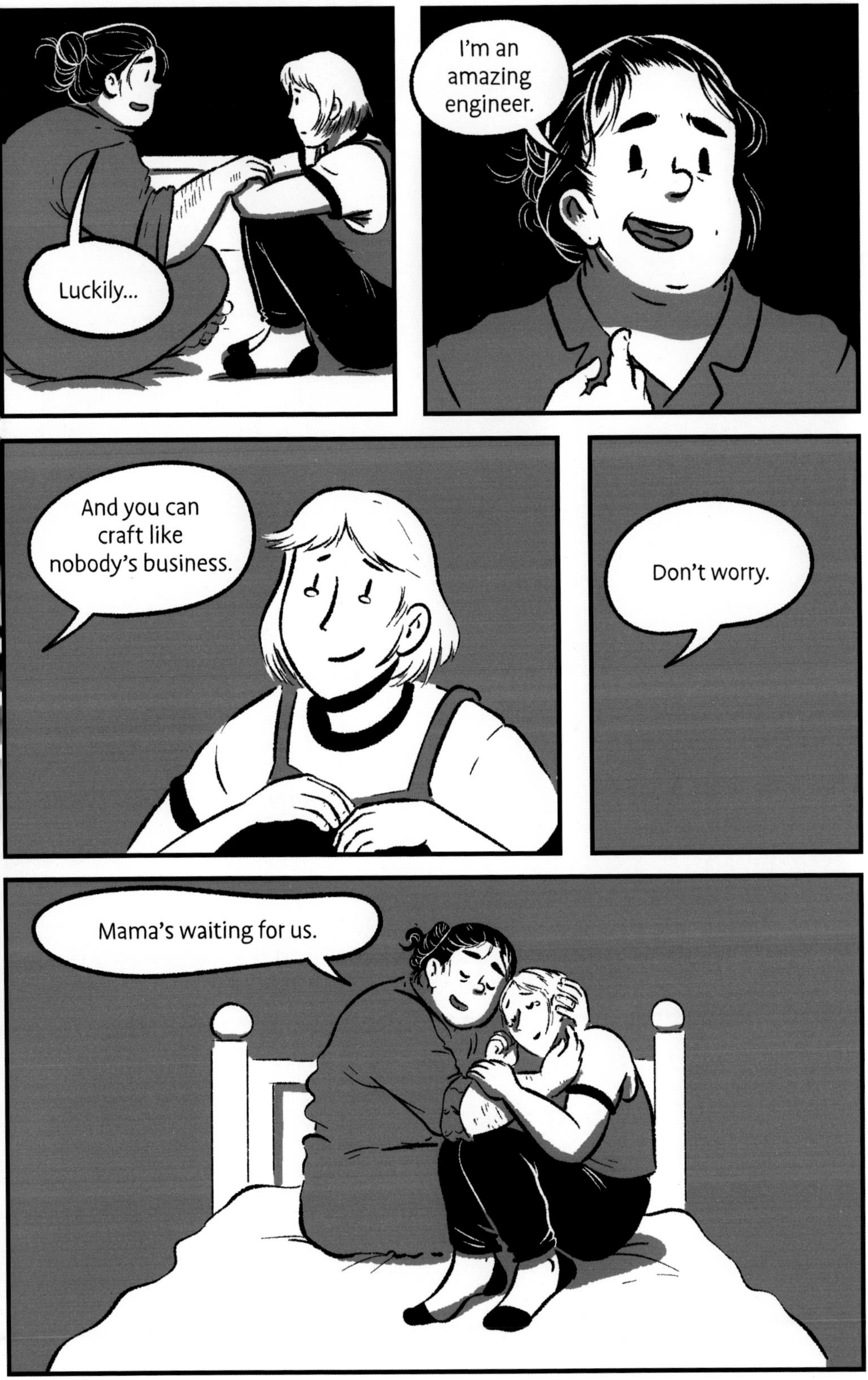
Luckily...
I'm an amazing engineer.
And you can craft like nobody's business.
Don't worry.
Mama's waiting for us.

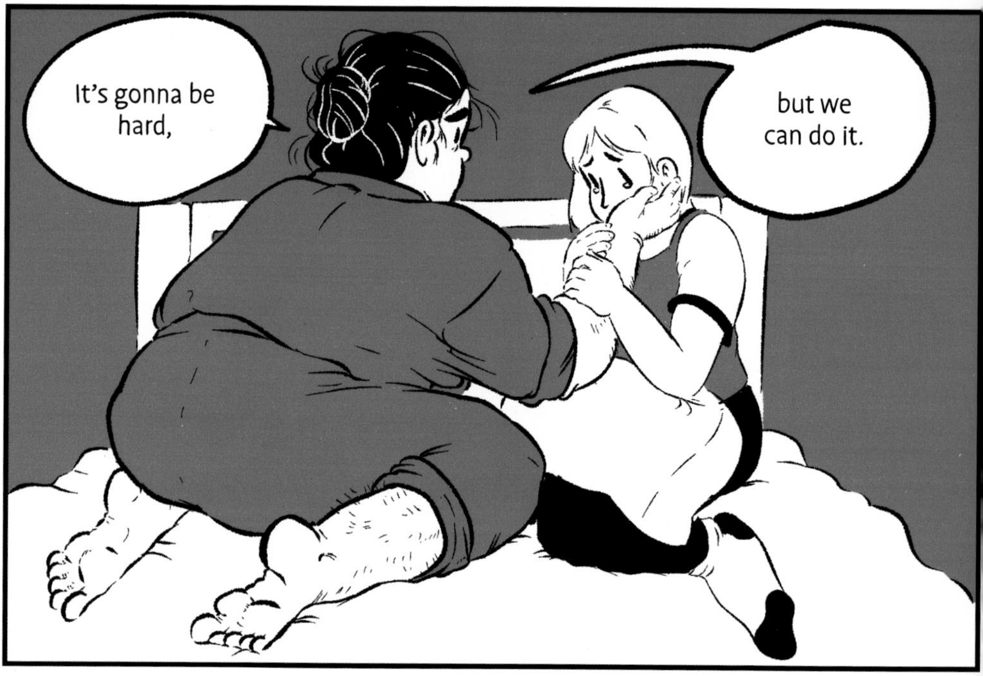
It's gonna be hard,
but we can do it.

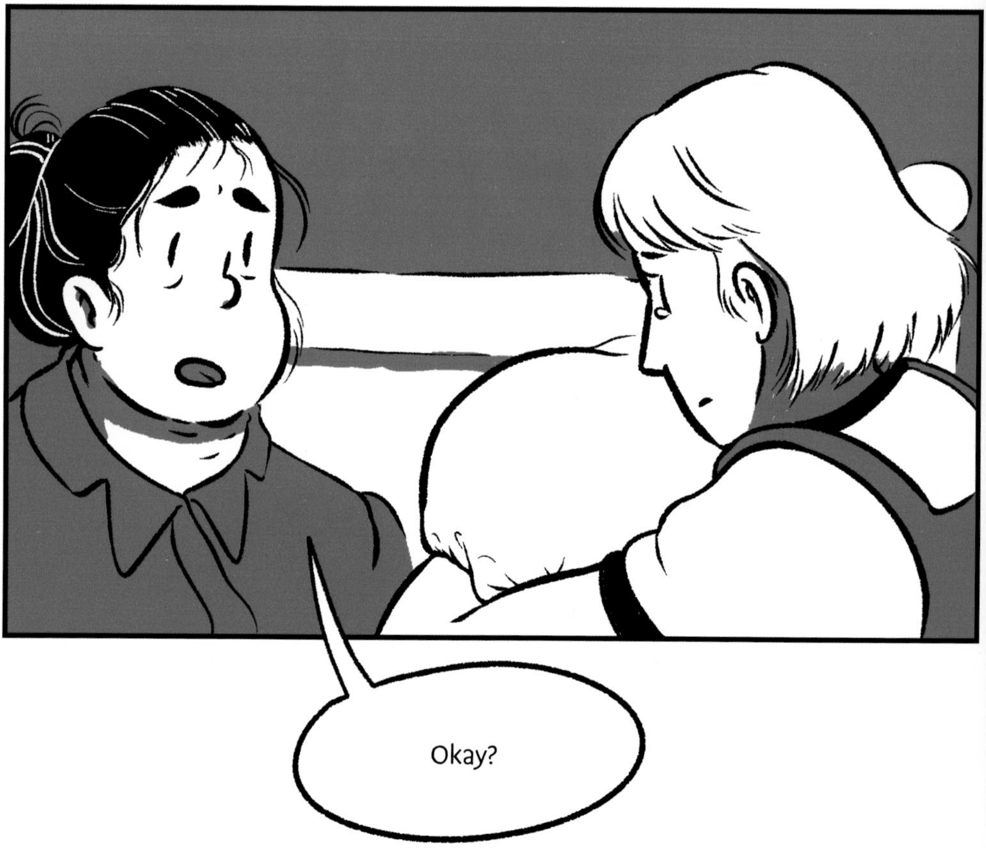
Okay?

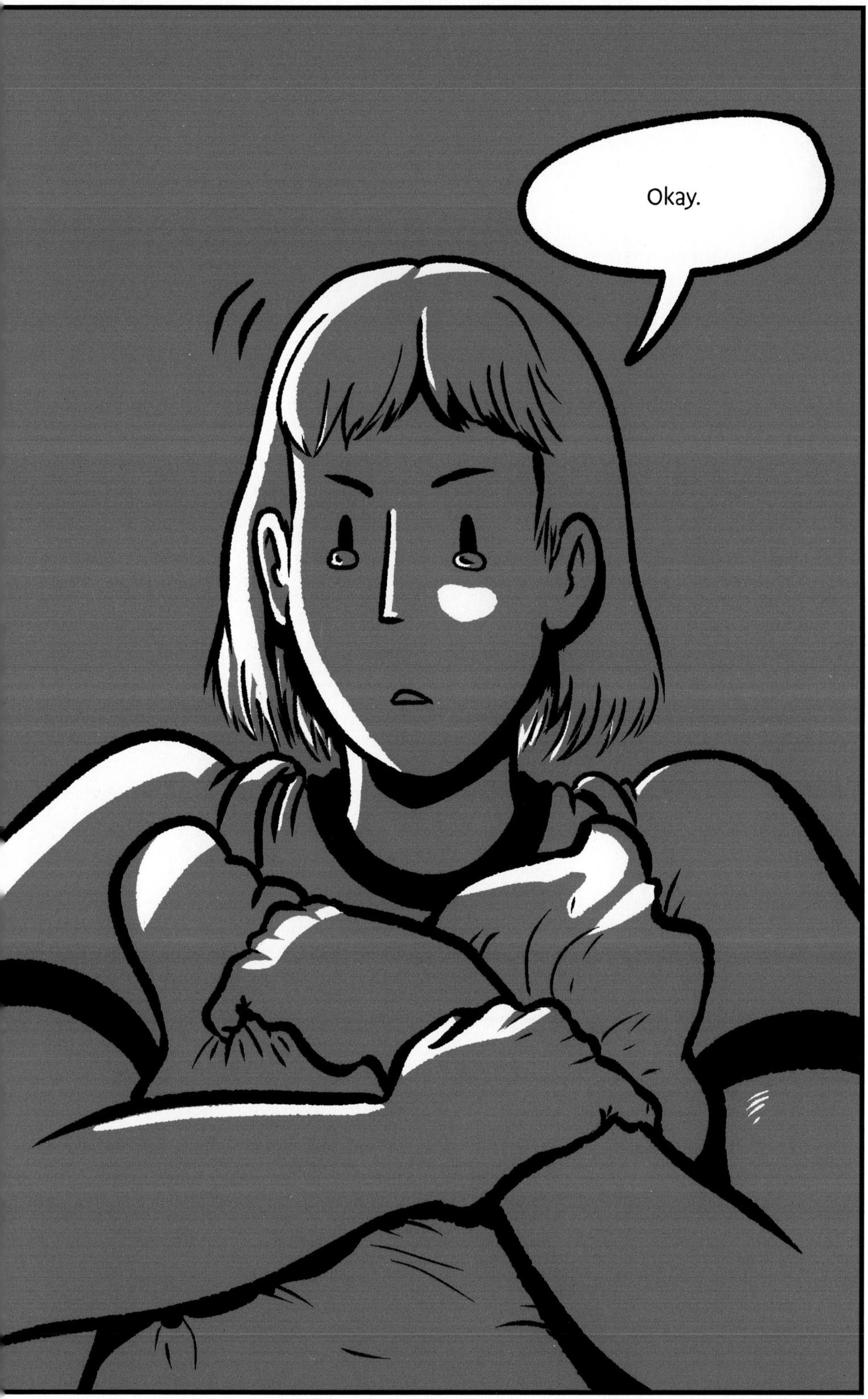
Okay.

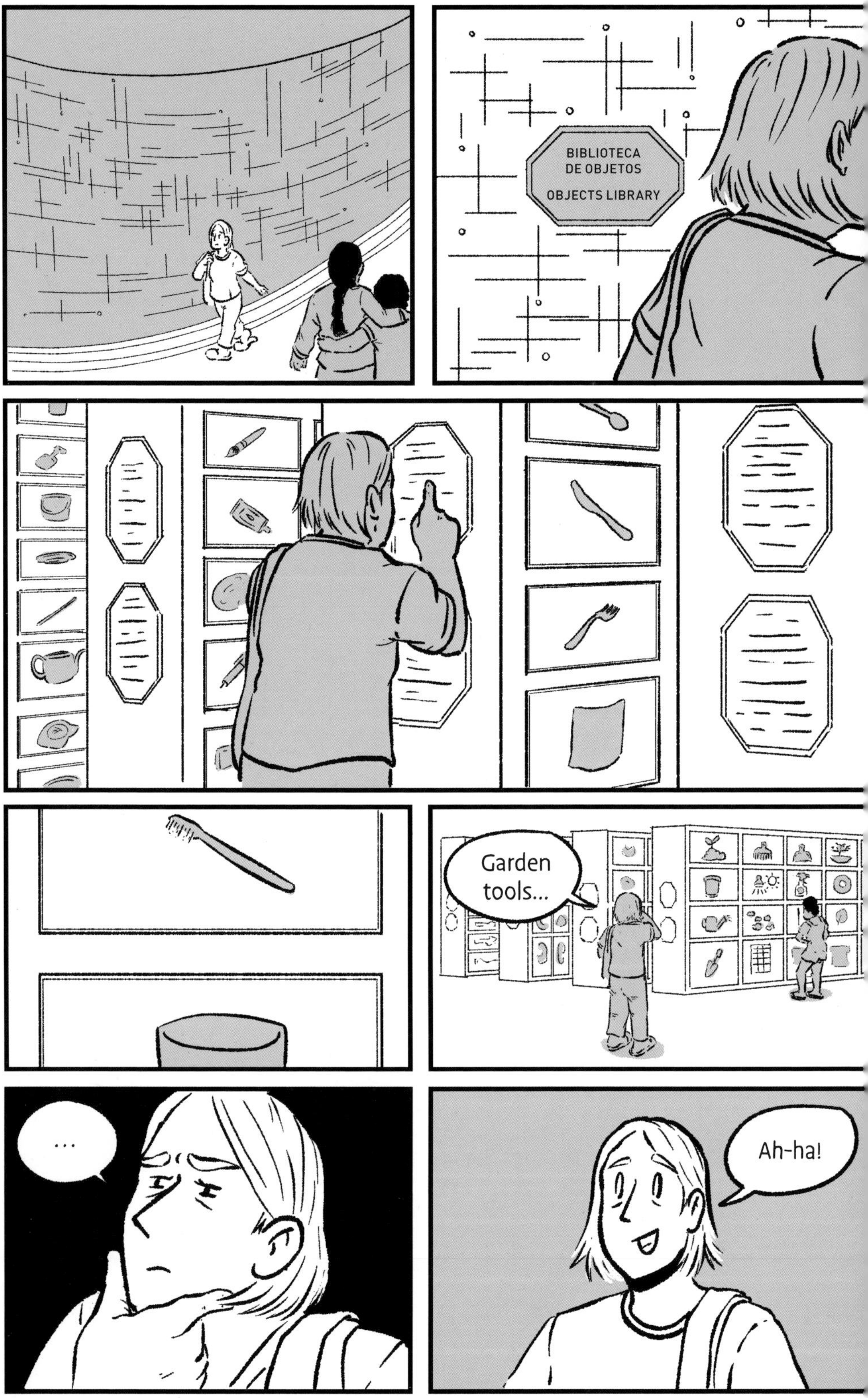

BIBLIOTECA
DE OBJETOS
OBJECTS LIBRARY
Garden tools...
...
Ah-ha!

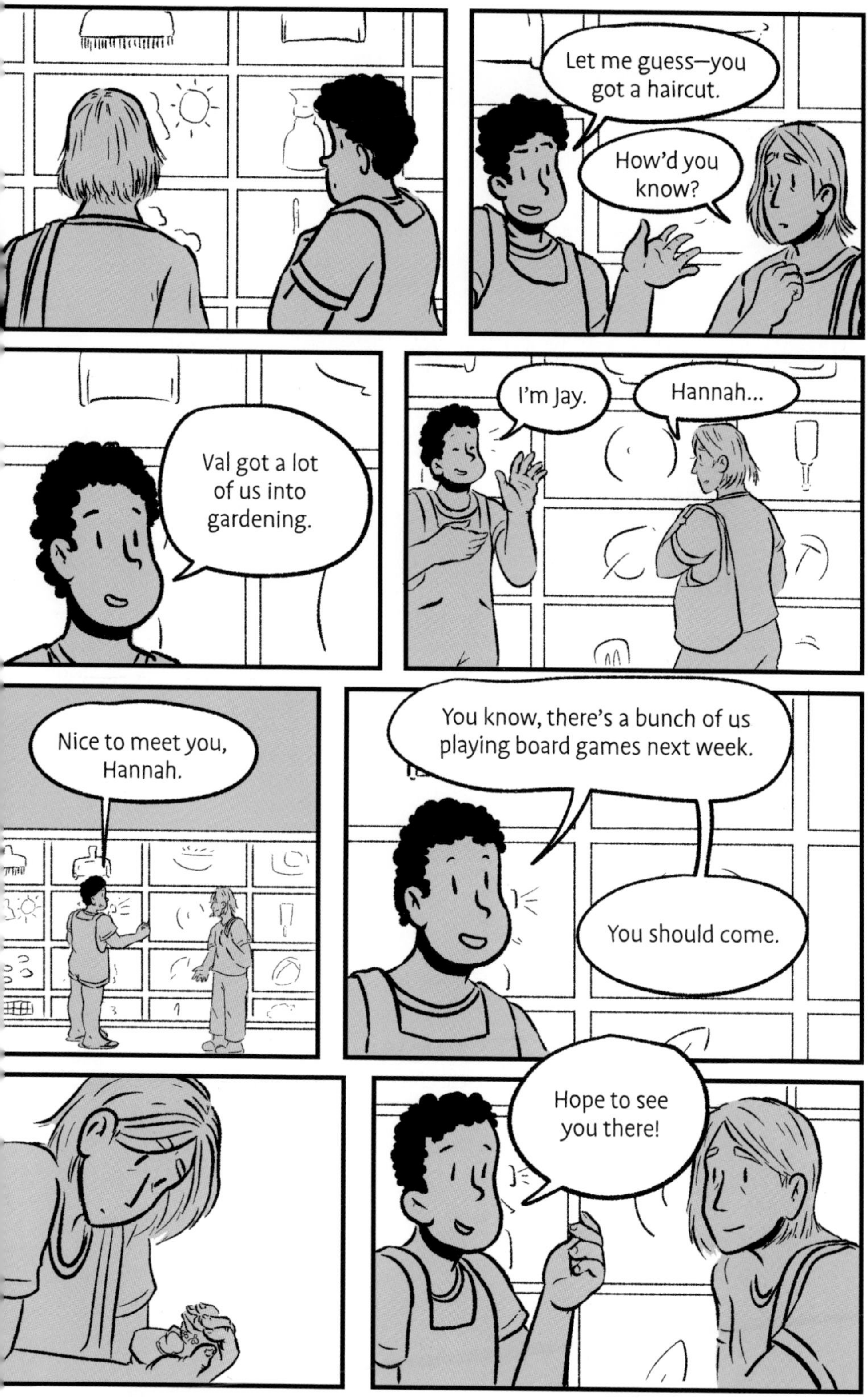
Let me guess—you got a haircut.
How'd you know?
Val got a lot of us into gardening.
I'm Jay.
Hannah...
Nice to meet you, Hannah.
You know, there's a bunch of us playing board games next week.
You should come.
Hope to see you there!

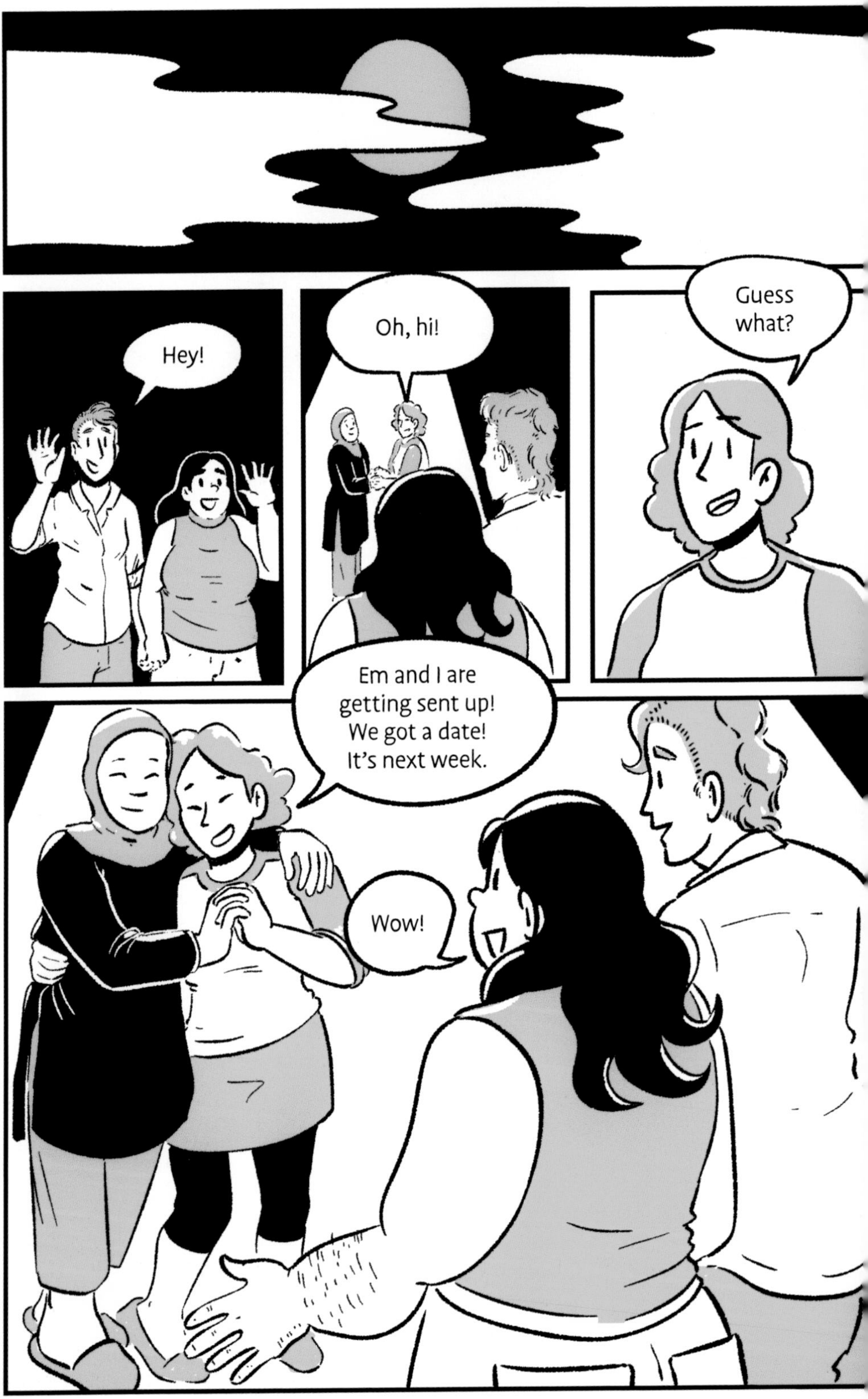

Hey!
Oh, hi!
Guess what?
Em and I are getting sent up! We got a date! It's next week.
Wow!

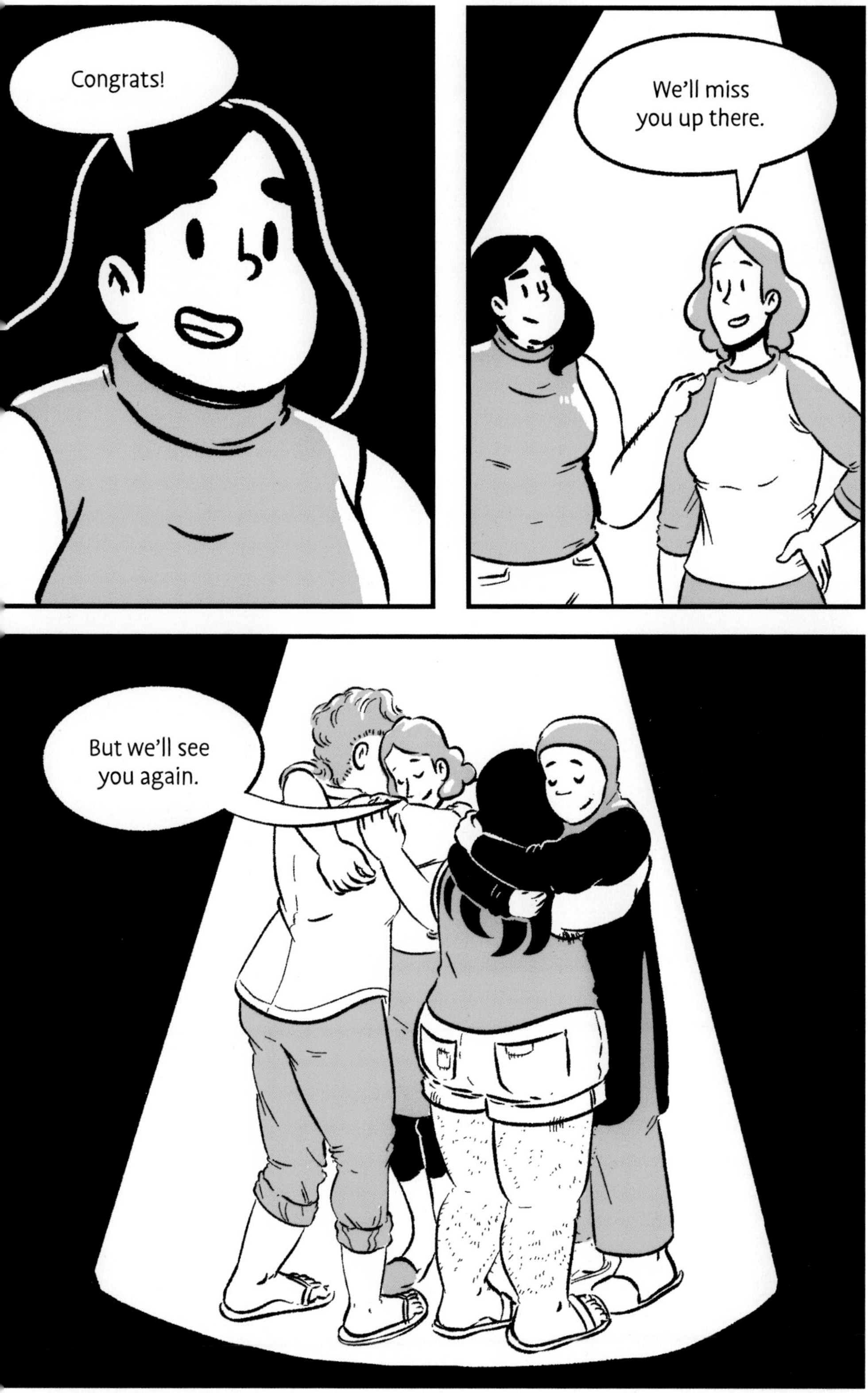
Congrats!
We'll miss you up there.
But we'll see you again.

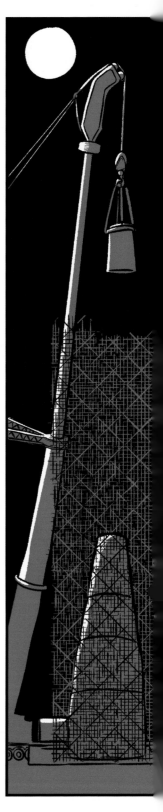

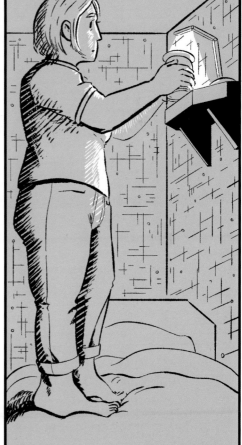

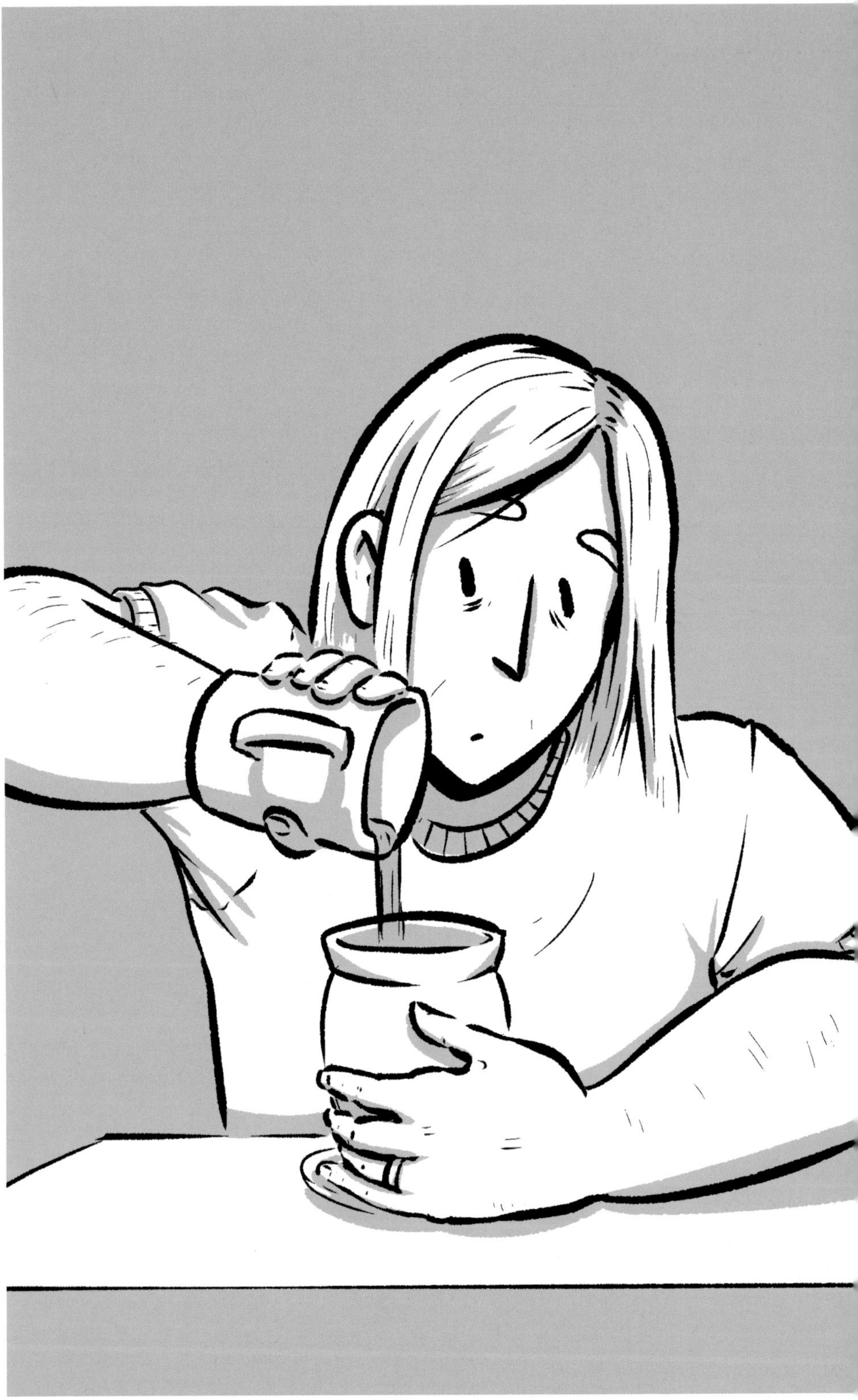

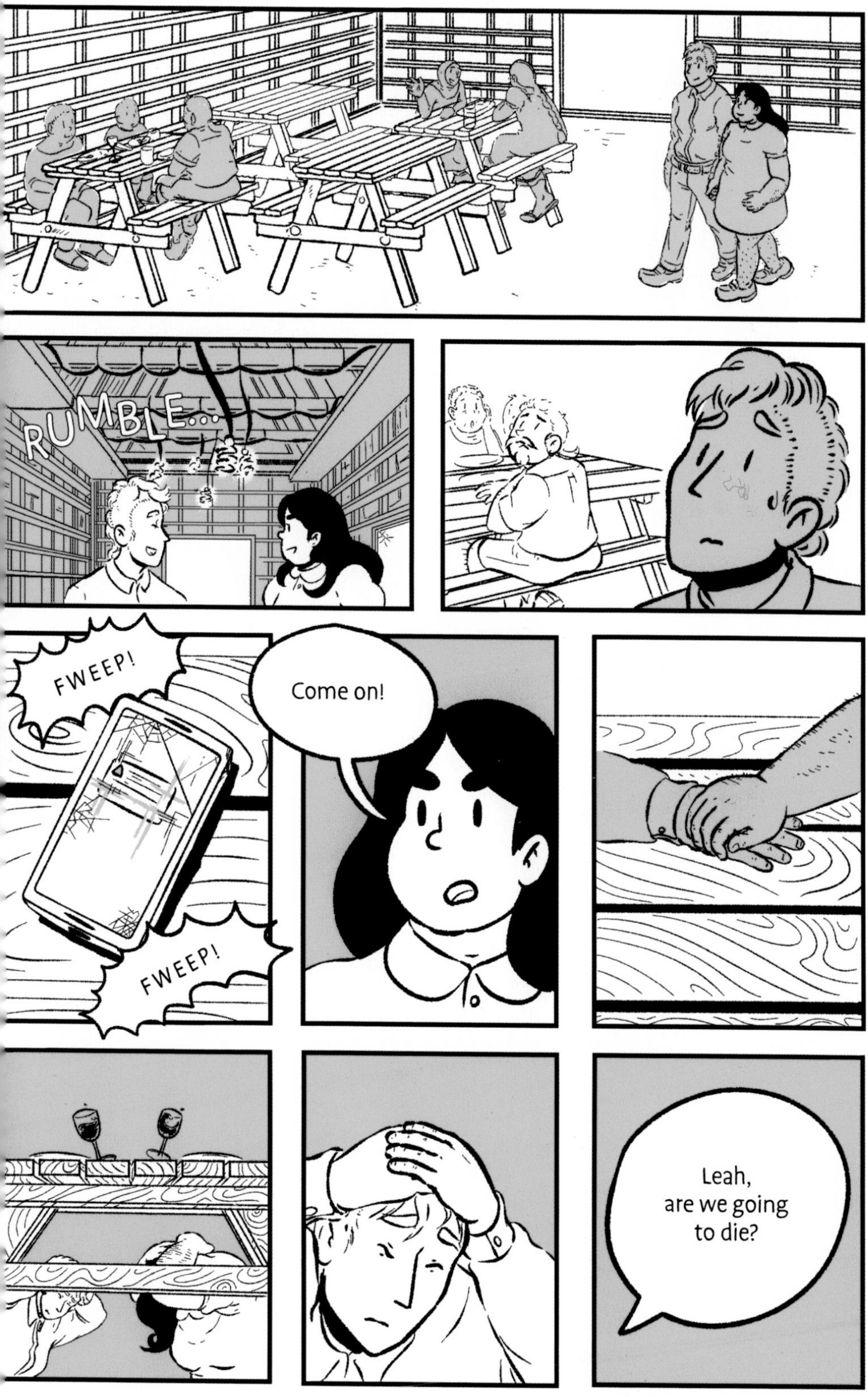
RUMBLE...
FWEEP!
FWEEP!
Come on!
Leah,
are we going
to die?

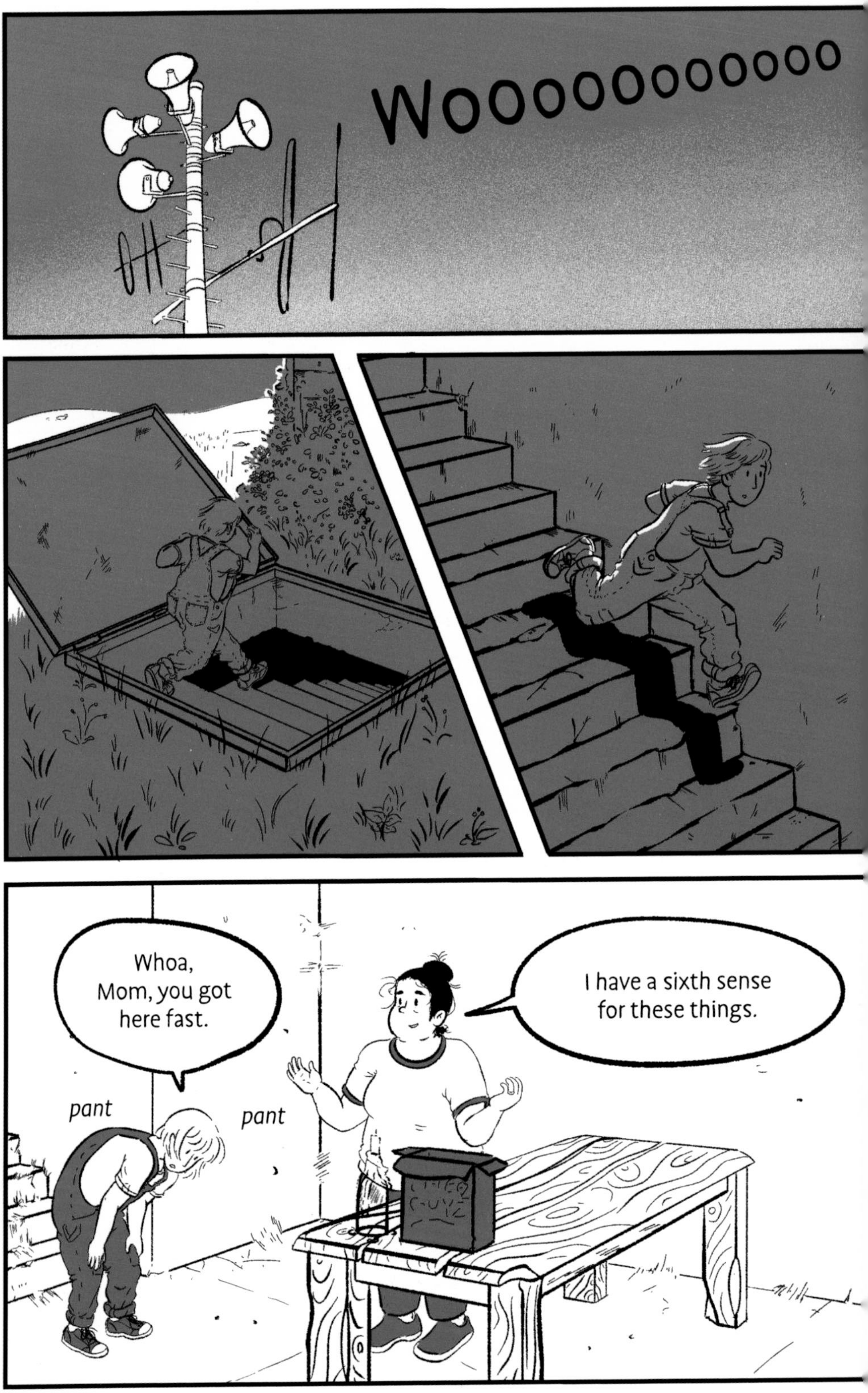
Wooooooooooo
Whoa, Mom, you got here fast.
pant
pant
I have a sixth sense for these things.

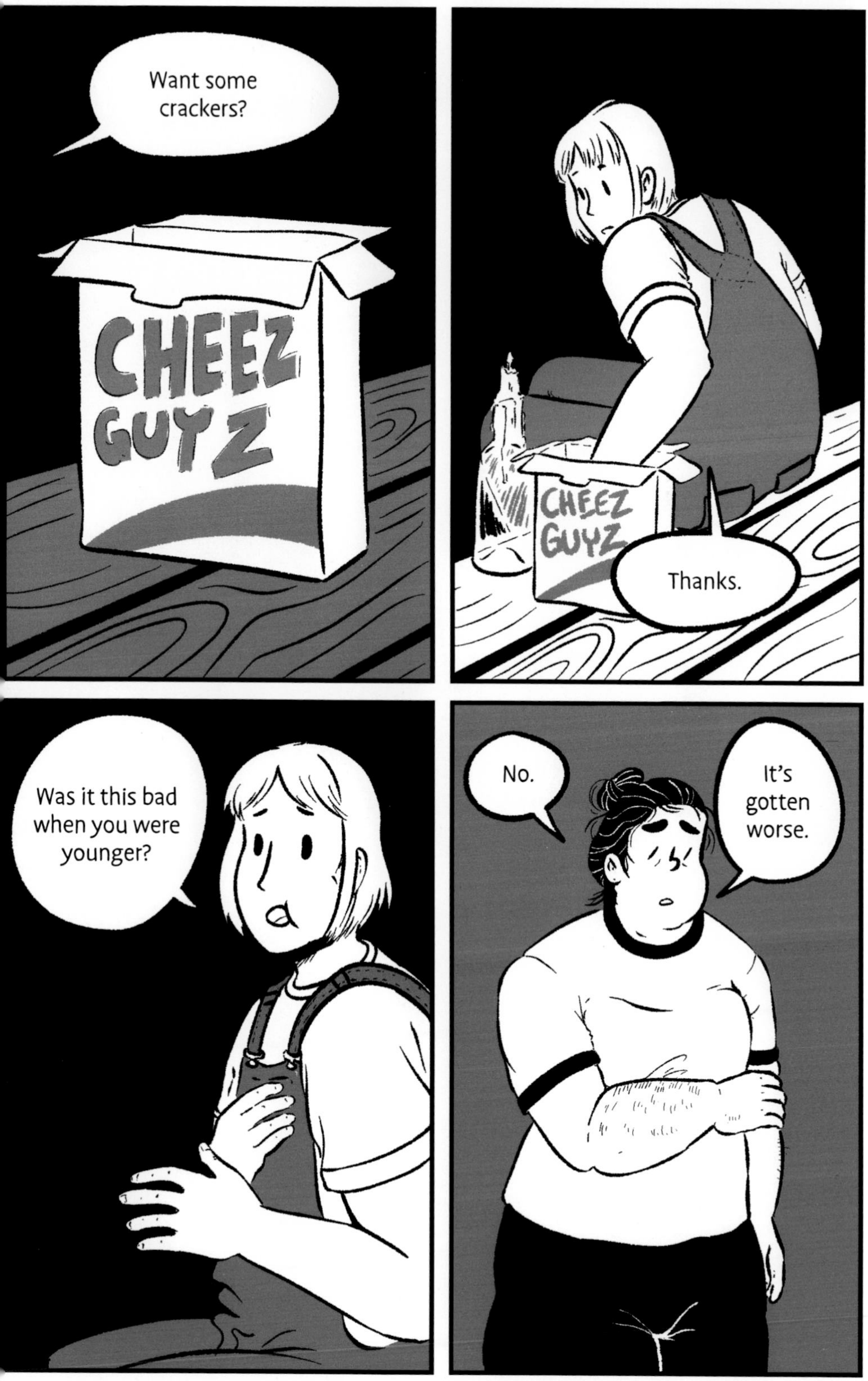
Want some crackers?
CHEEZ GUYZ
CHEEZ GUYZ
Thanks.
Was it this bad when you were younger?
No.
It's gotten worse.

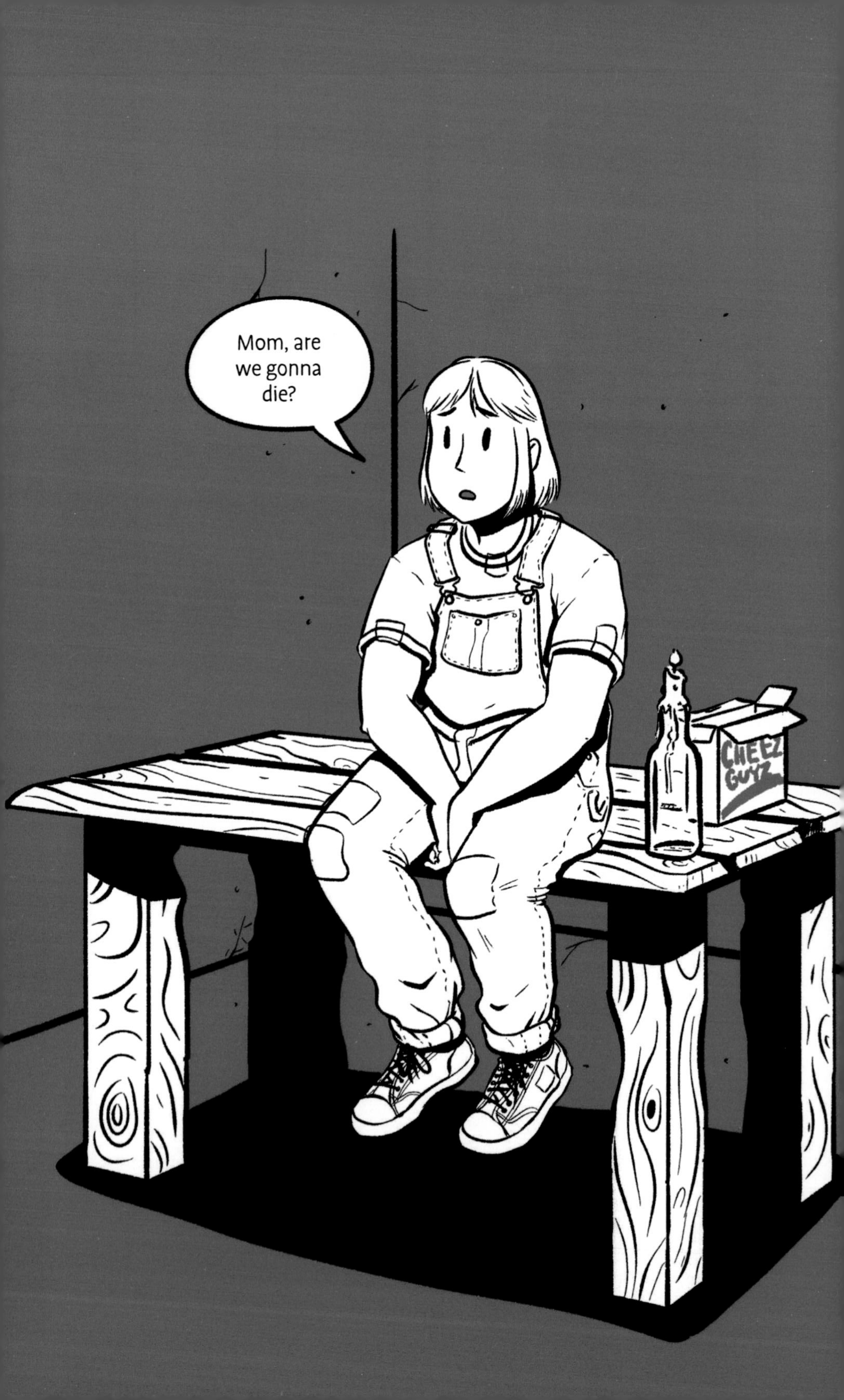
Mom, are we gonna die?
CHEEZ GUYZ

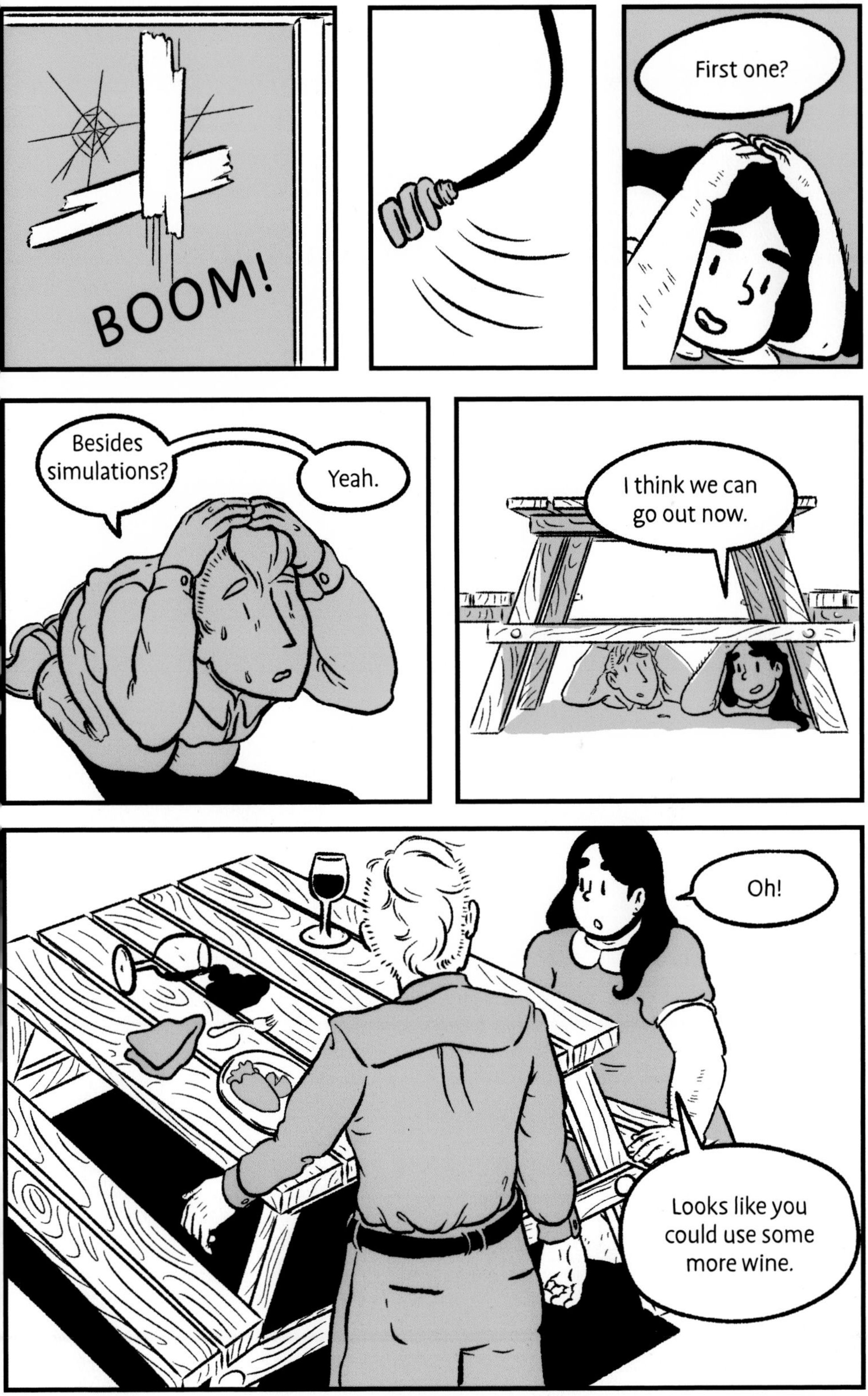
BOOM!
First one?
Besides simulations?
Yeah.
I think we can go out now.
Oh!
Looks like you could use some more wine.

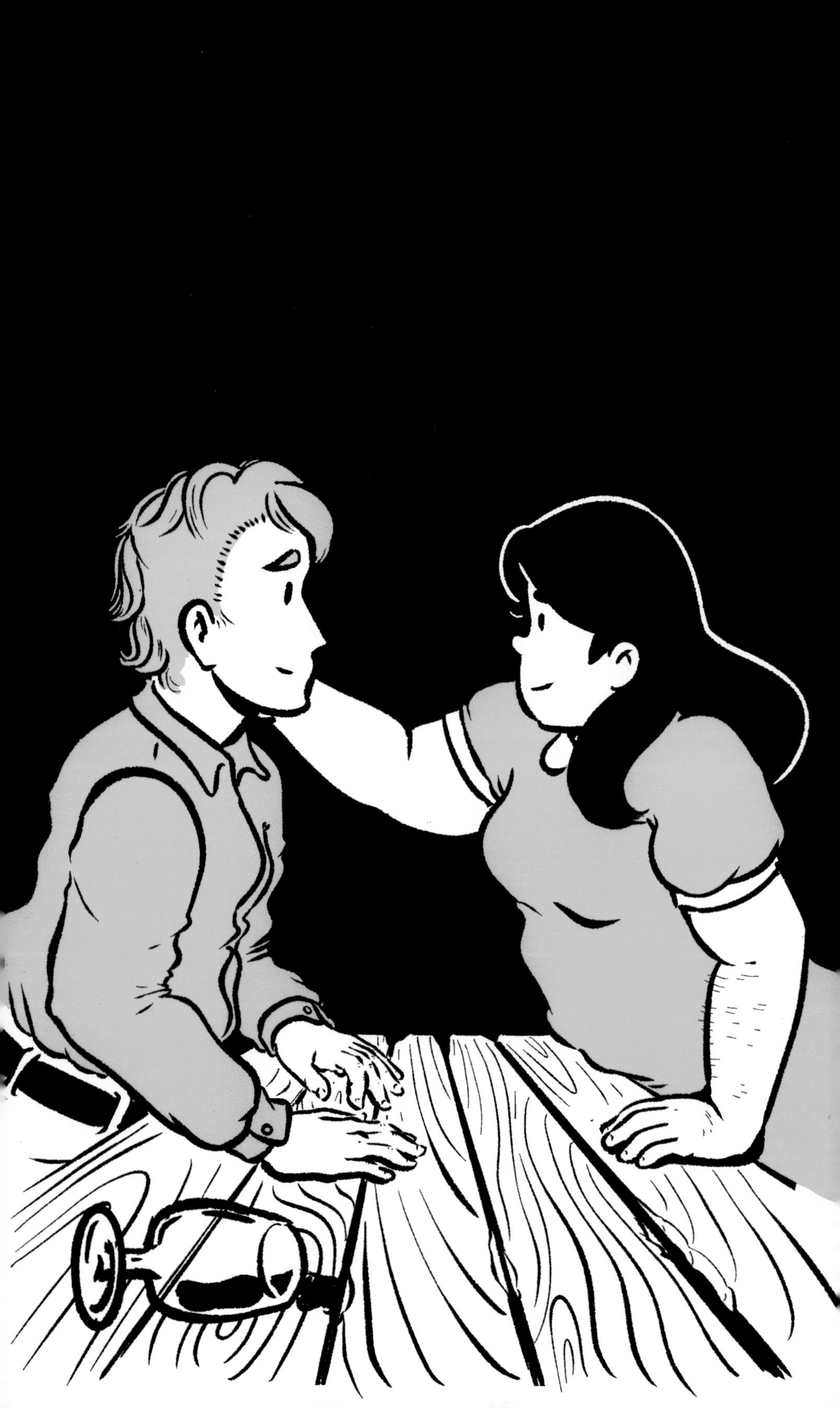

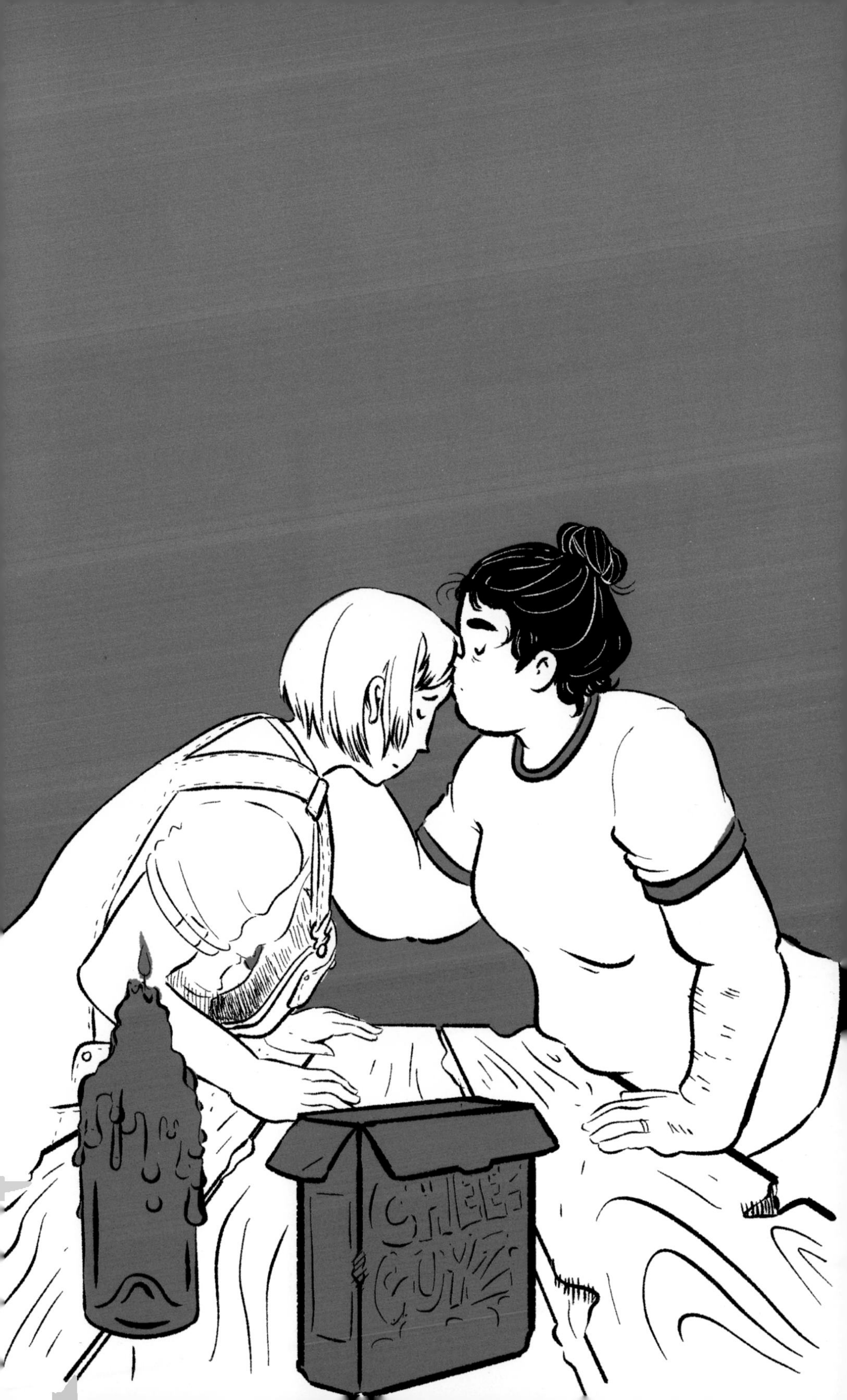
CHEES
GUYZ

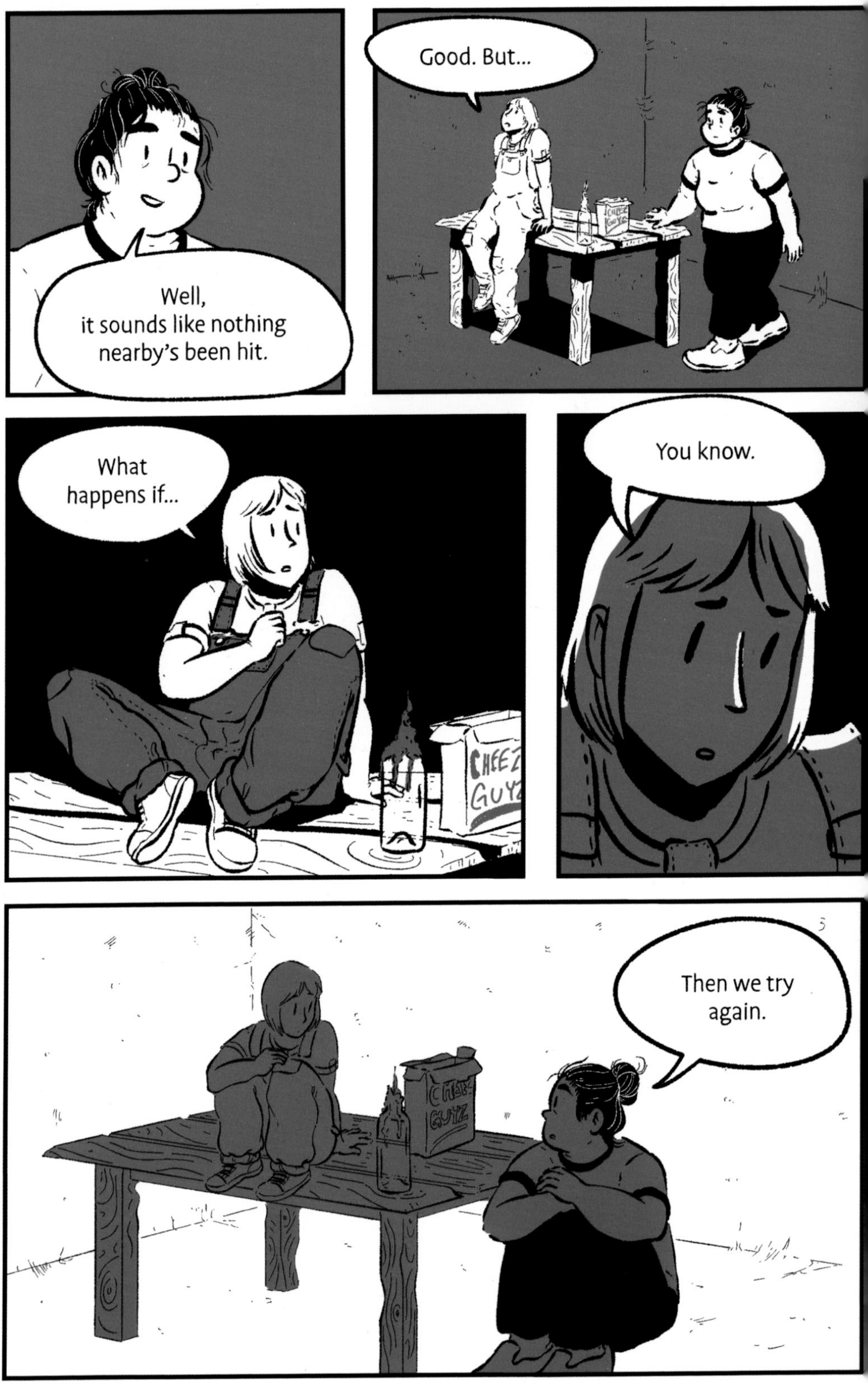
Well,
it sounds like nothing
nearby's been hit.
Good. But...
What
happens if...
You know.
CHEEZ GUYZ
Then we try
again.

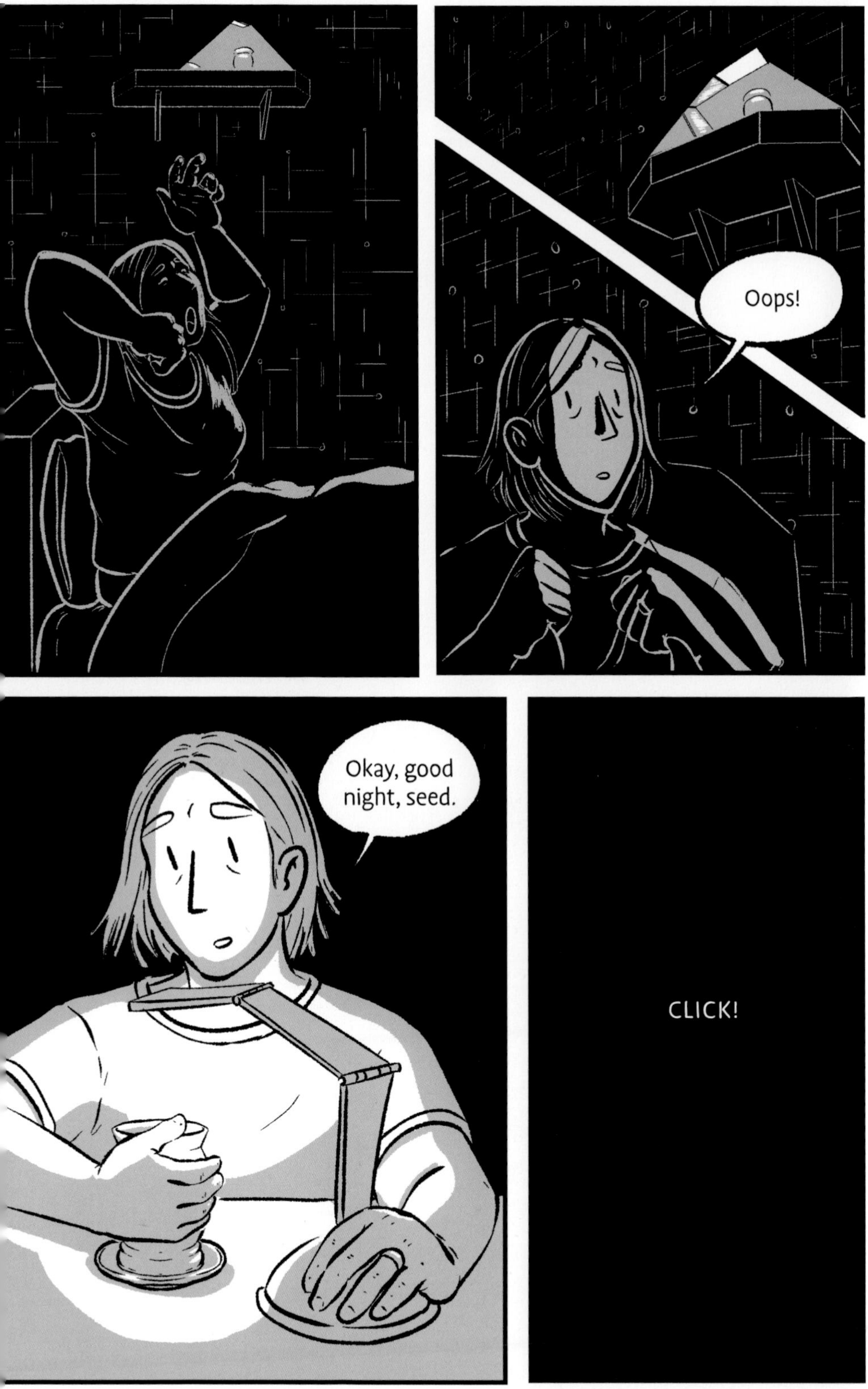
Oops!
Okay, good night, seed.
CLICK!

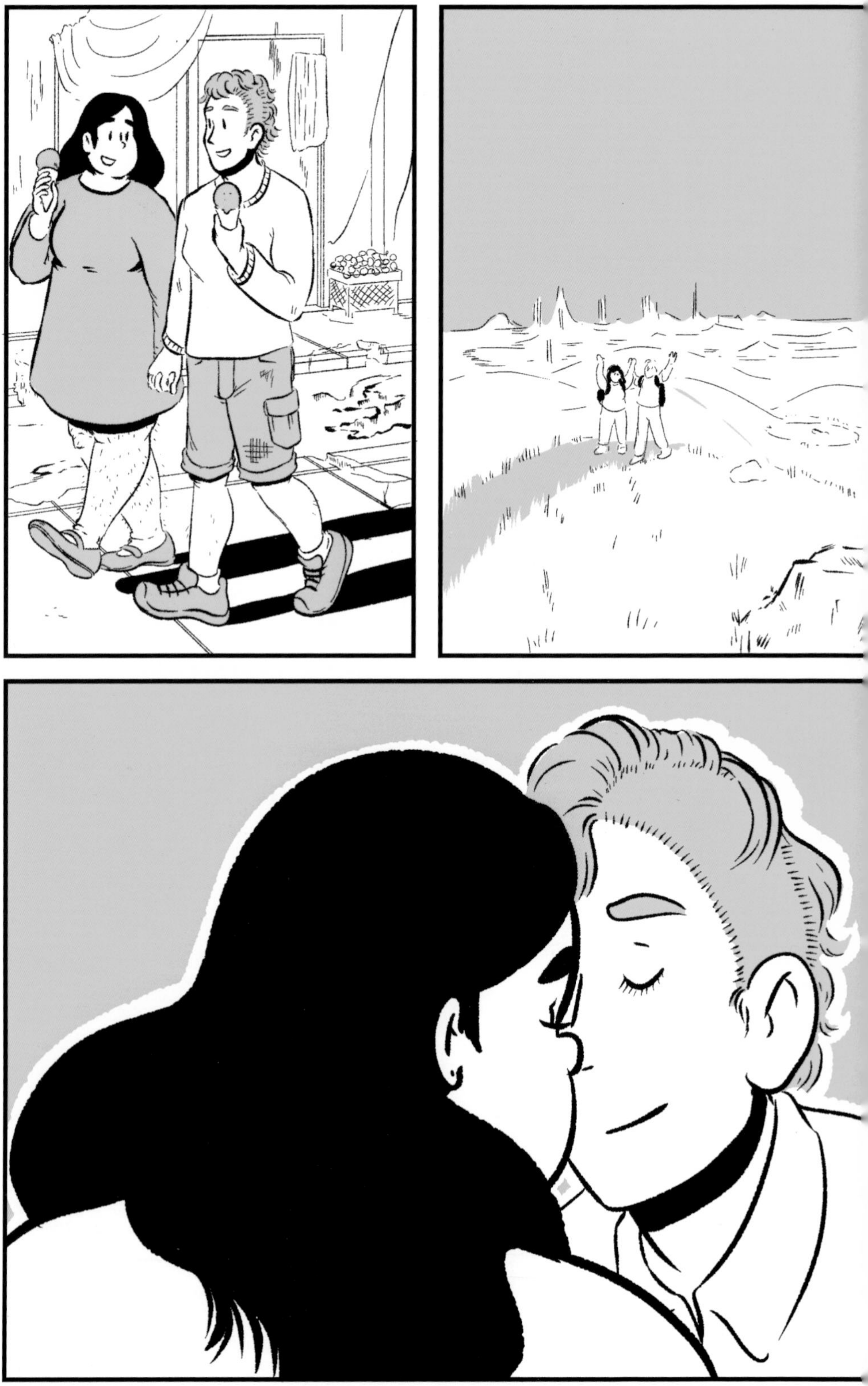

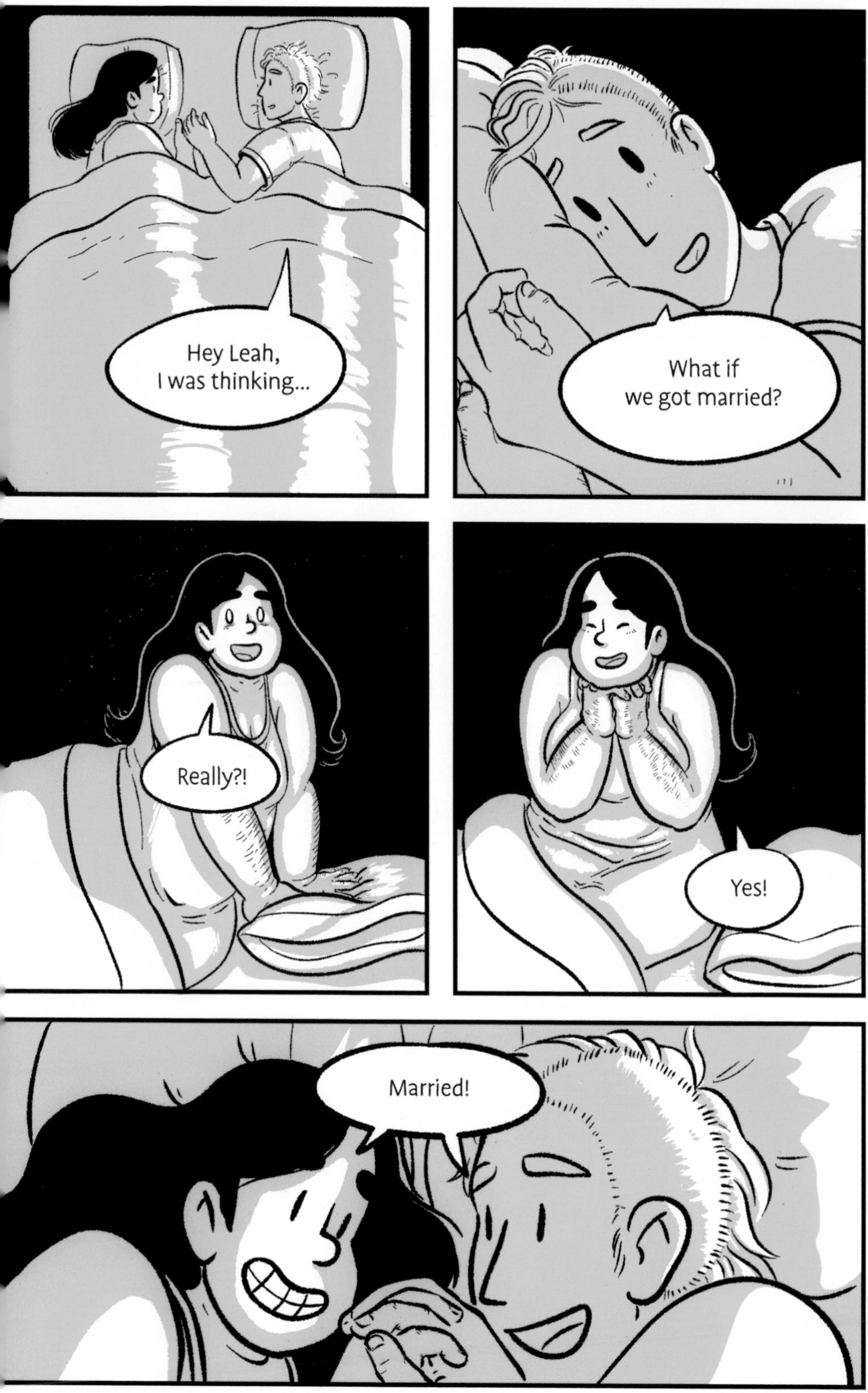
Hey Leah,
I was thinking...
What if
we got married?
Really?!
Yes!
Married!

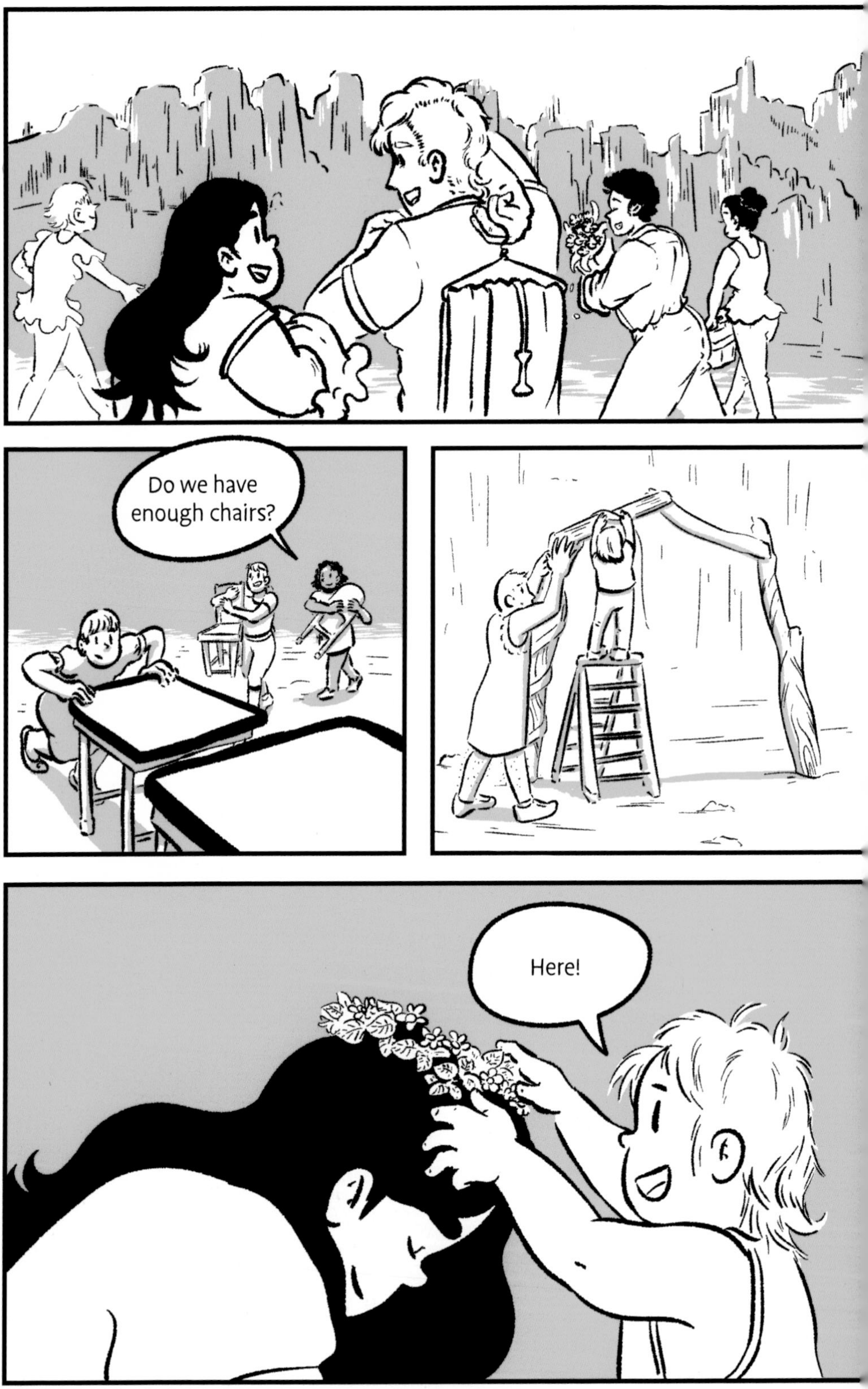
Do we have enough chairs?
Here!

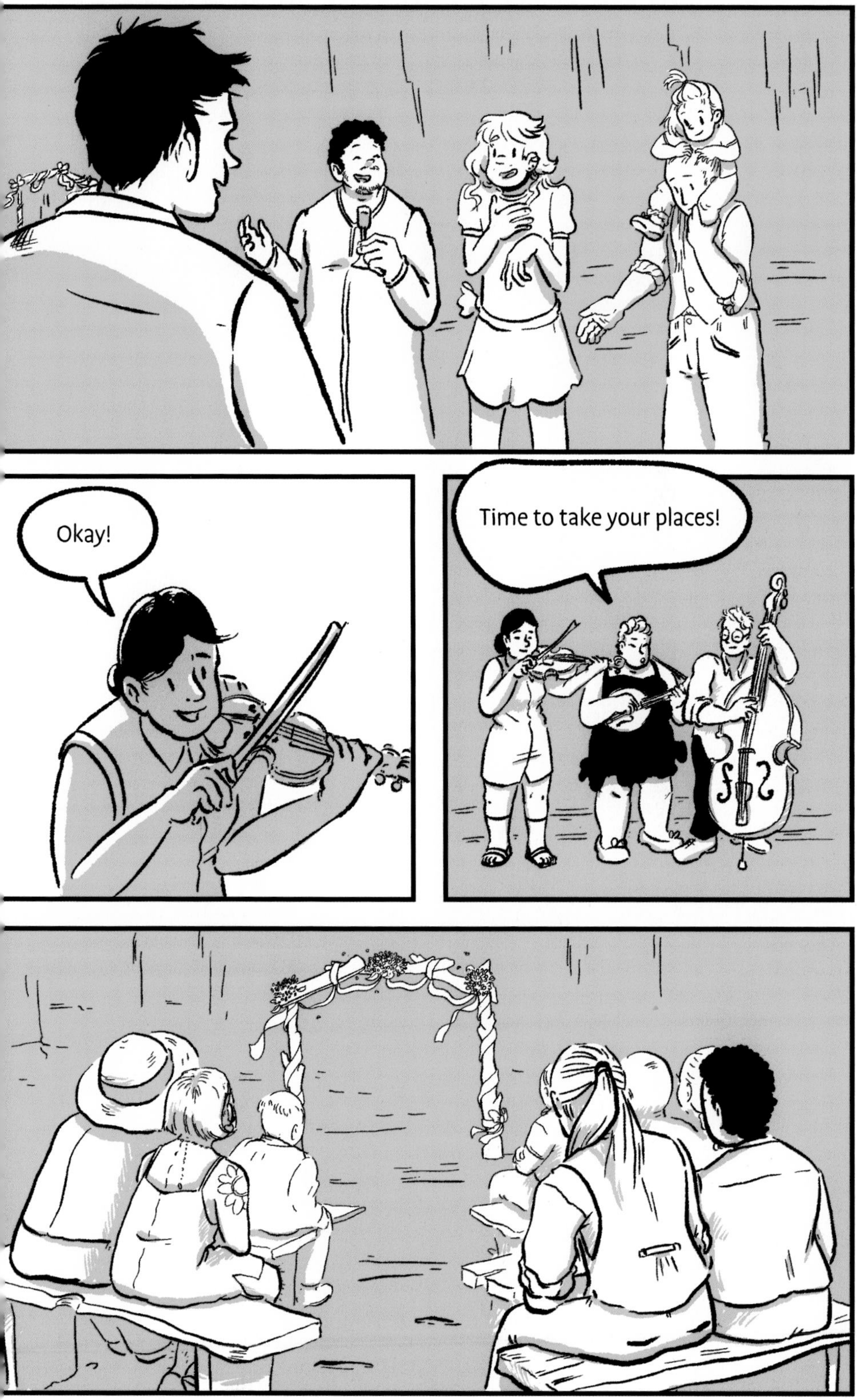
Okay!
Time to take your places!

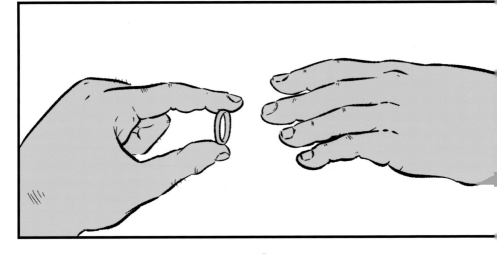

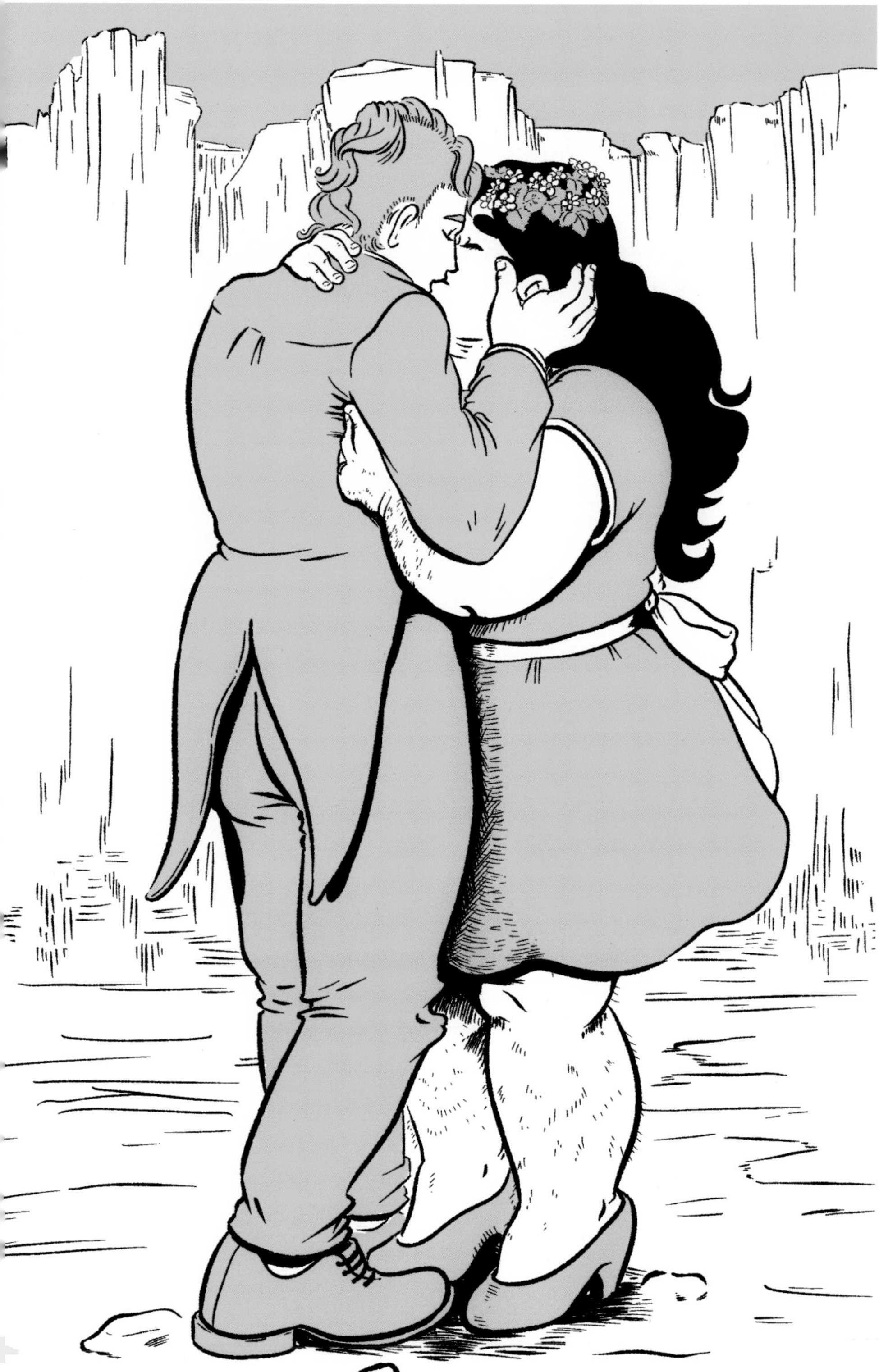

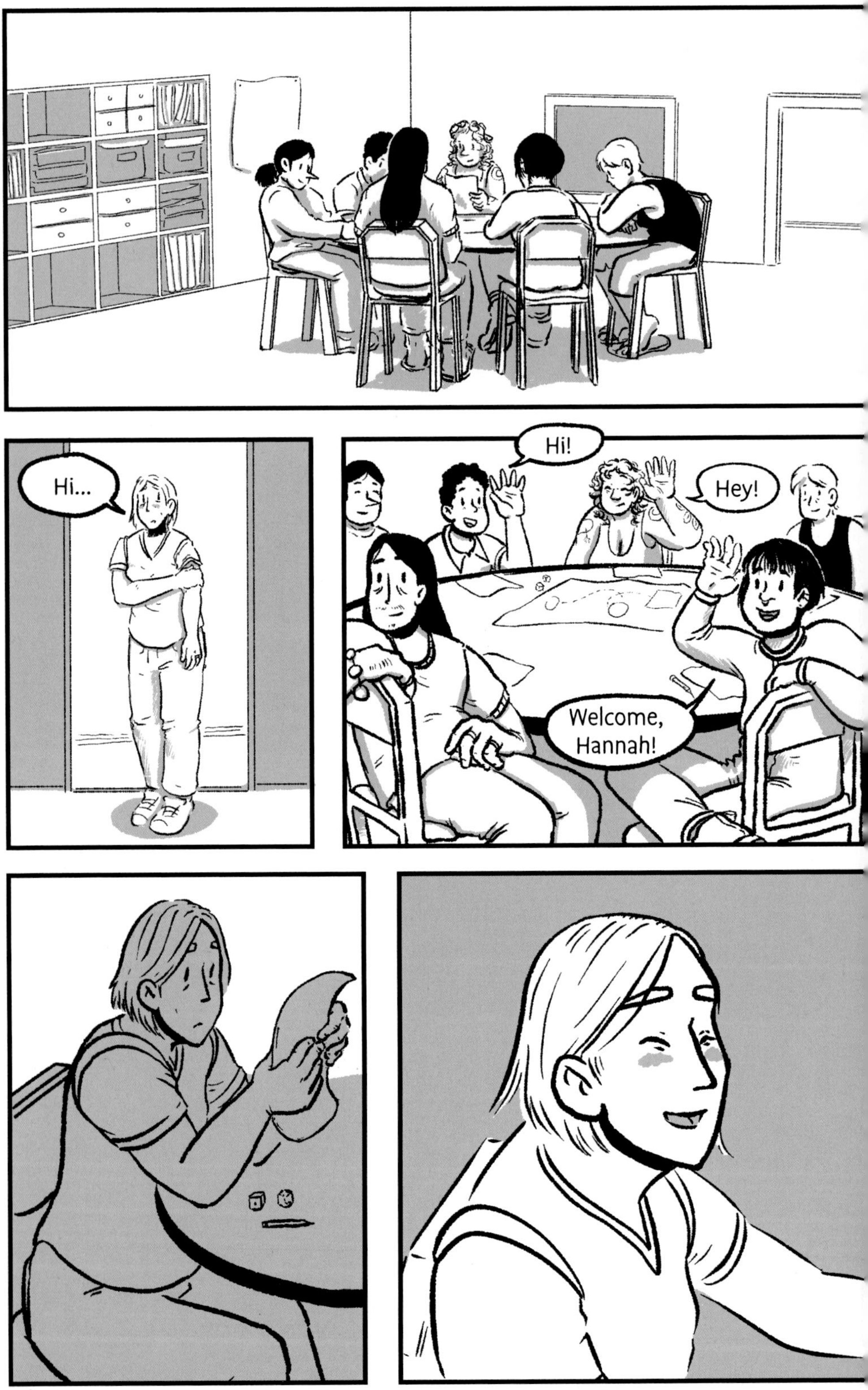
Hi...
Hi!
Hey!
Welcome,
Hannah!

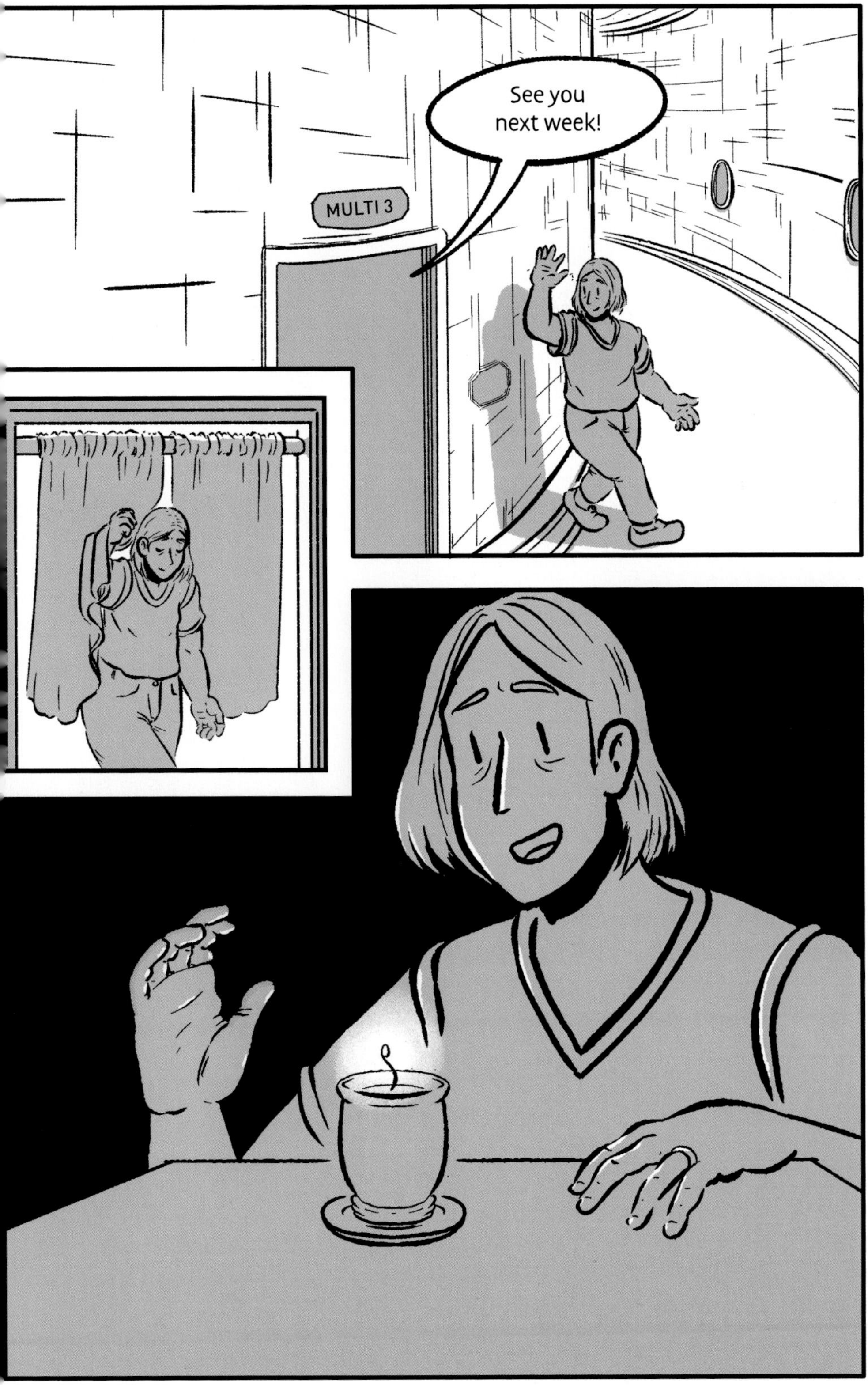
See you next week!
MULTI 3

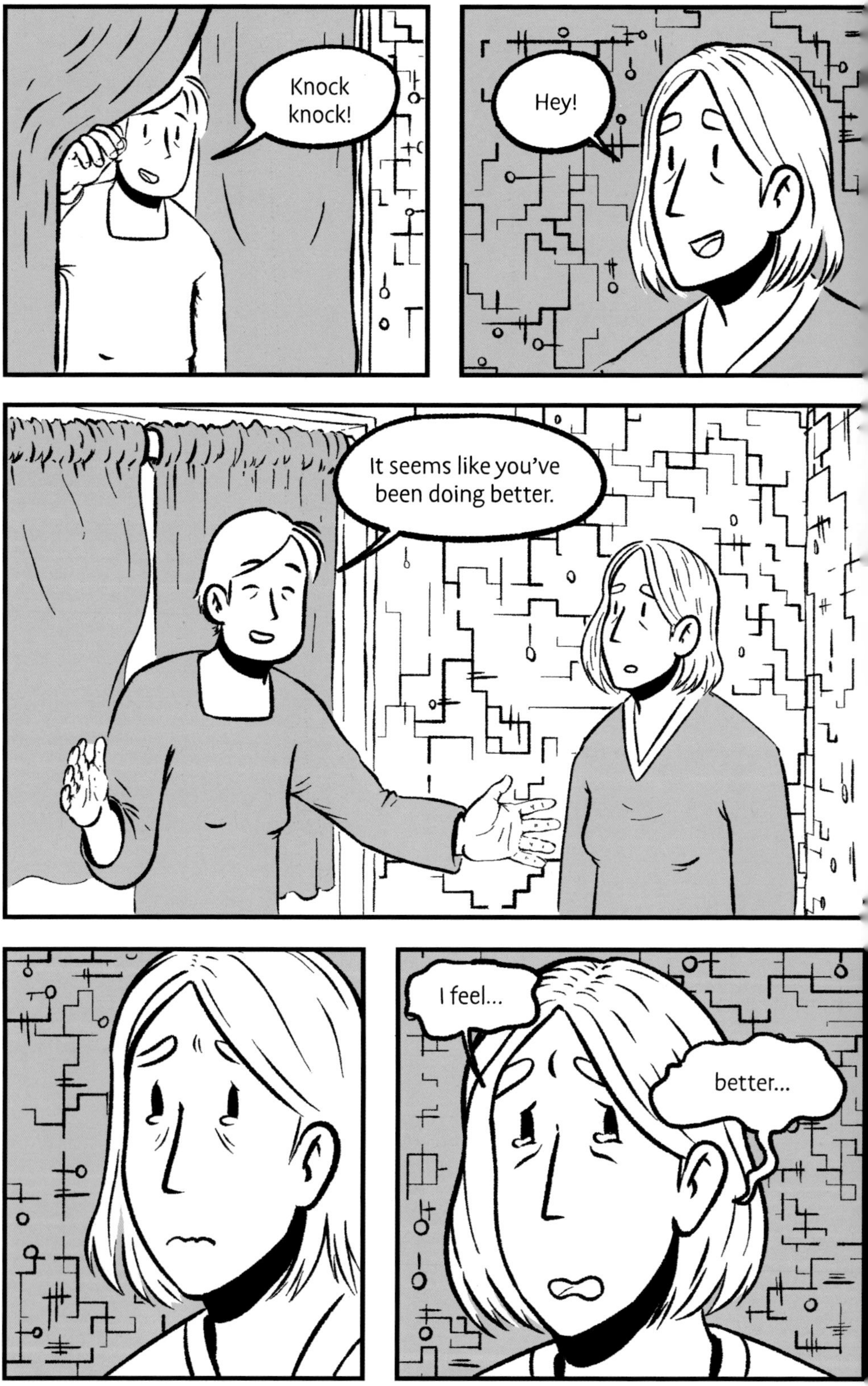
Knock knock!
Hey!
It seems like you've been doing better.
I feel...
better...

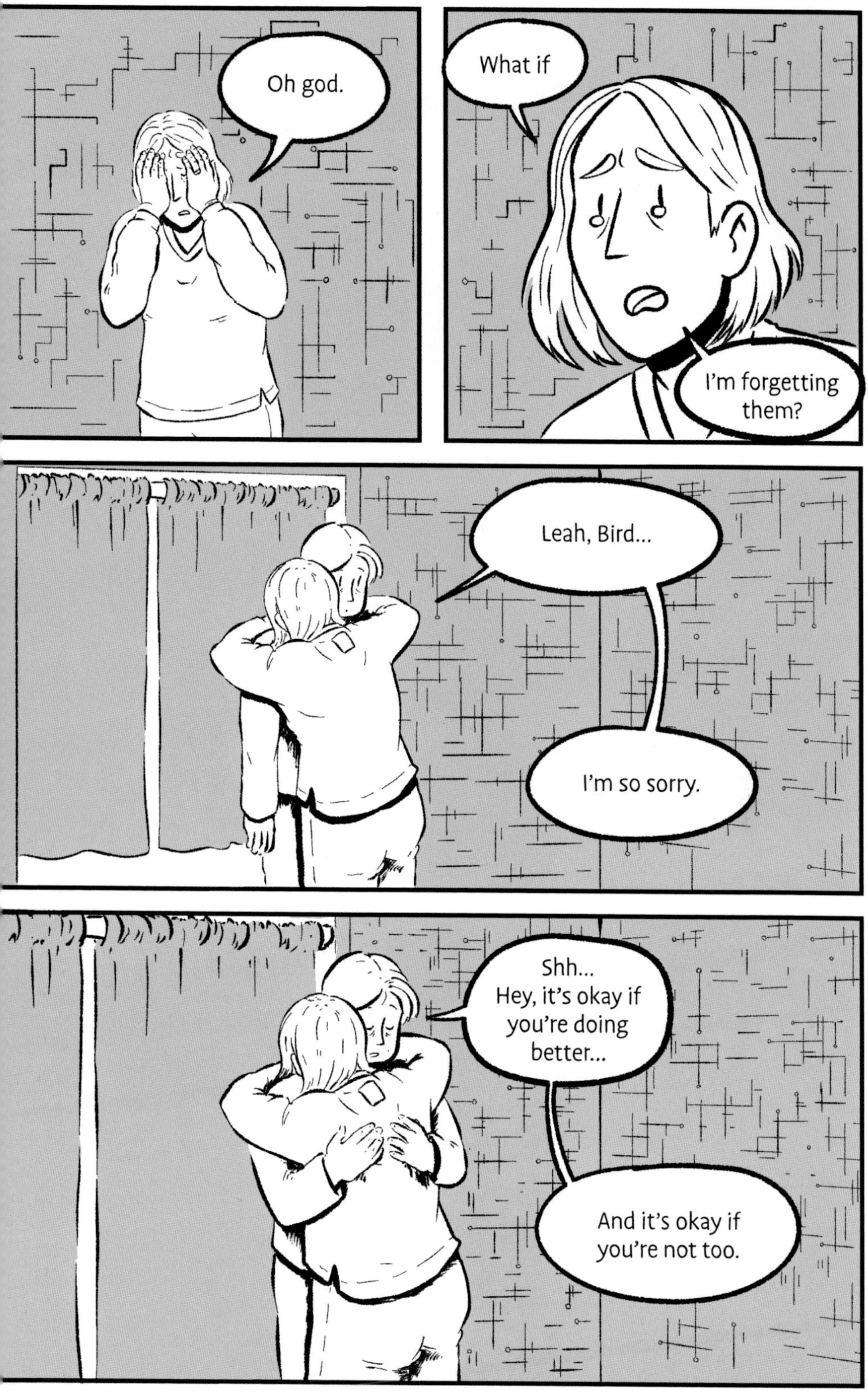
Oh god.
What if
I'm forgetting them?
Leah, Bird...
I'm so sorry.
Shh...
Hey, it's okay if you're doing better...
And it's okay if you're not too.

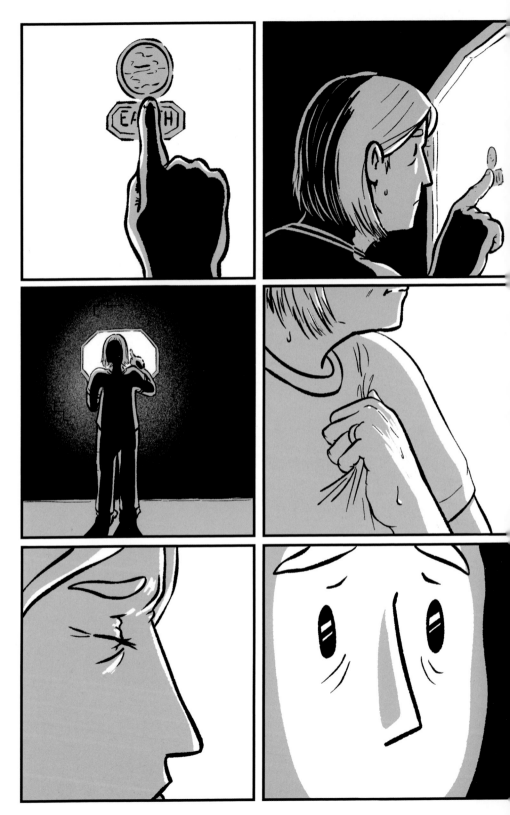

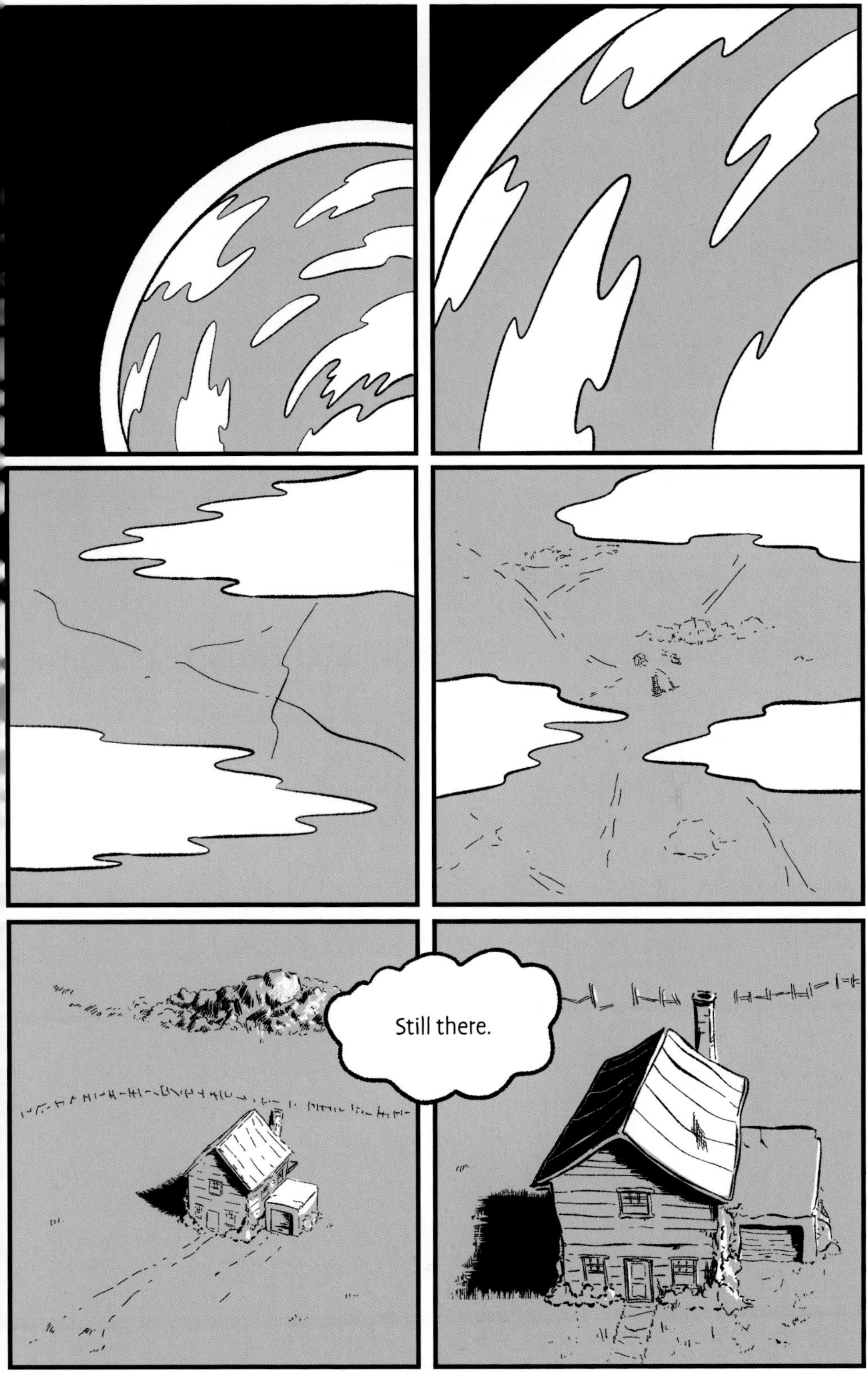
Still there.

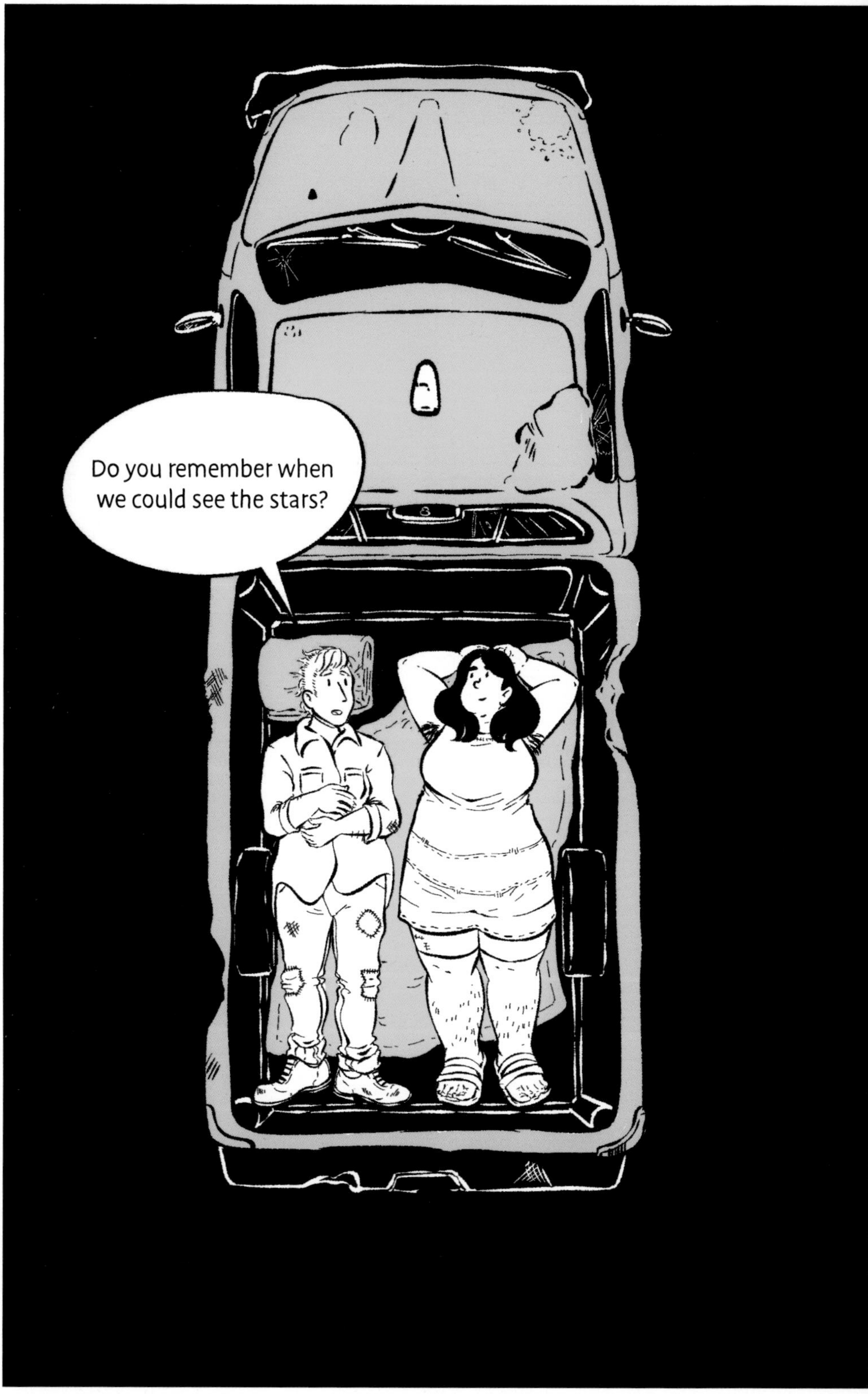
Do you remember when we could see the stars?

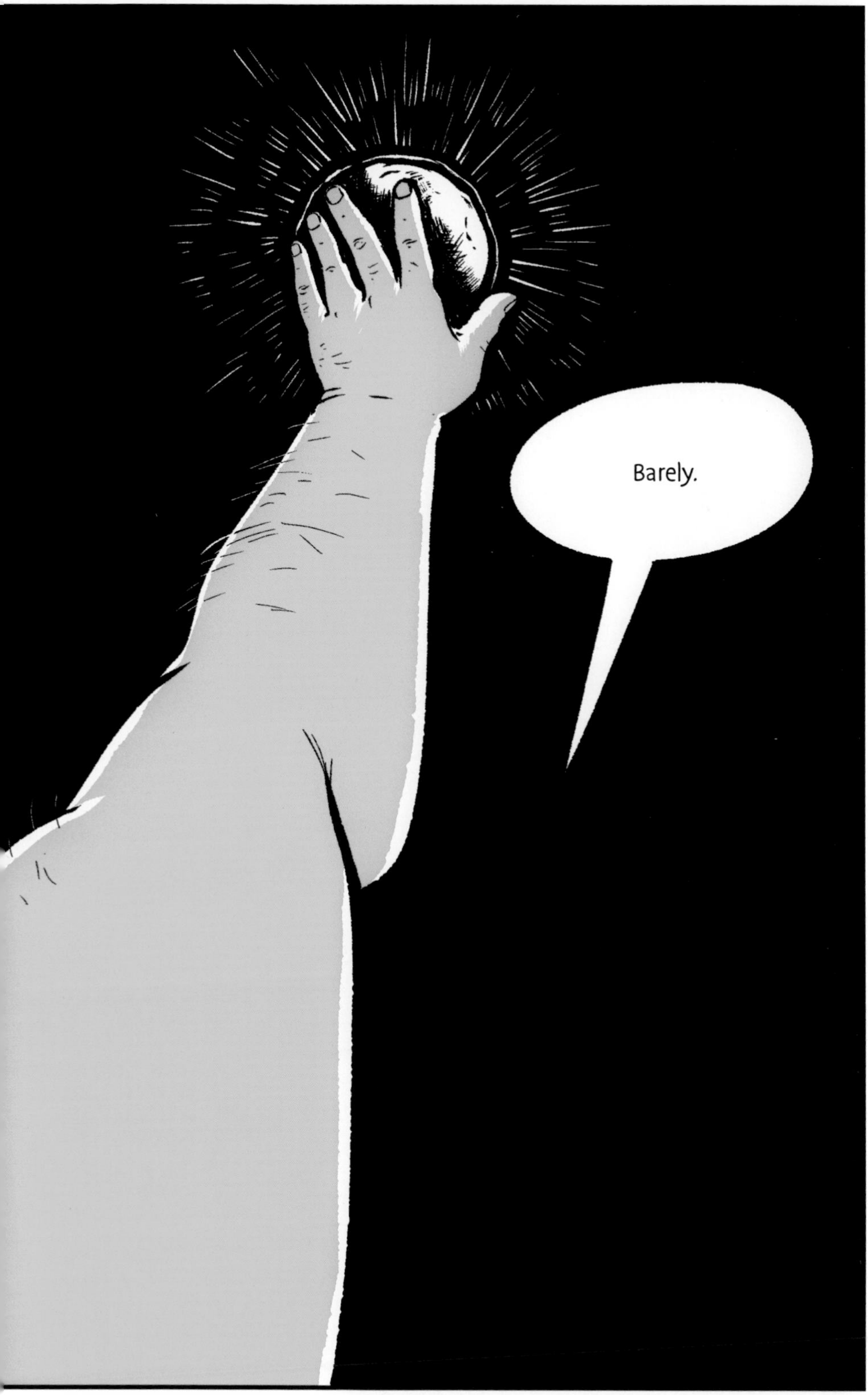
Barely.

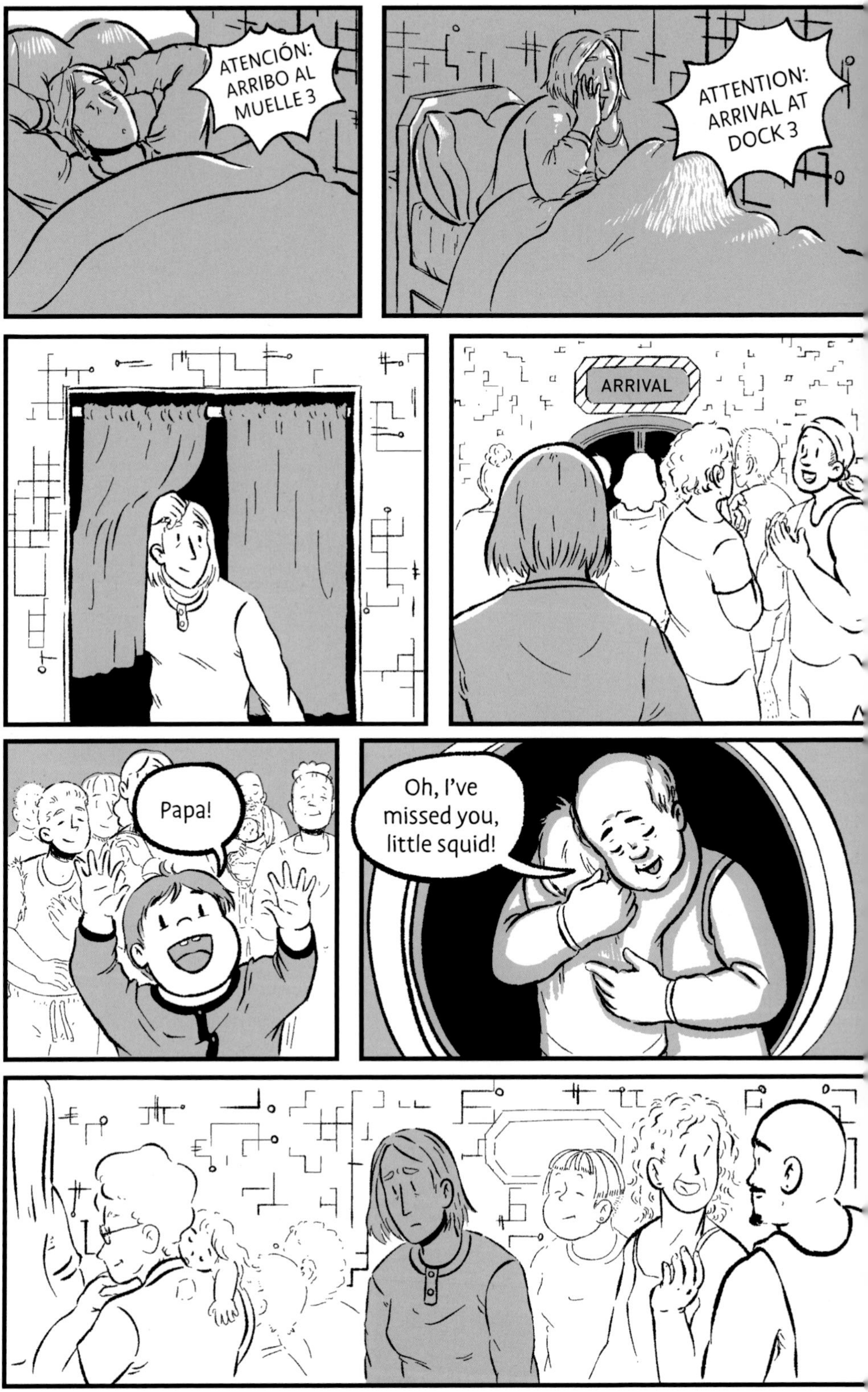
ATENCIÓN: ARRIBO AL MUELLE 3
ATTENTION: ARRIVAL AT DOCK 3
ARRIVAL
Papa!
Oh, I've missed you, little squid!

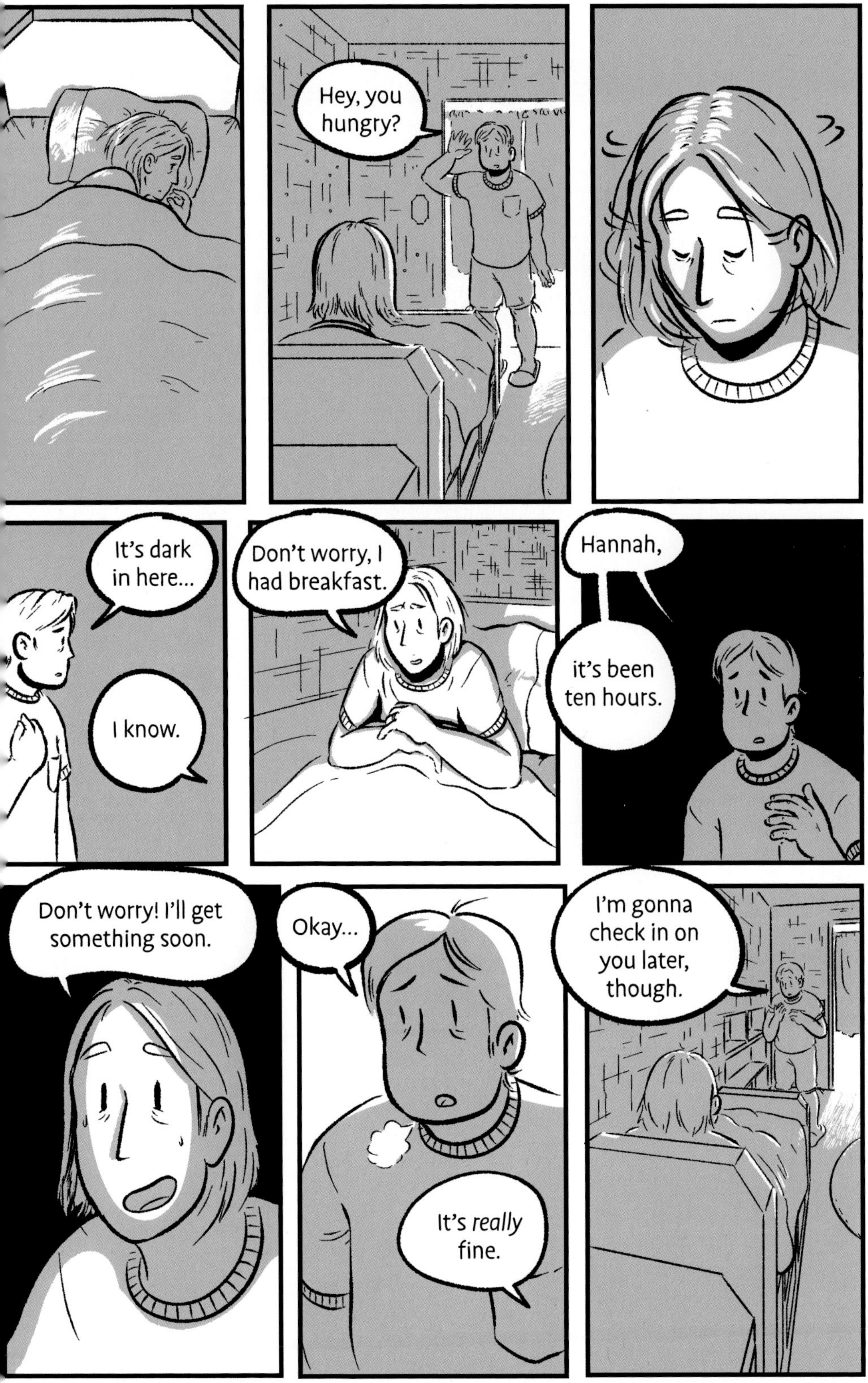
Hey, you hungry?
It's dark in here...
I know.
Don't worry, I had breakfast.
Hannah,
it's been ten hours.
Don't worry! I'll get something soon.
Okay...
It's *really* fine.
I'm gonna check in on you later, though.

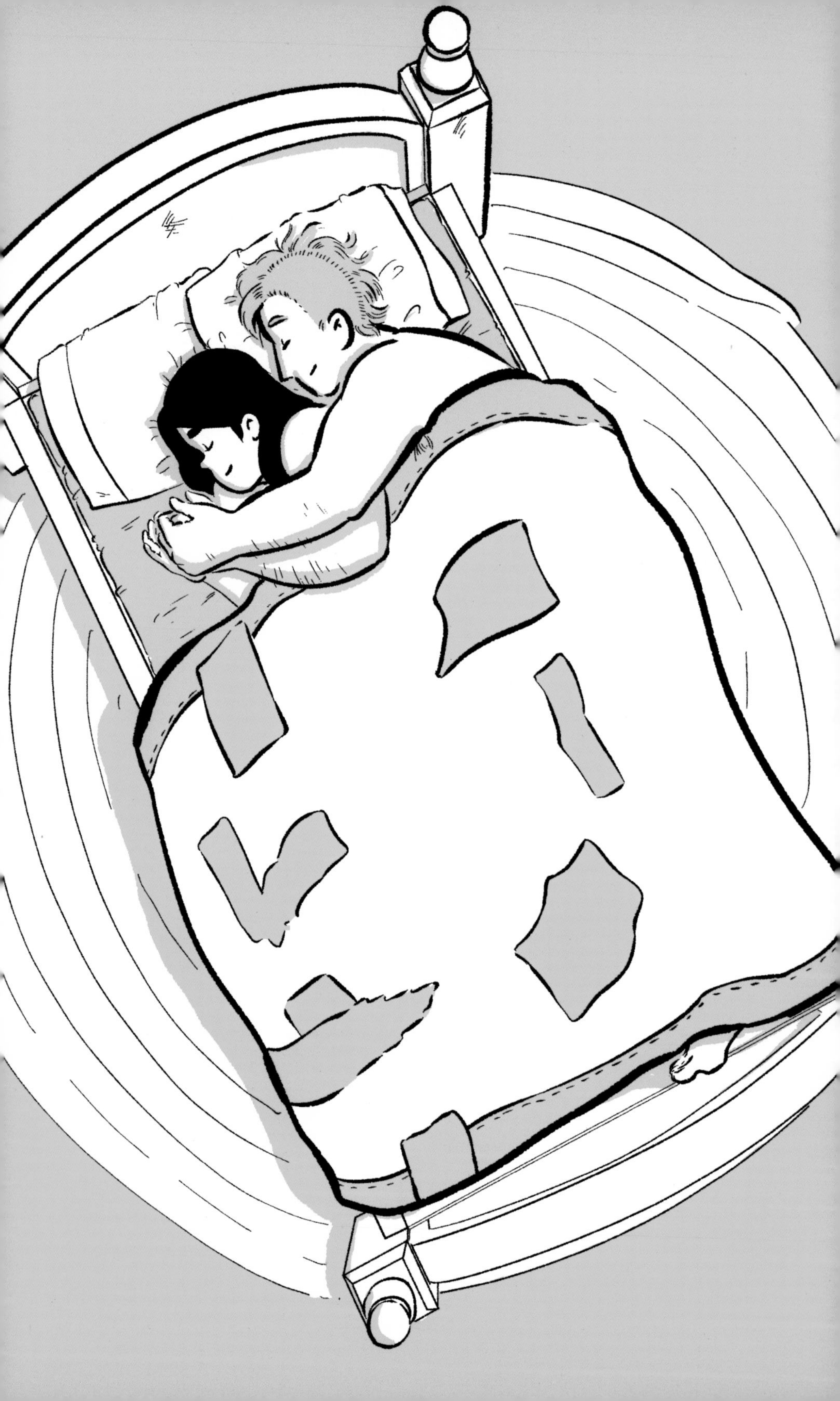

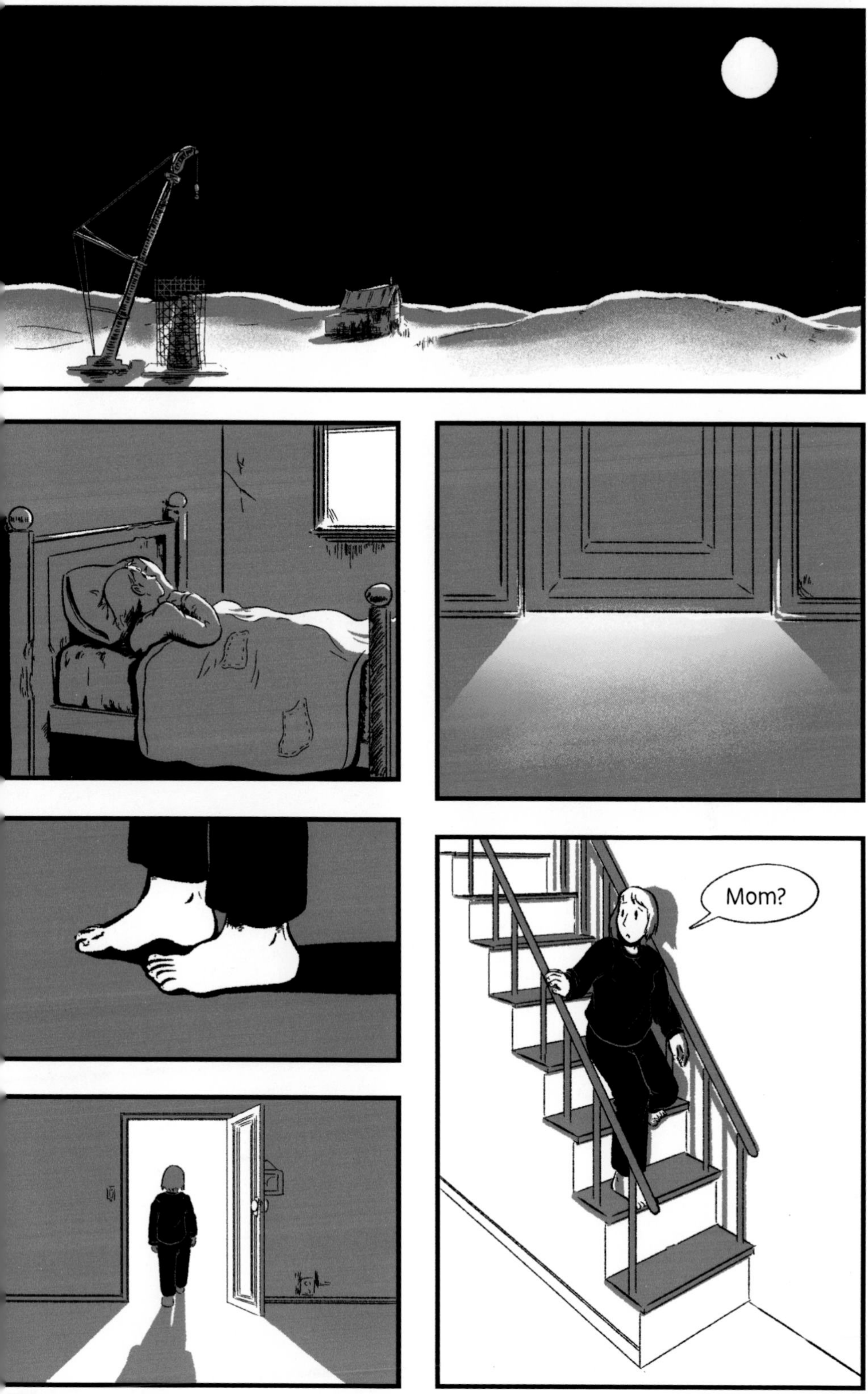
Mom?

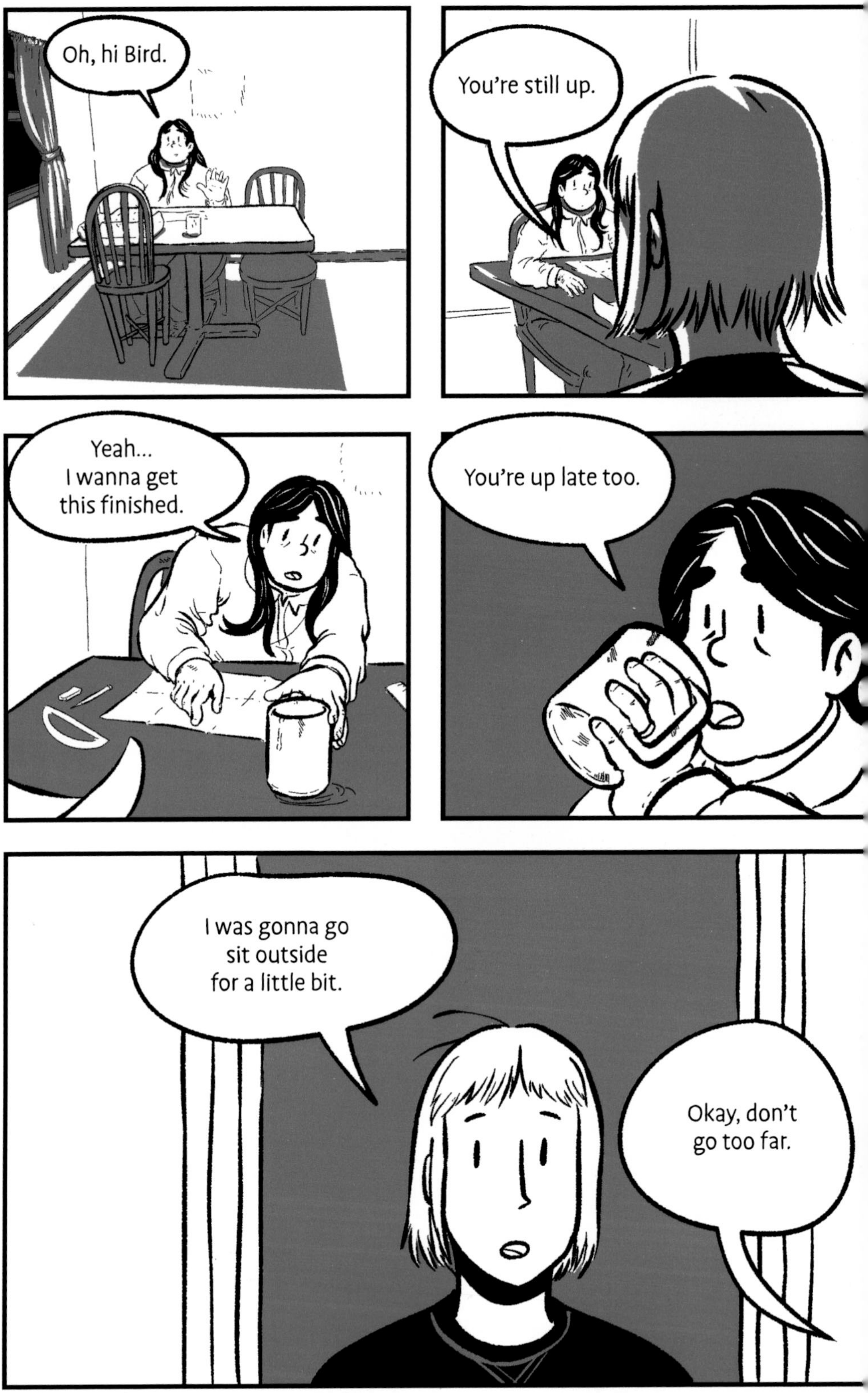
Oh, hi Bird.
You're still up.
Yeah...
I wanna get
this finished.
You're up late too.
I was gonna go
sit outside
for a little bit.
Okay, don't
go too far.

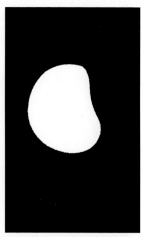

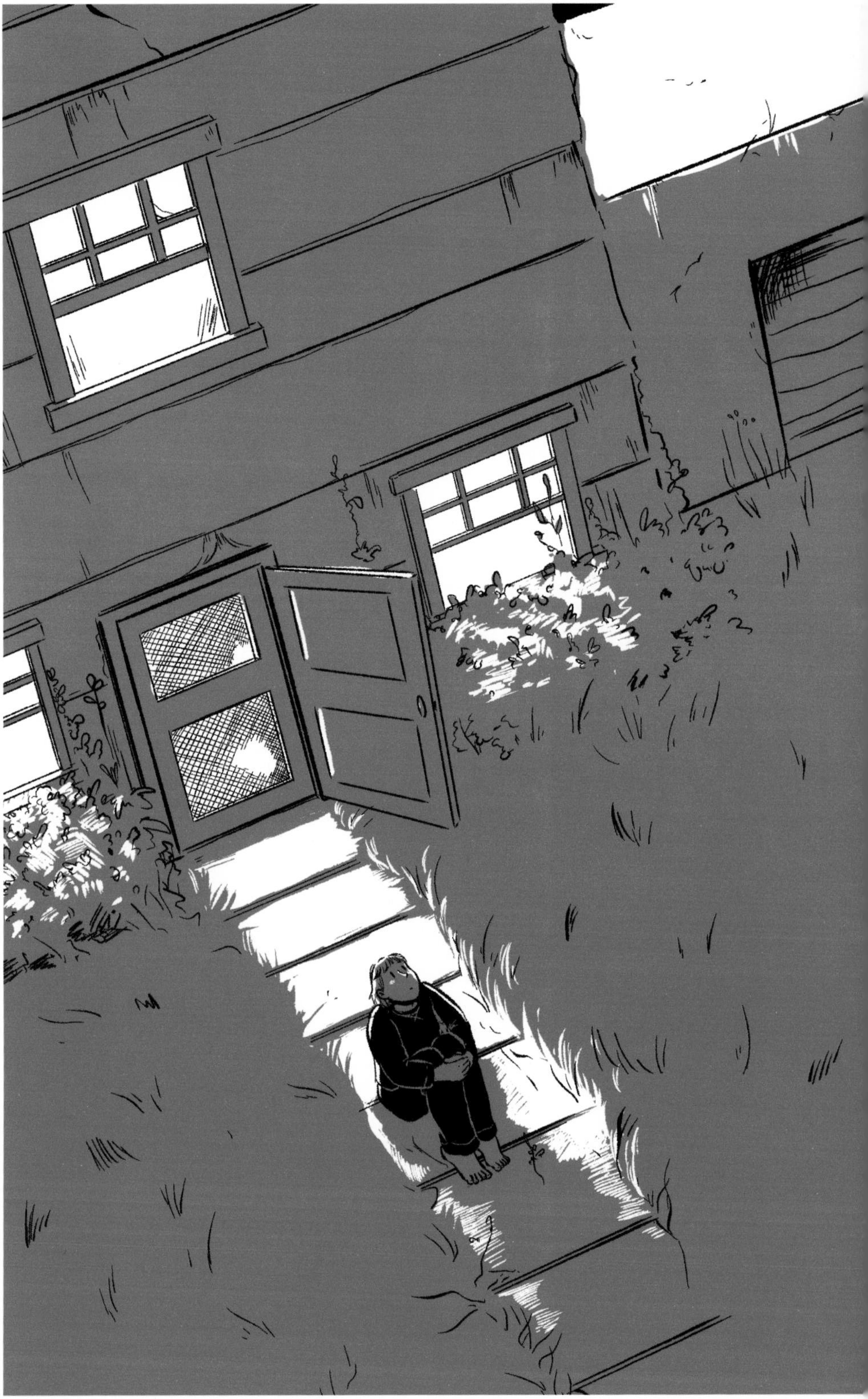

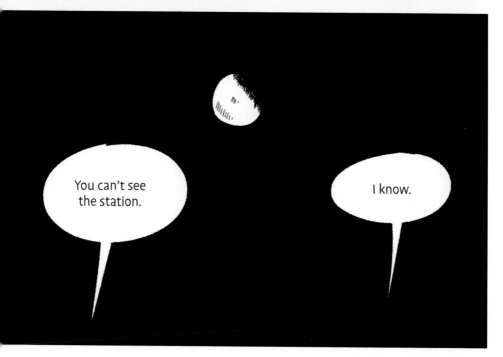

You can't see the station.

I know.

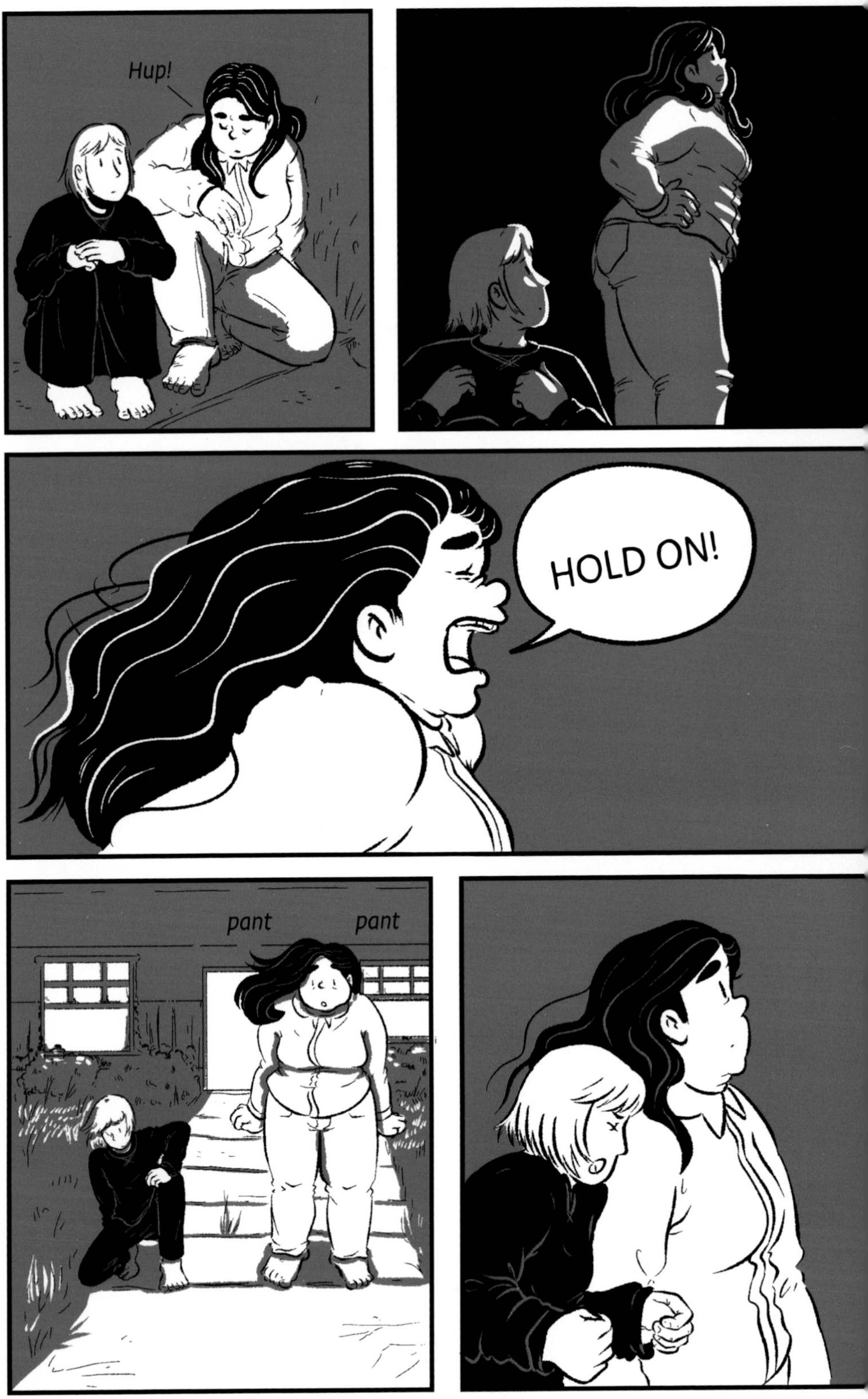
Hup!
HOLD ON!
pant
pant

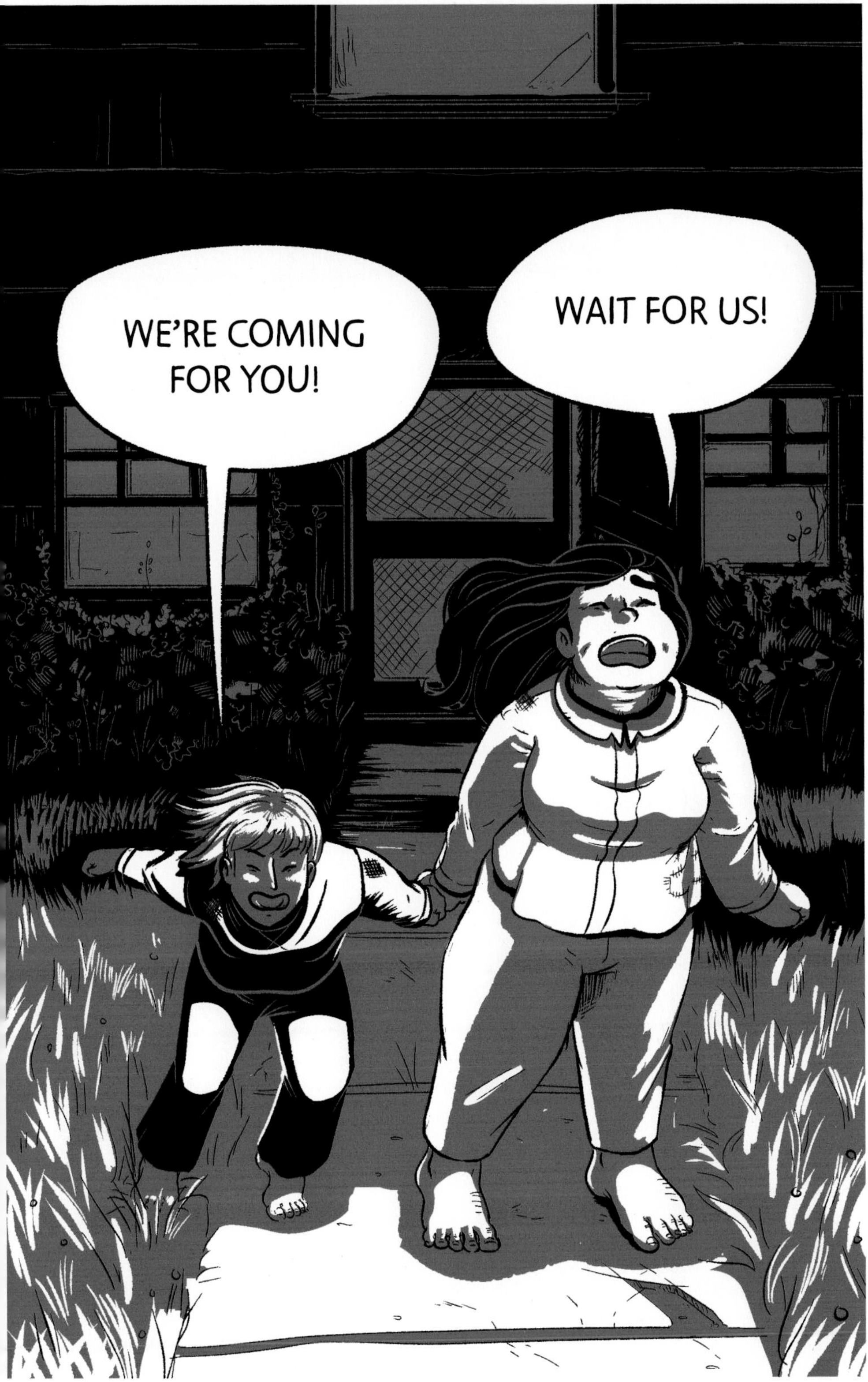
WE'RE COMING FOR YOU!
WAIT FOR US!

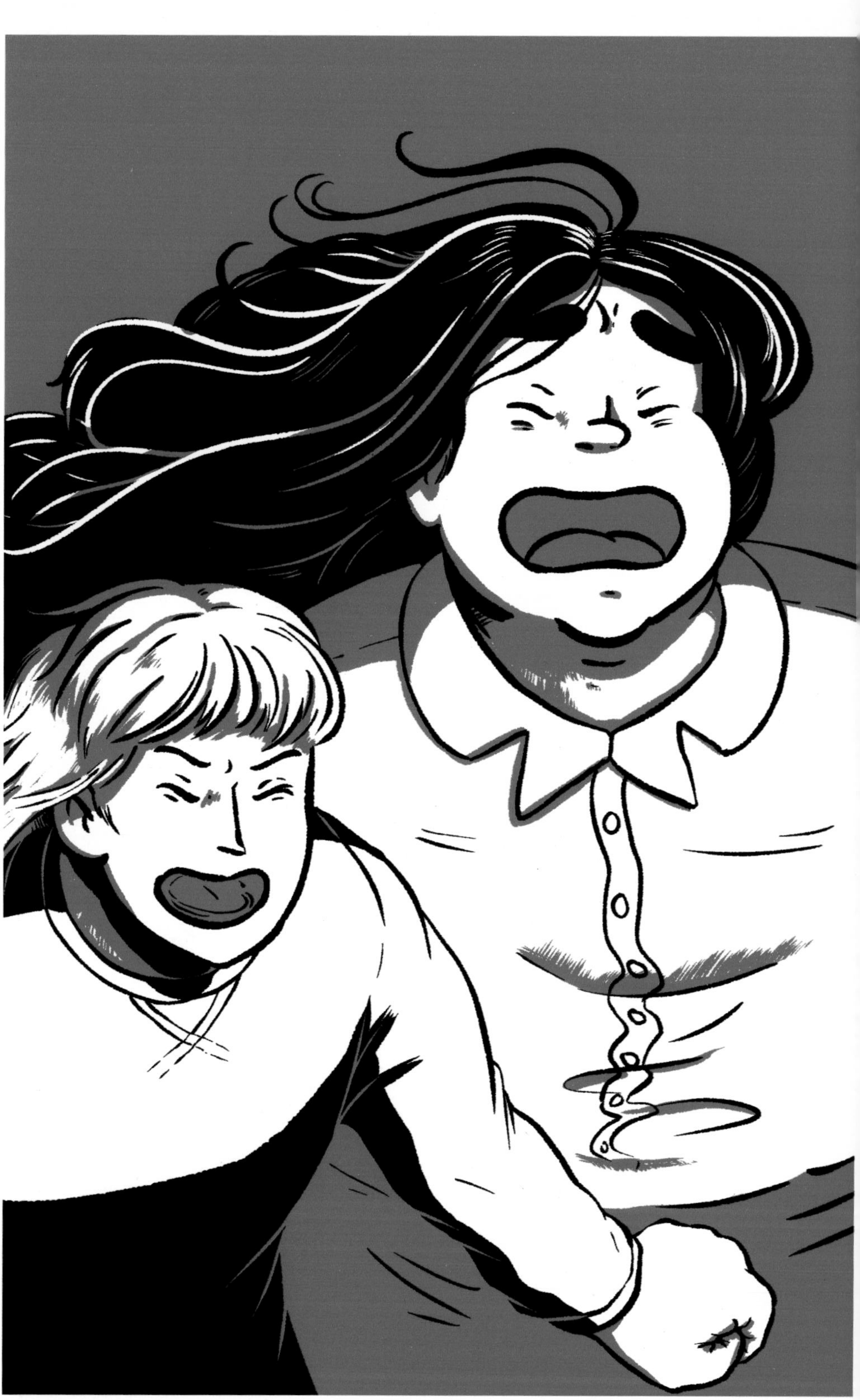

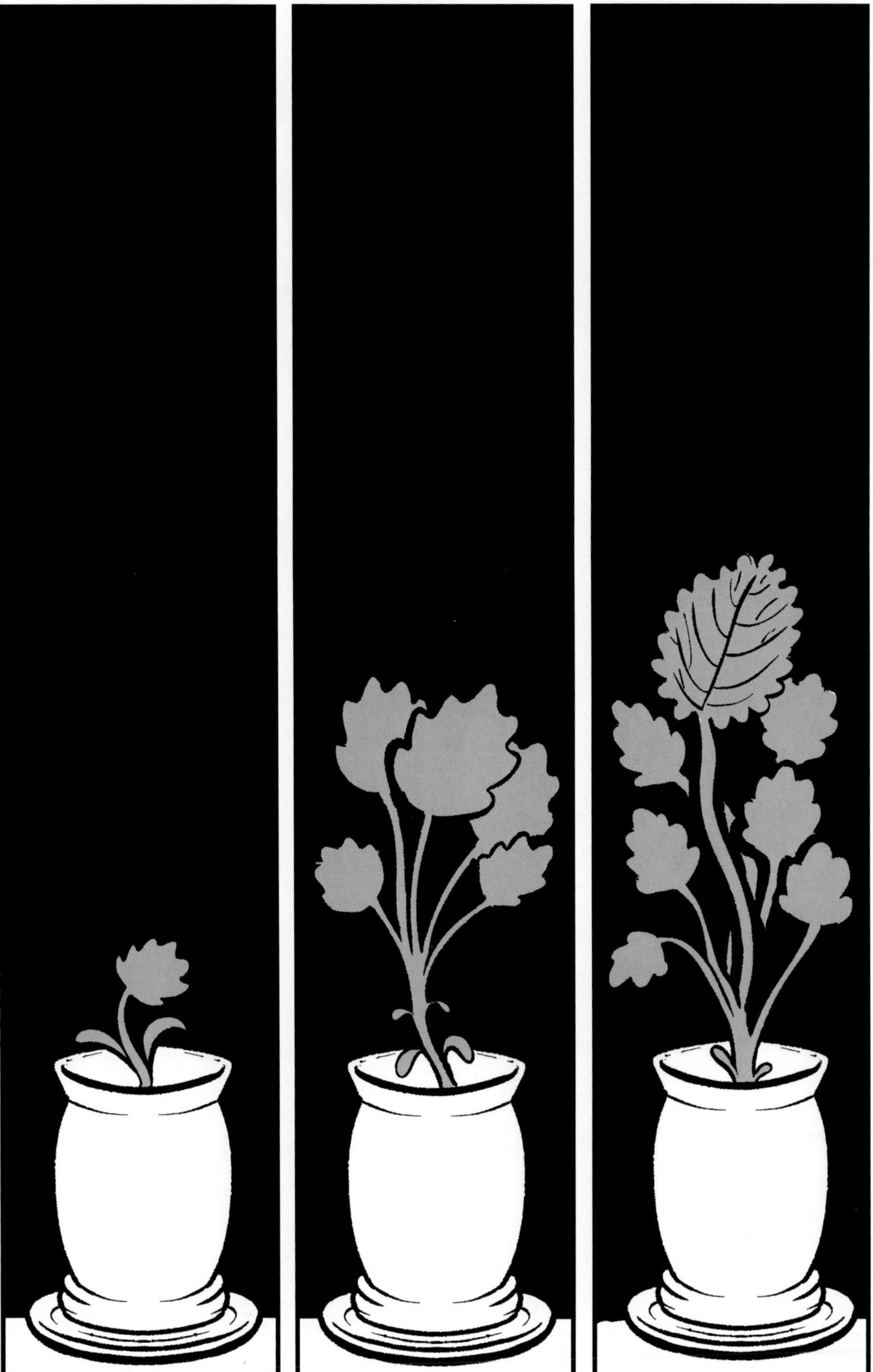

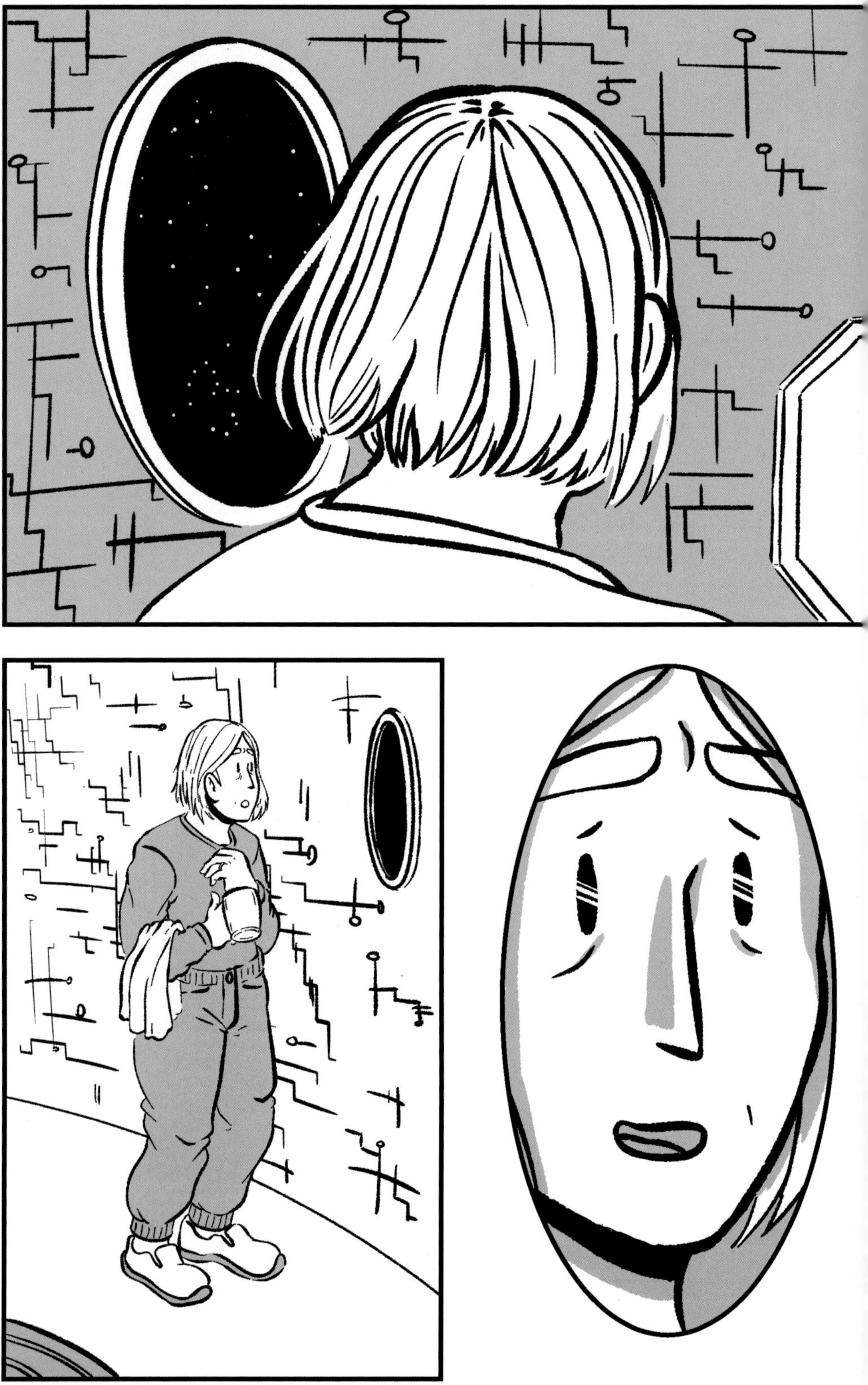

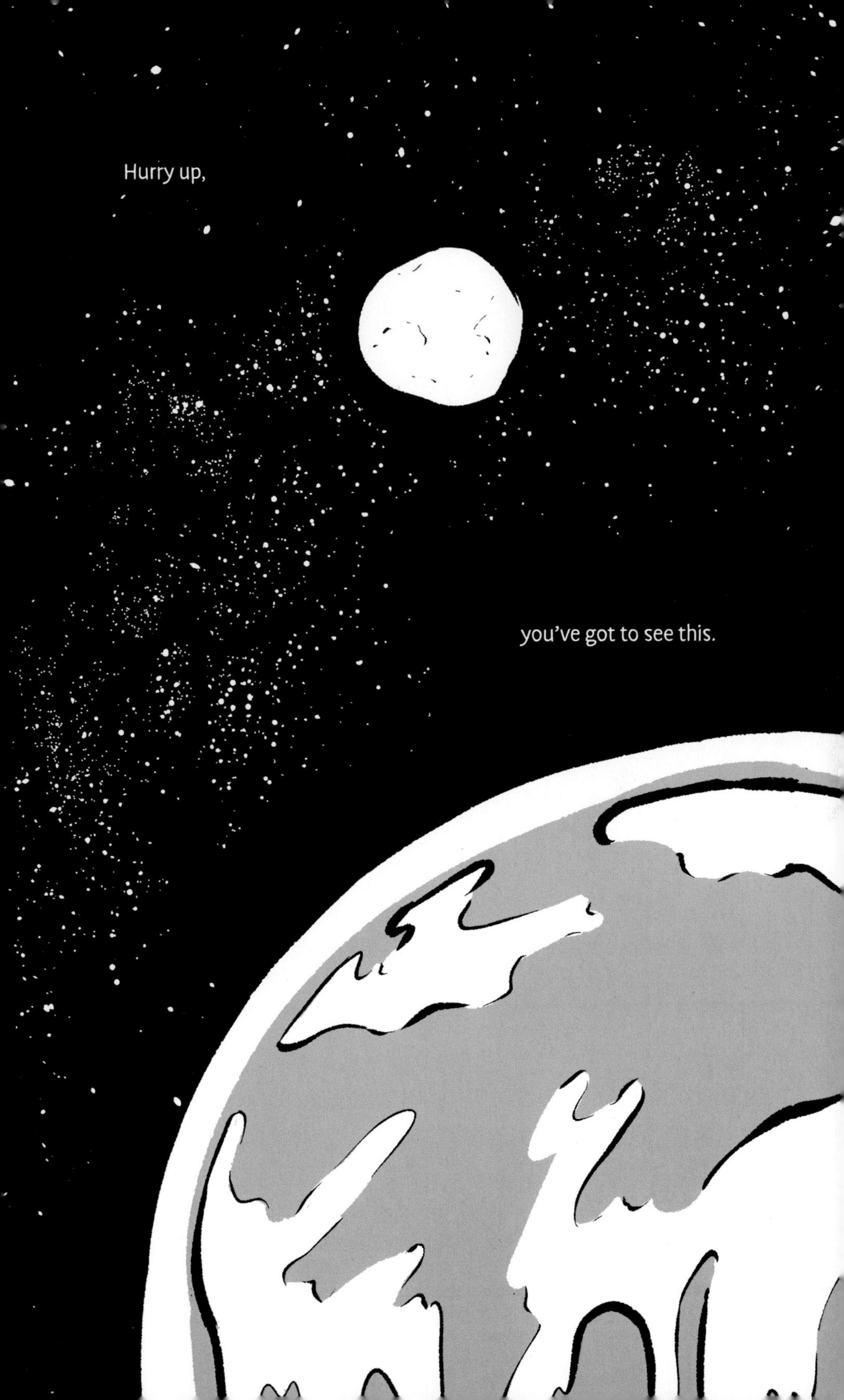
Hurry up,
you’ve got to see this.

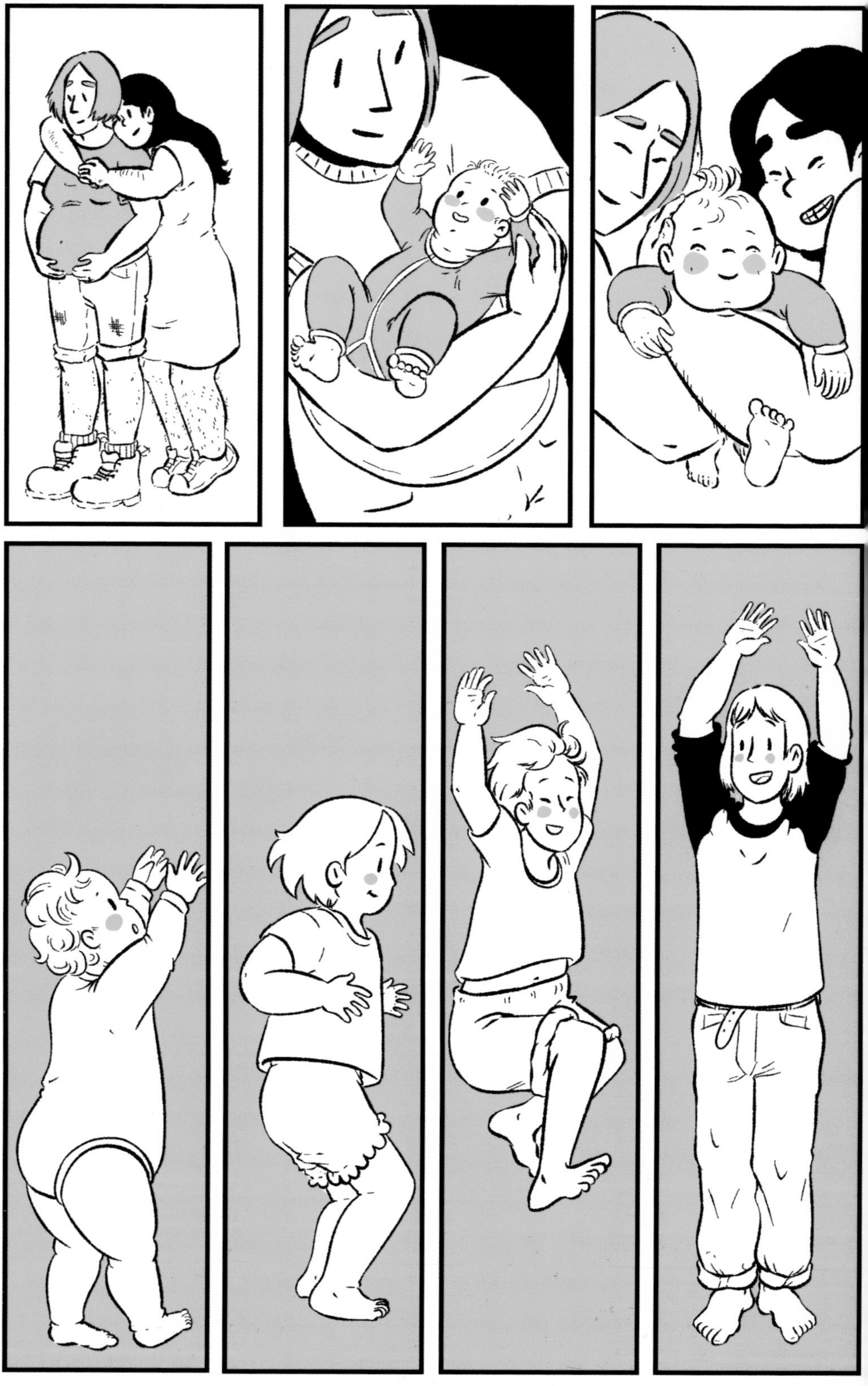

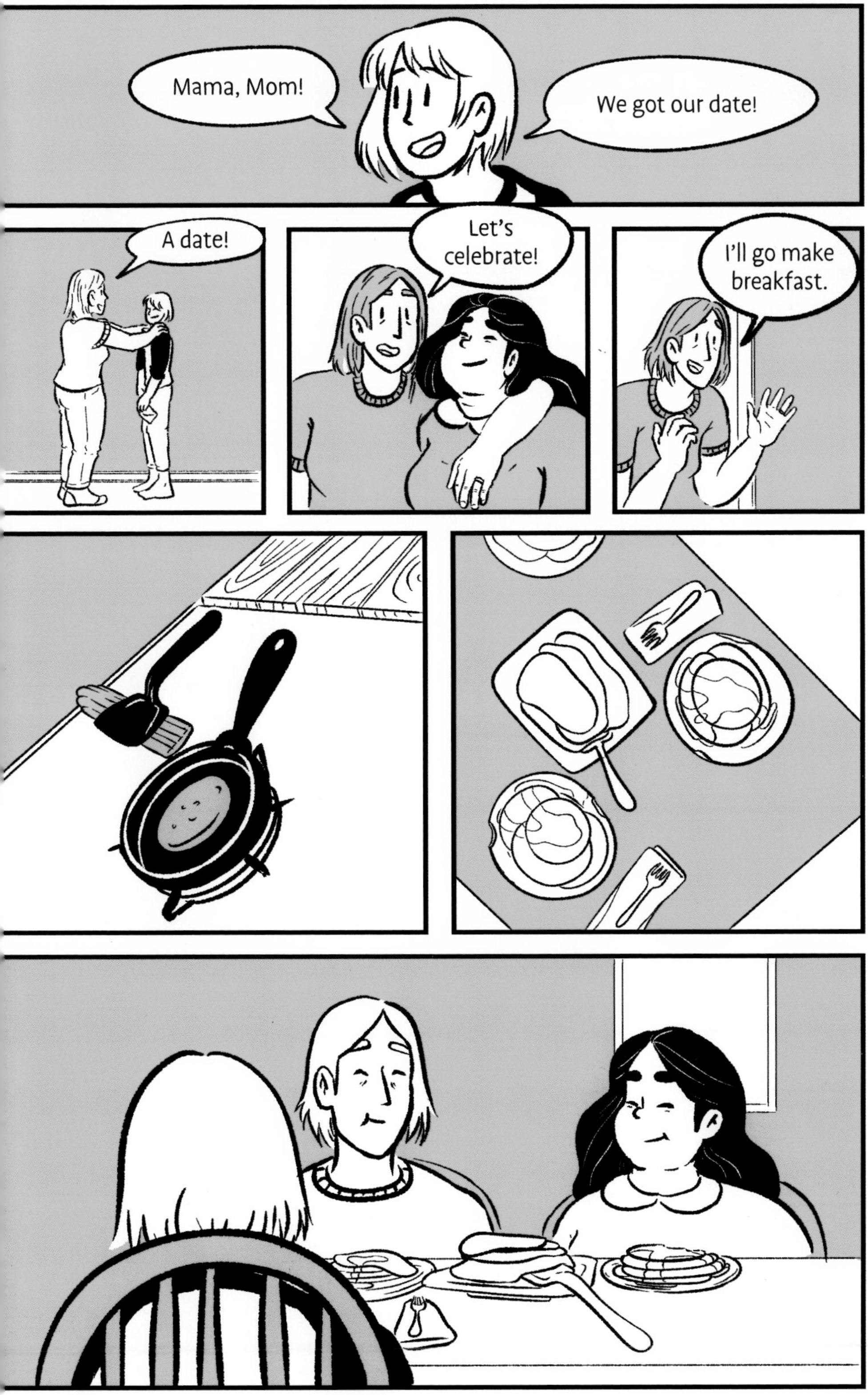
Mama, Mom!
We got our date!
A date!
Let's celebrate!
I'll go make breakfast.

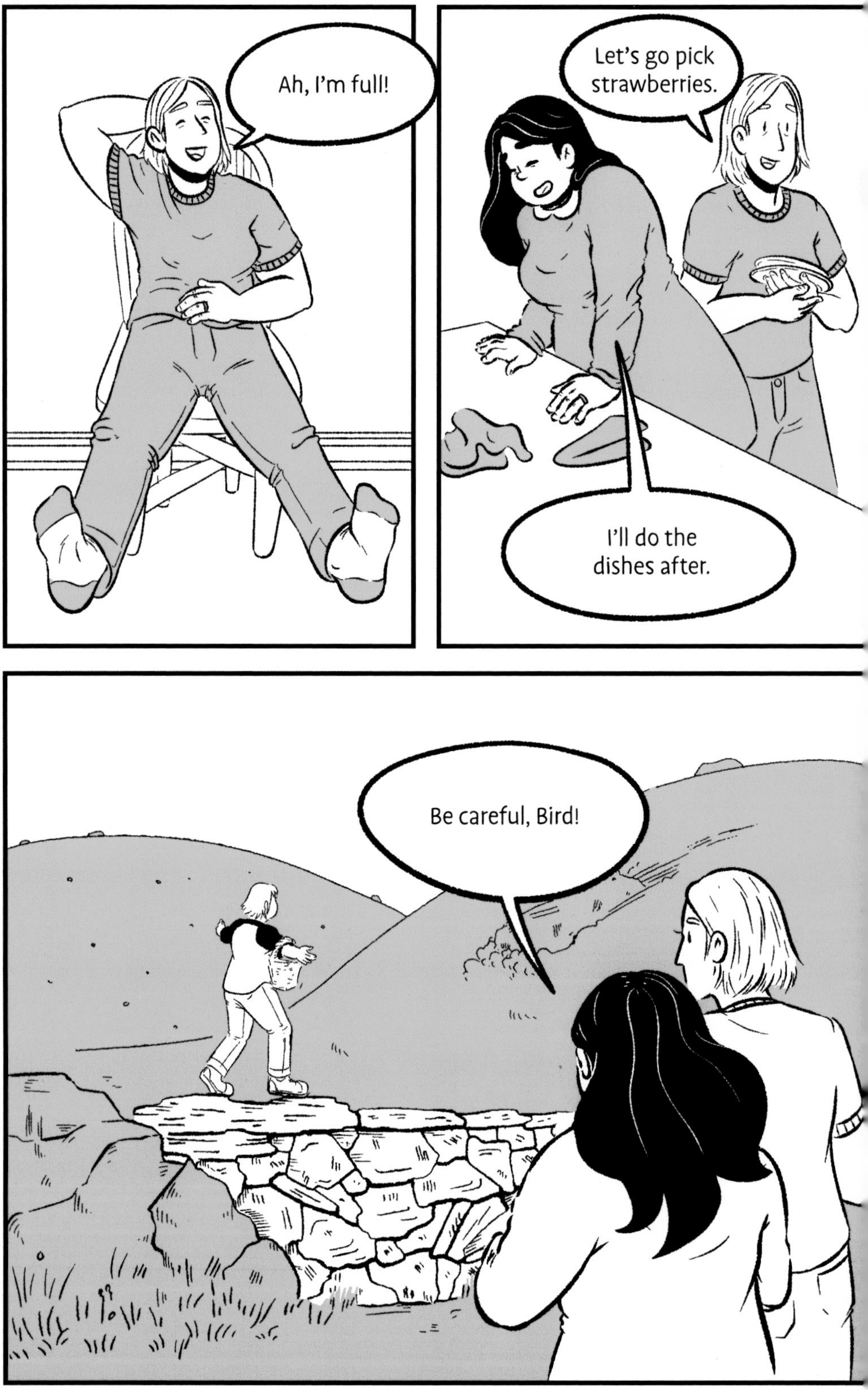
Ah, I'm full!
Let's go pick strawberries.
I'll do the dishes after.
Be careful, Bird!

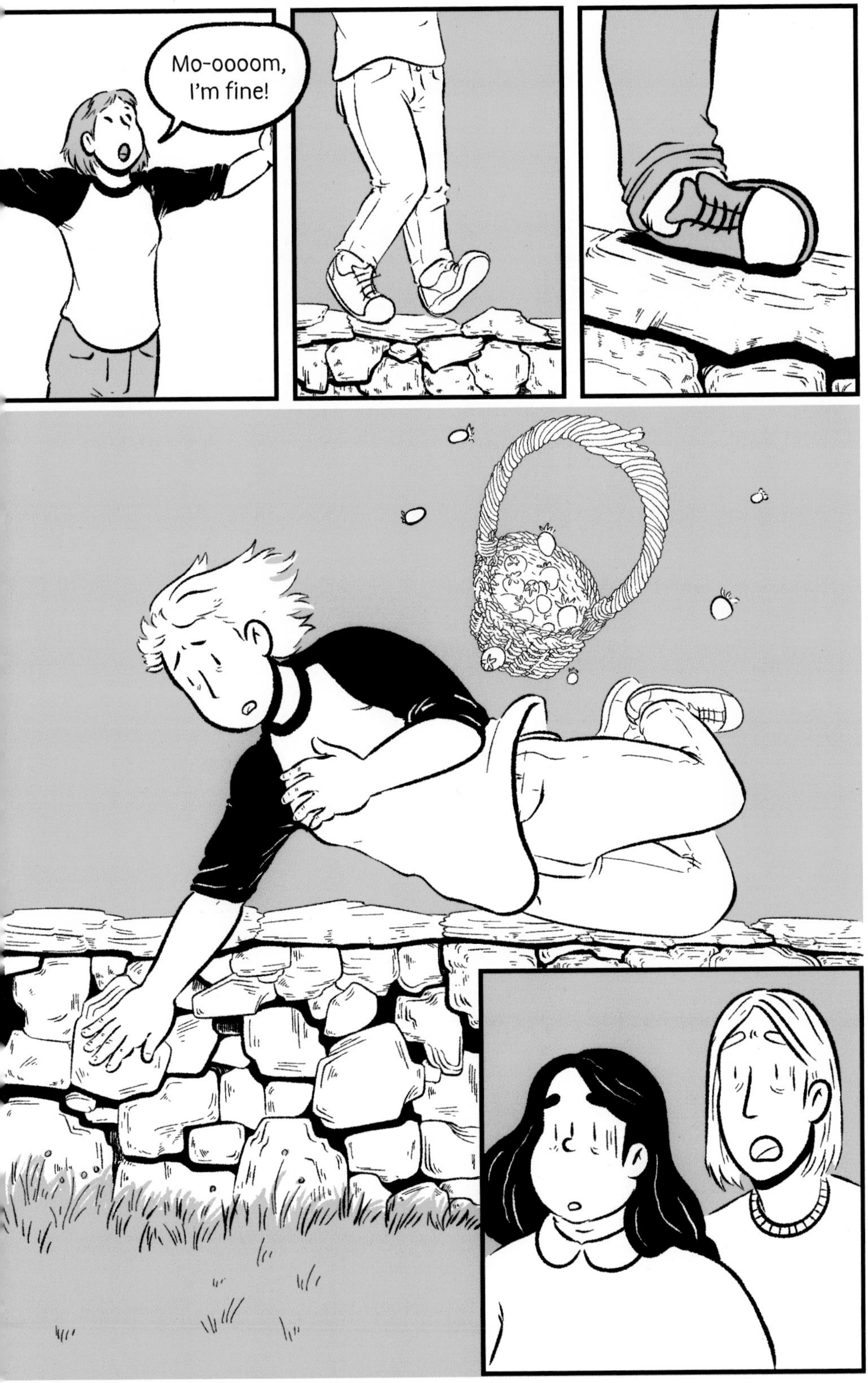
Mo-oooom,
I'm fine!

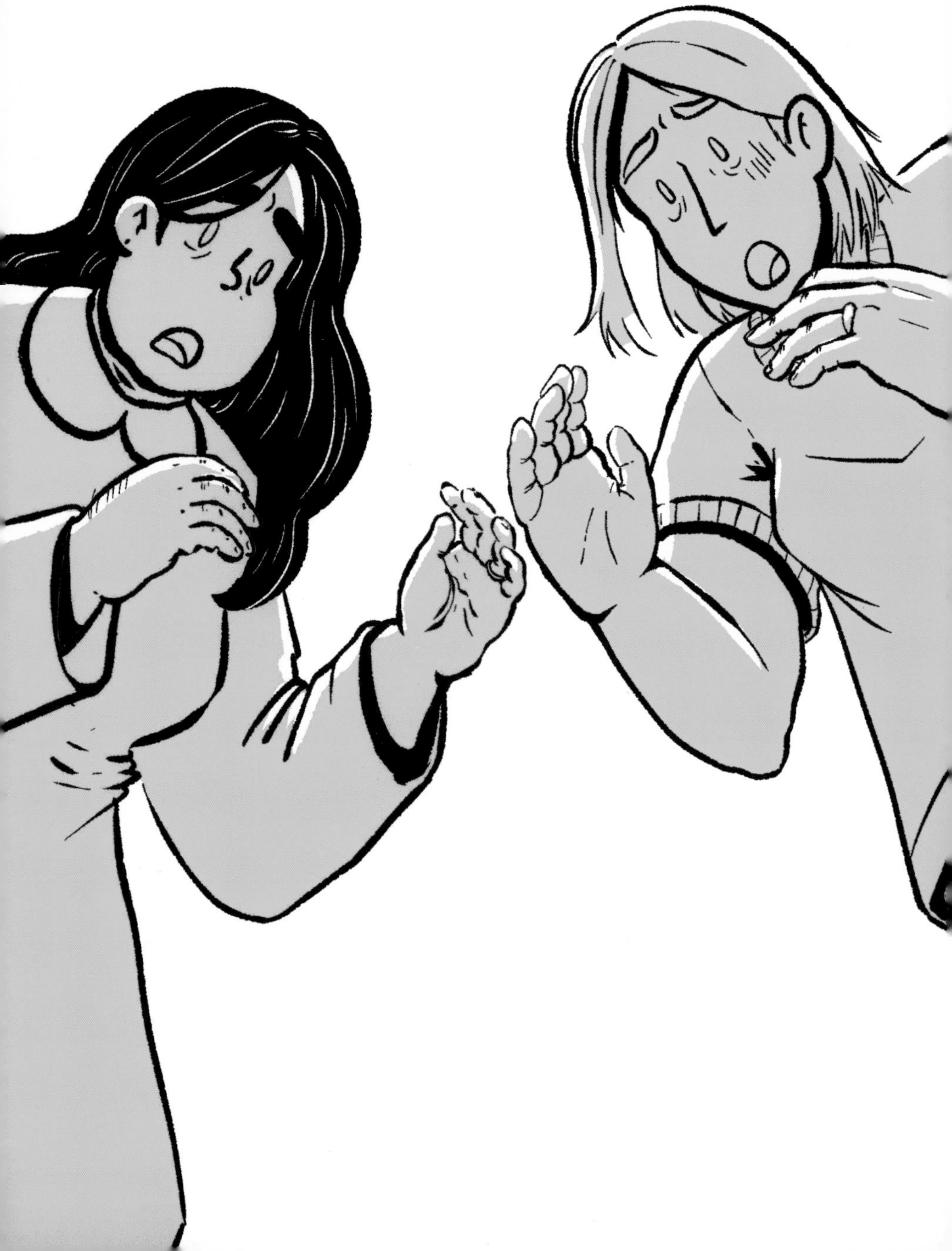

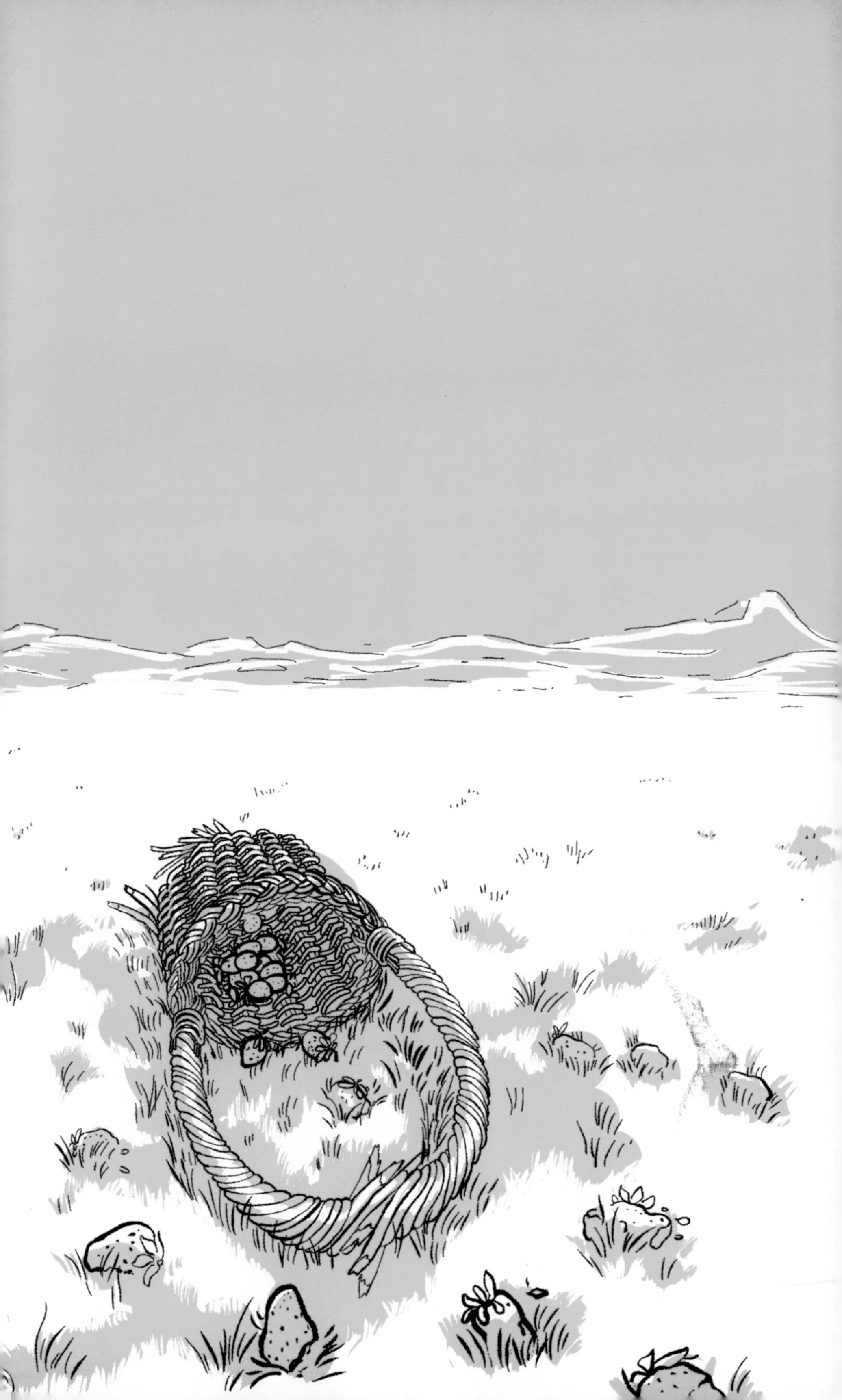

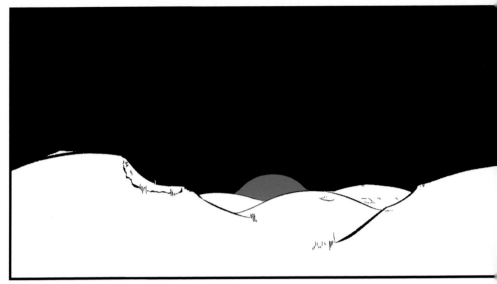

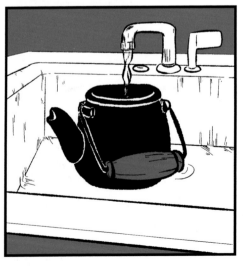

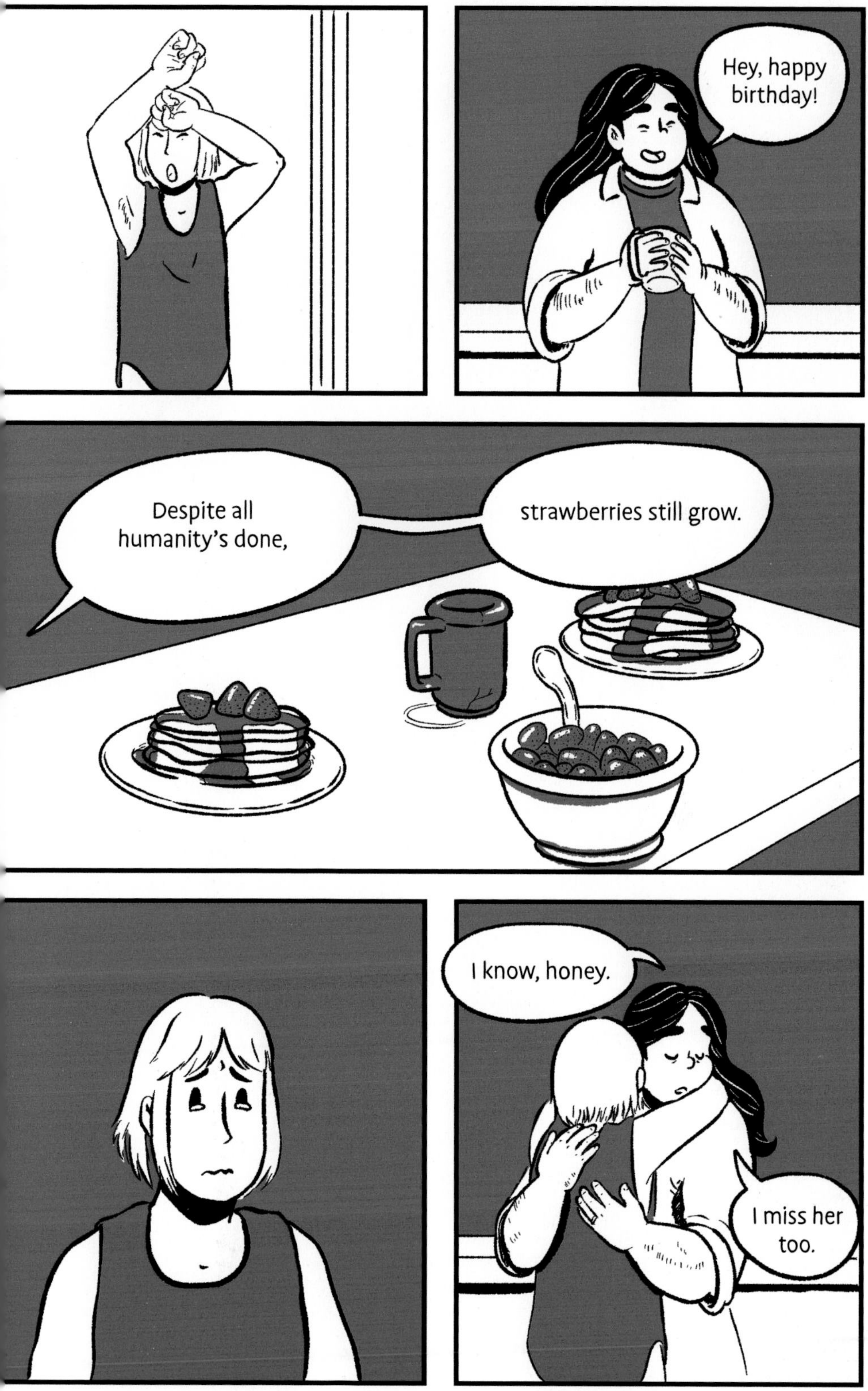
Hey, happy birthday!
Despite all humanity's done,
strawberries still grow.
I know, honey.
I miss her too.

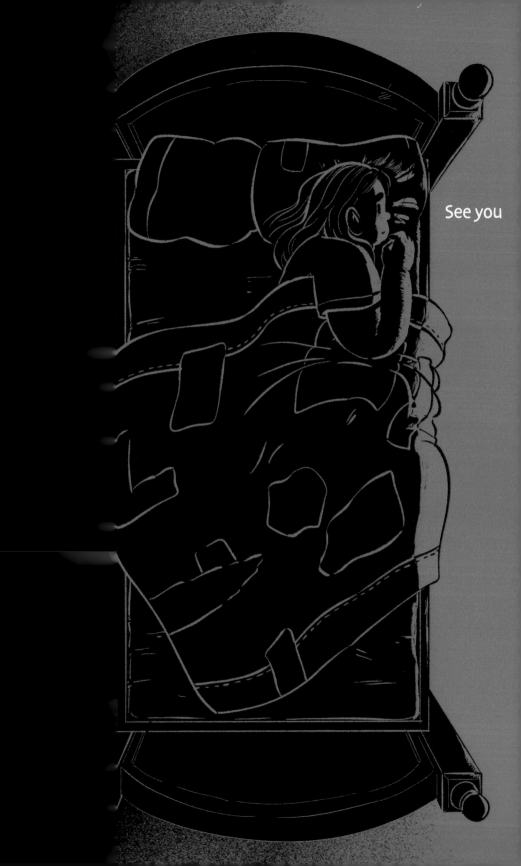

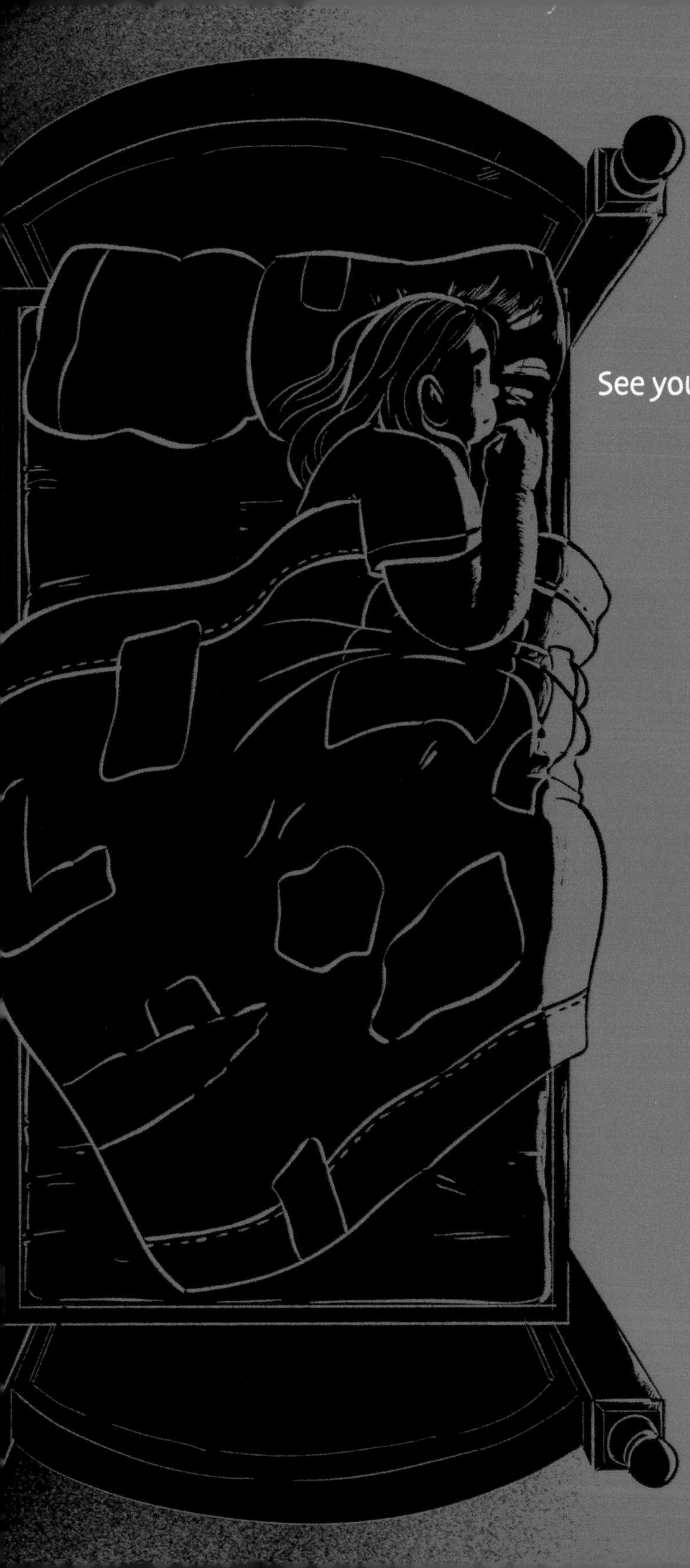
See you

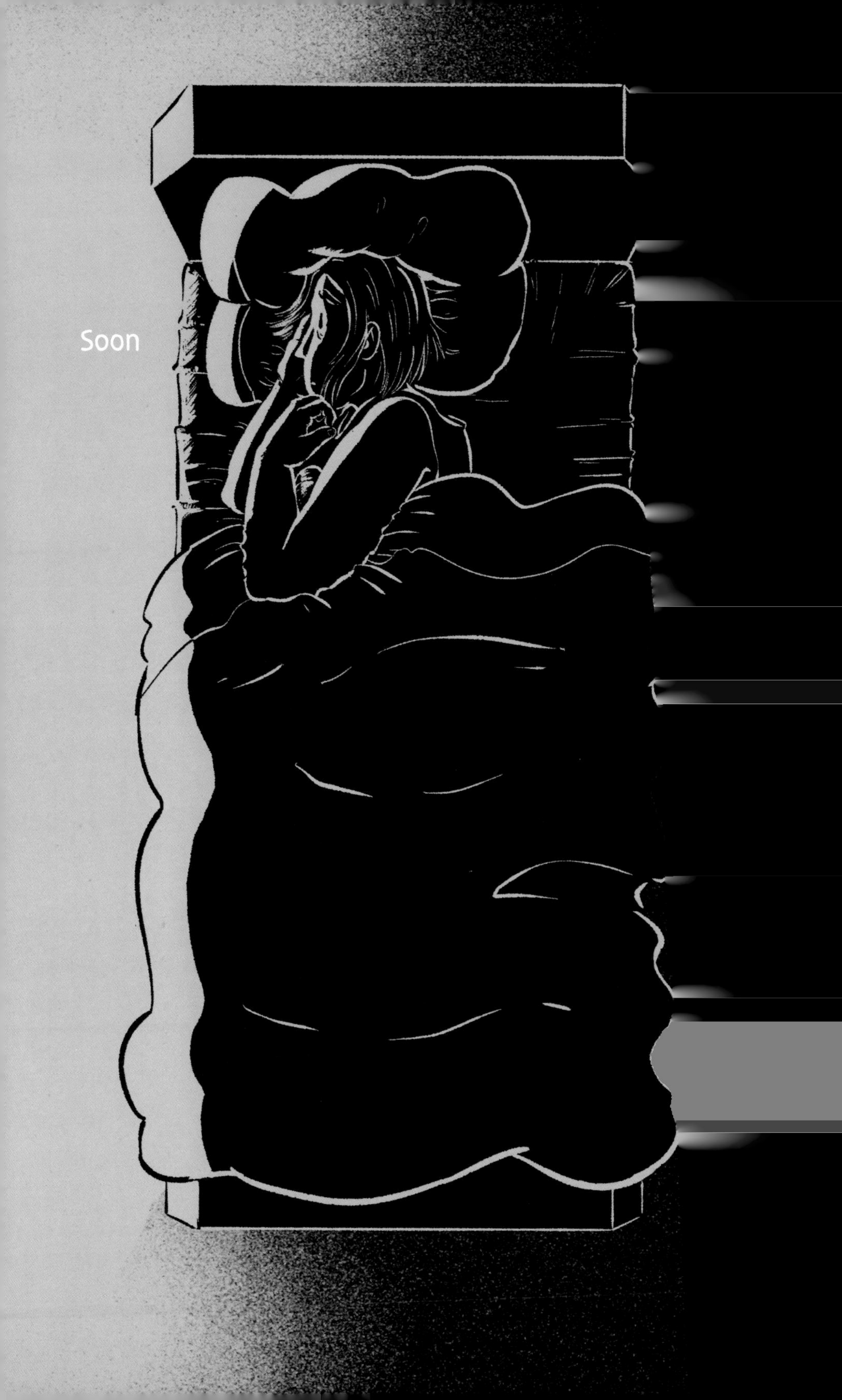
Soon

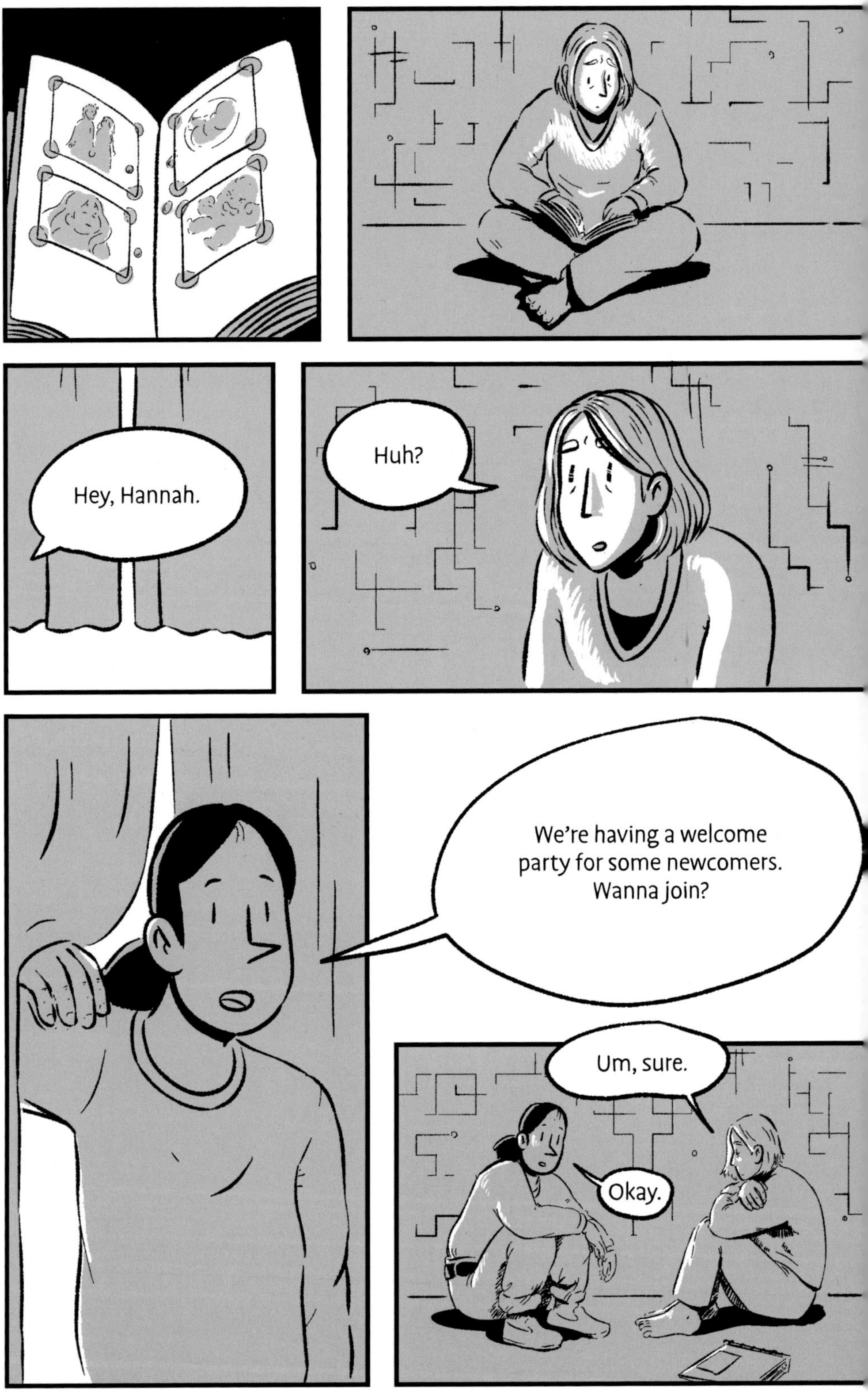
Hey, Hannah.
Huh?
We're having a welcome party for some newcomers. Wanna join?
Um, sure.
Okay.

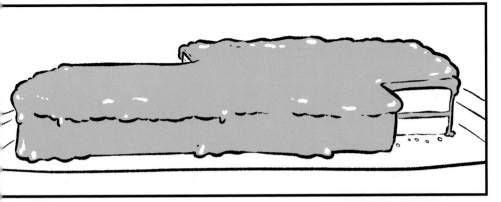

This is Lisa.
She's from Region X.

Oh! My wife and
daughter are there.
They'll be coming soon.

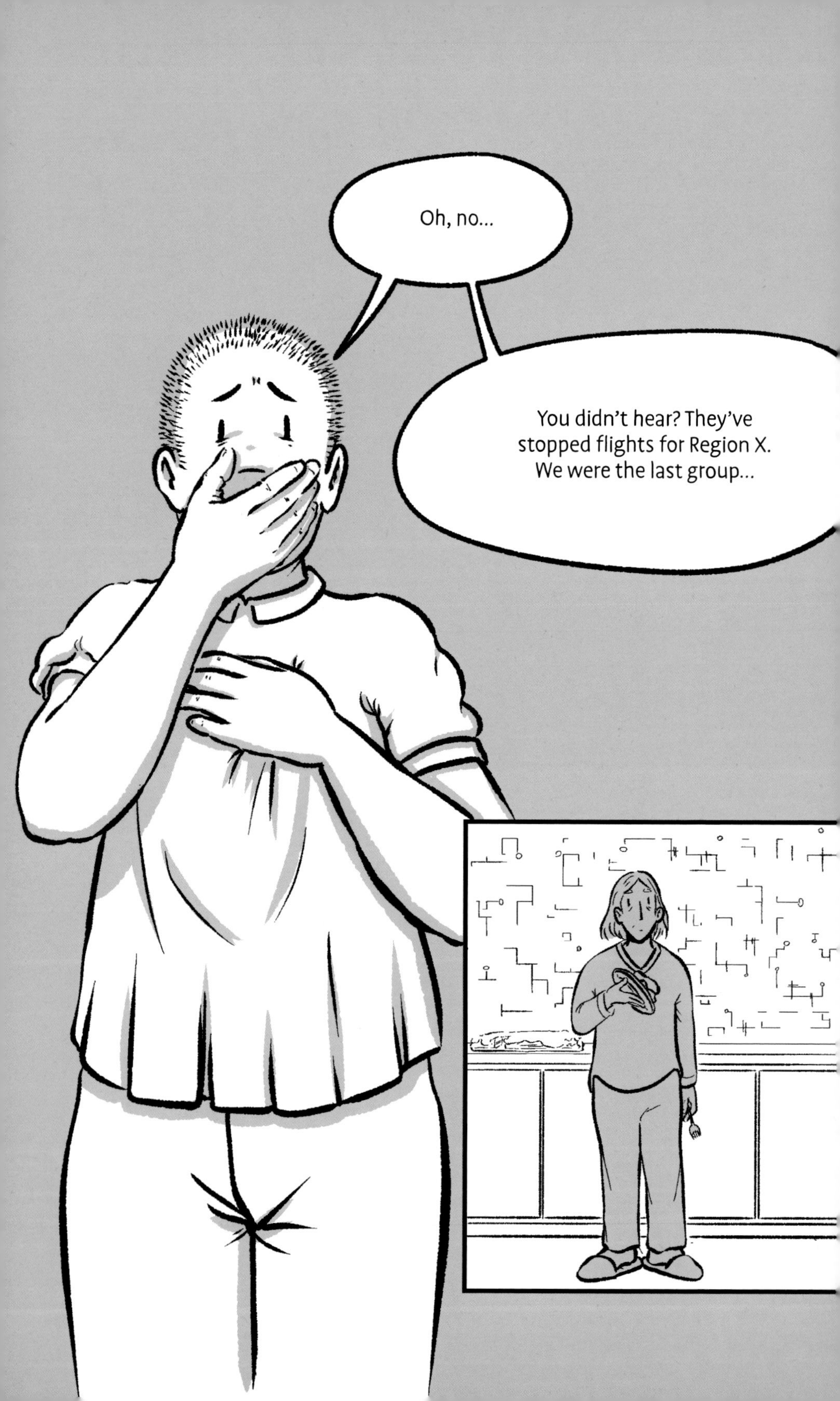
Oh, no...
You didn't hear? They've stopped flights for Region X. We were the last group...

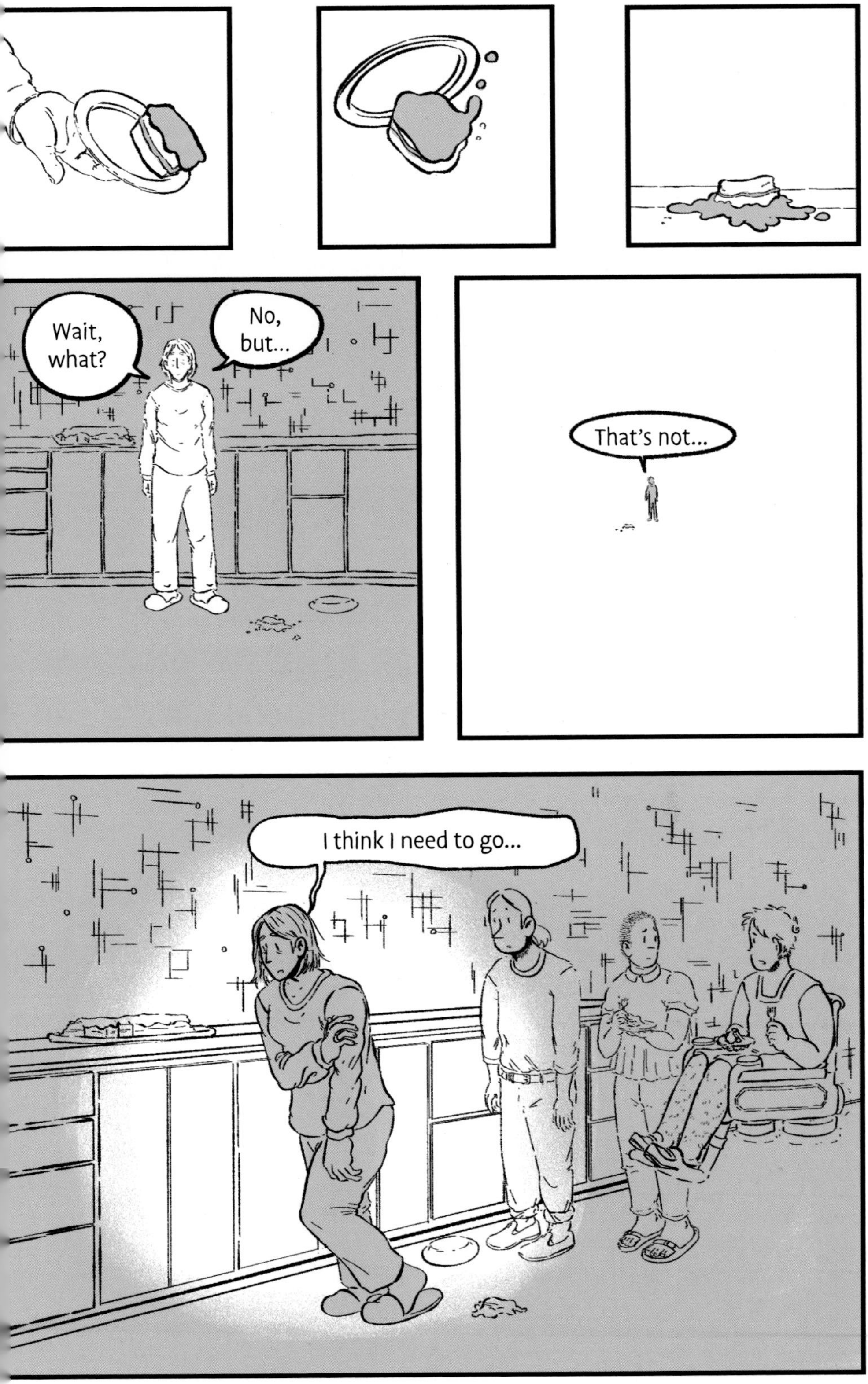
Wait, what?
No, but...
That's not...
I think I need to go...

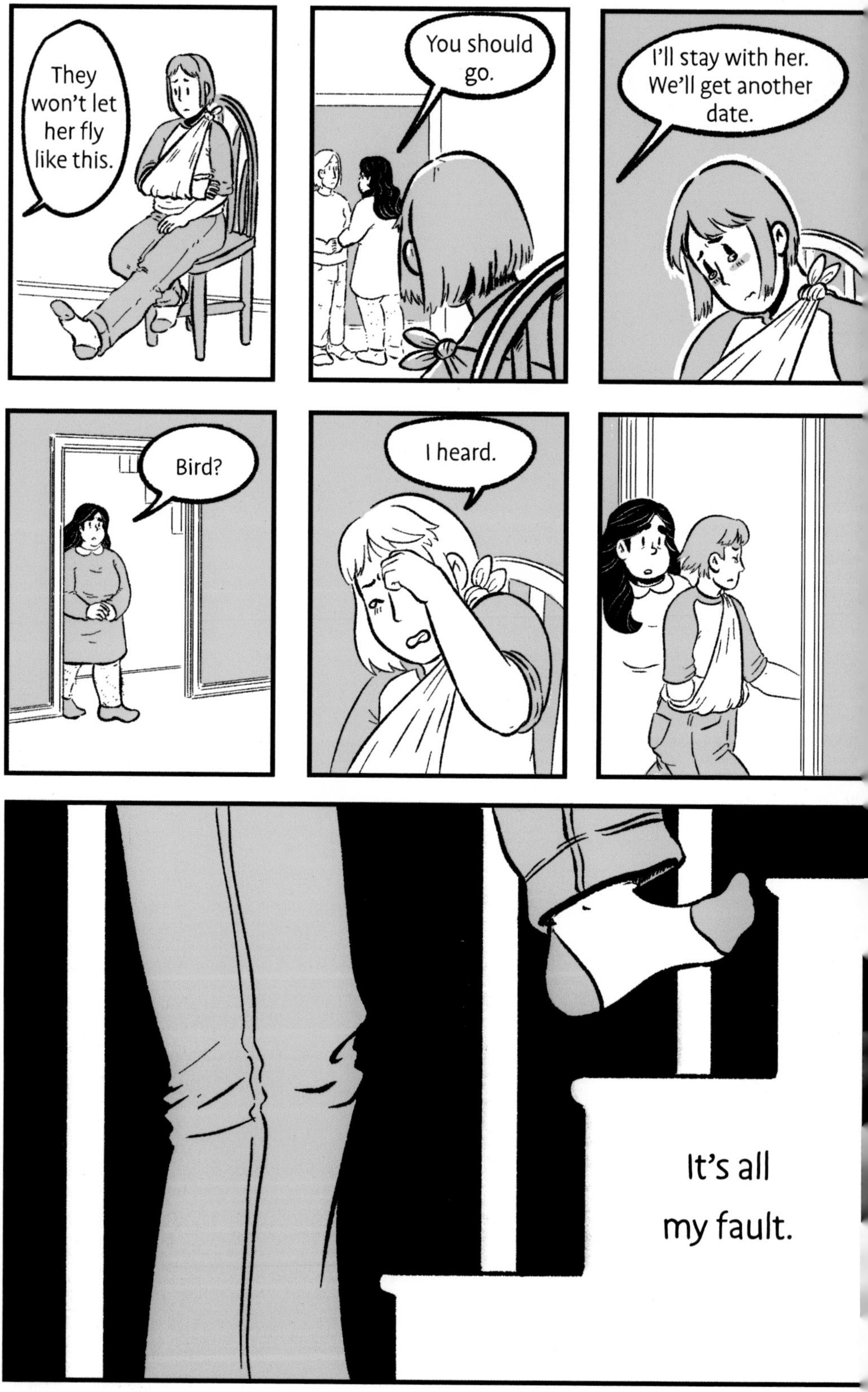
They won't let her fly like this.
You should go.
I'll stay with her. We'll get another date.
Bird?
I heard.
It's all my fault.

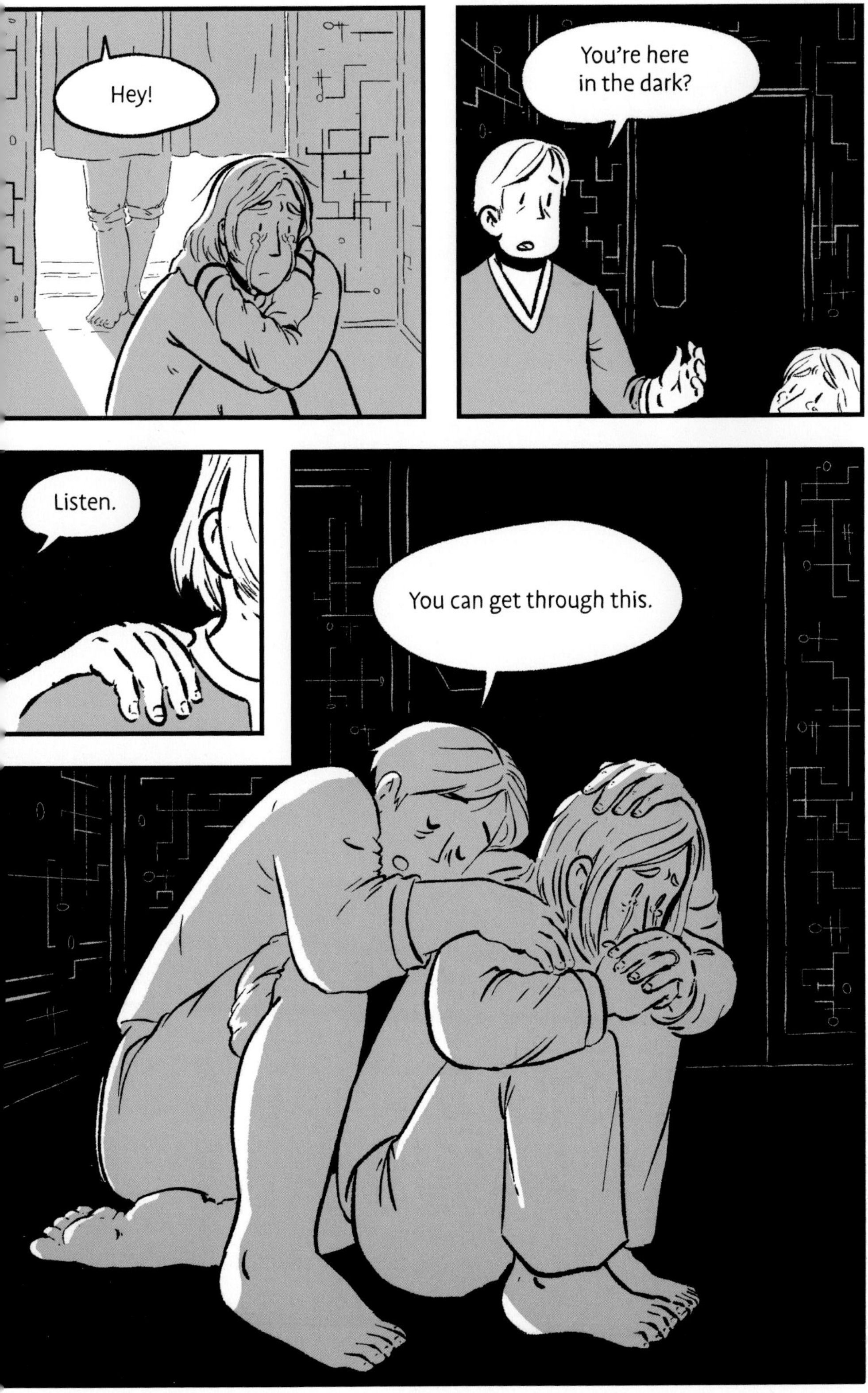
Hey!
You're here in the dark?
Listen.
You can get through this.

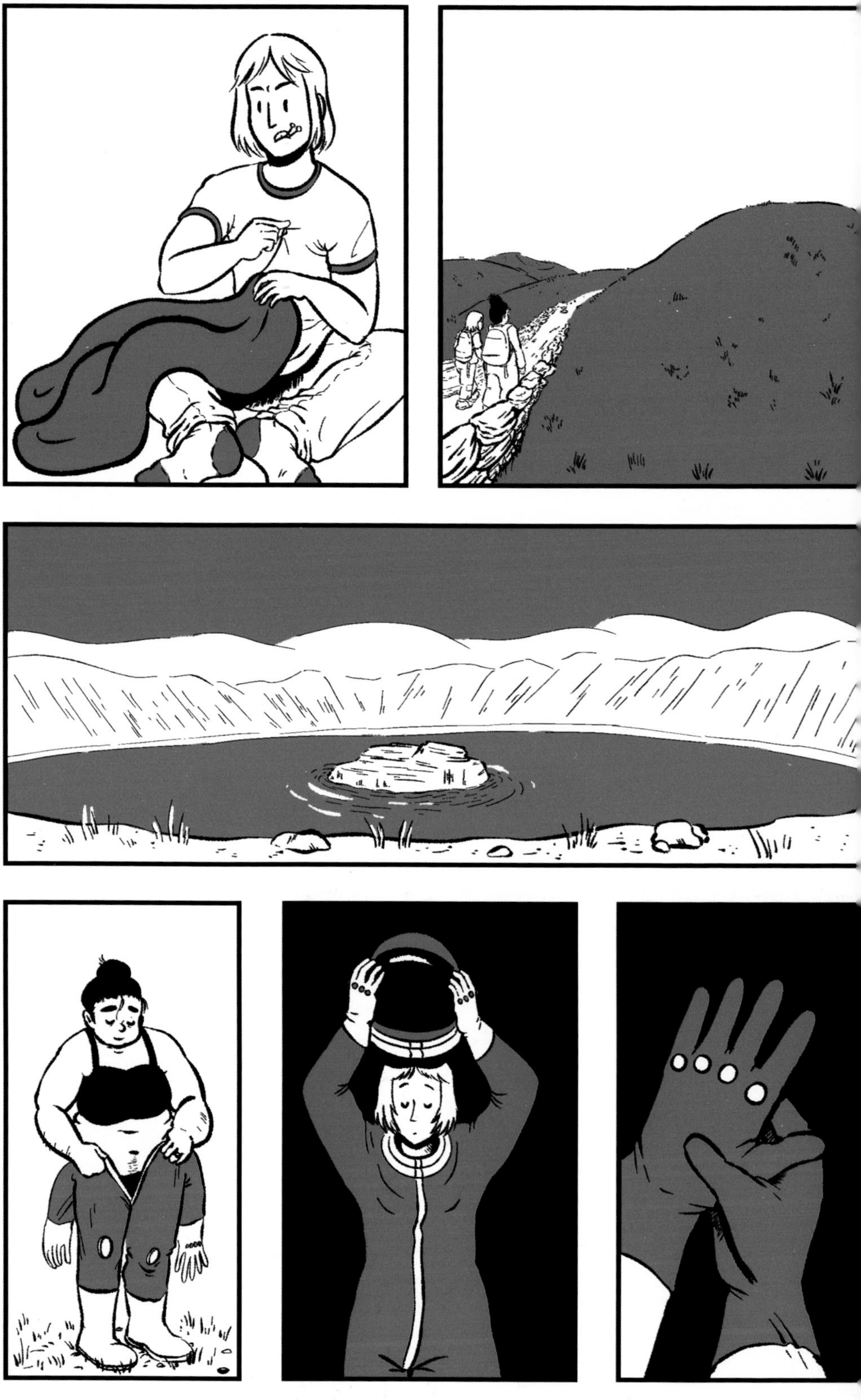

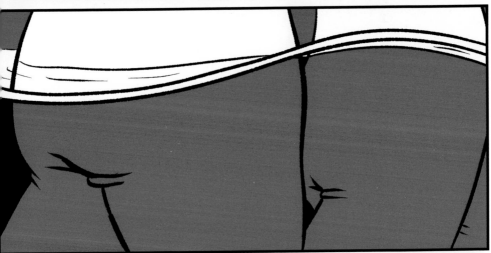

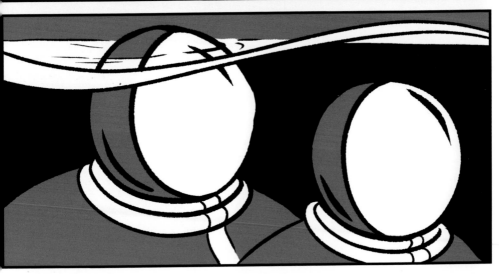

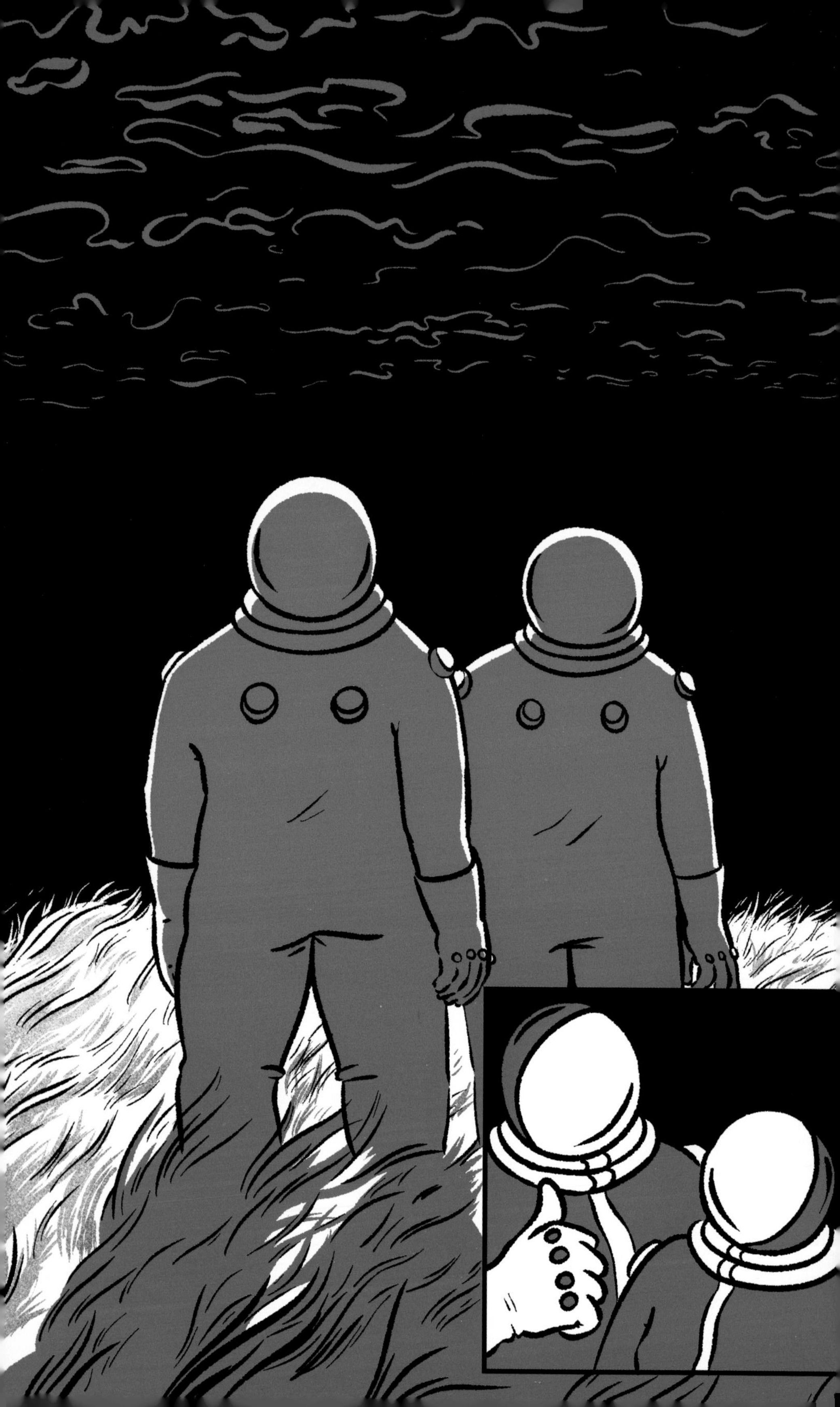

KITCH
COCIN

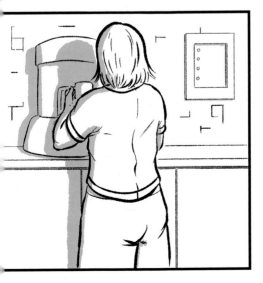

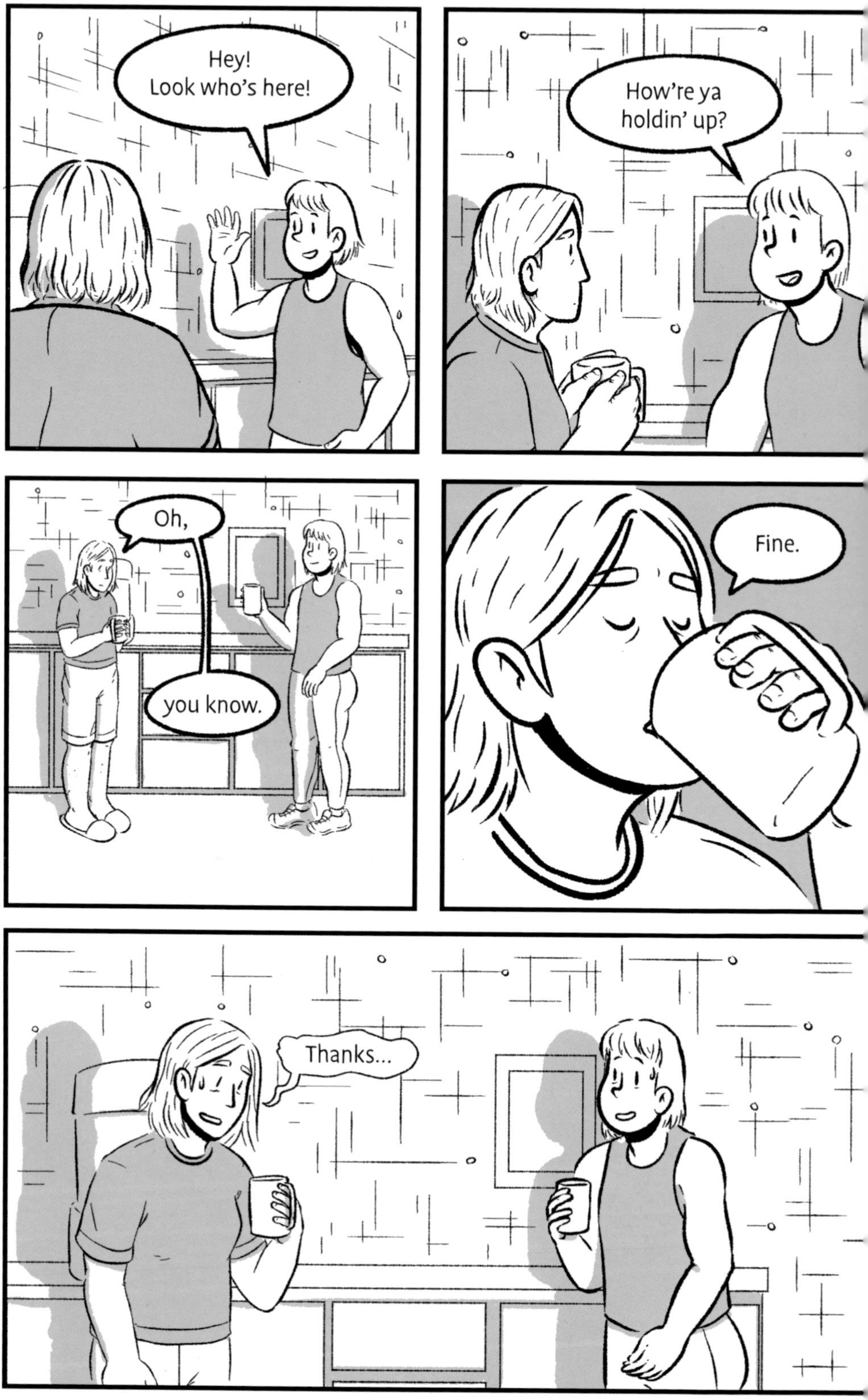
Hey!
Look who's here!
How're ya
holdin' up?
Oh,
you know.
Fine.
Thanks...

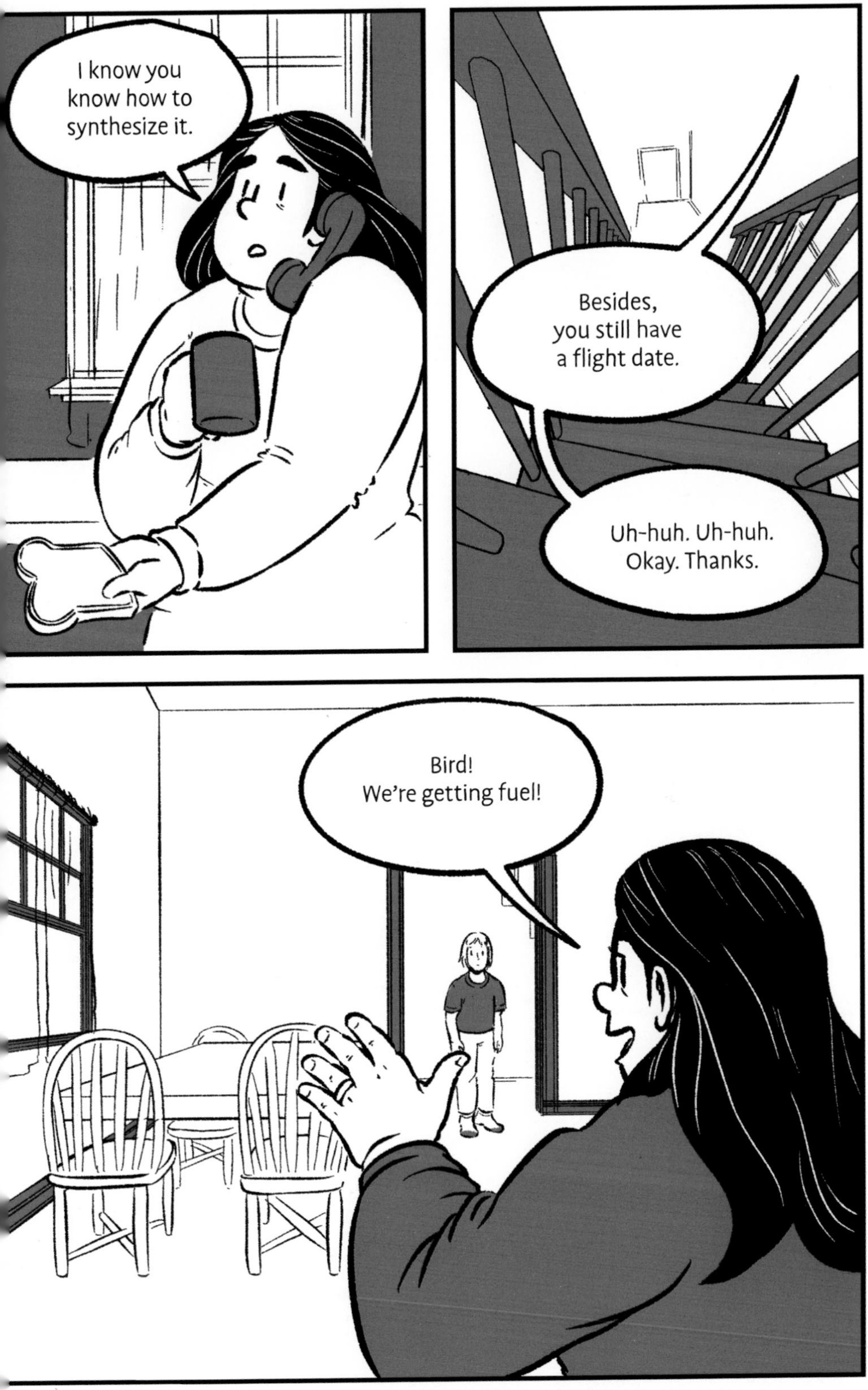
I know you know how to synthesize it.
Besides, you still have a flight date.
Uh-huh. Uh-huh. Okay. Thanks.
Bird! We're getting fuel!

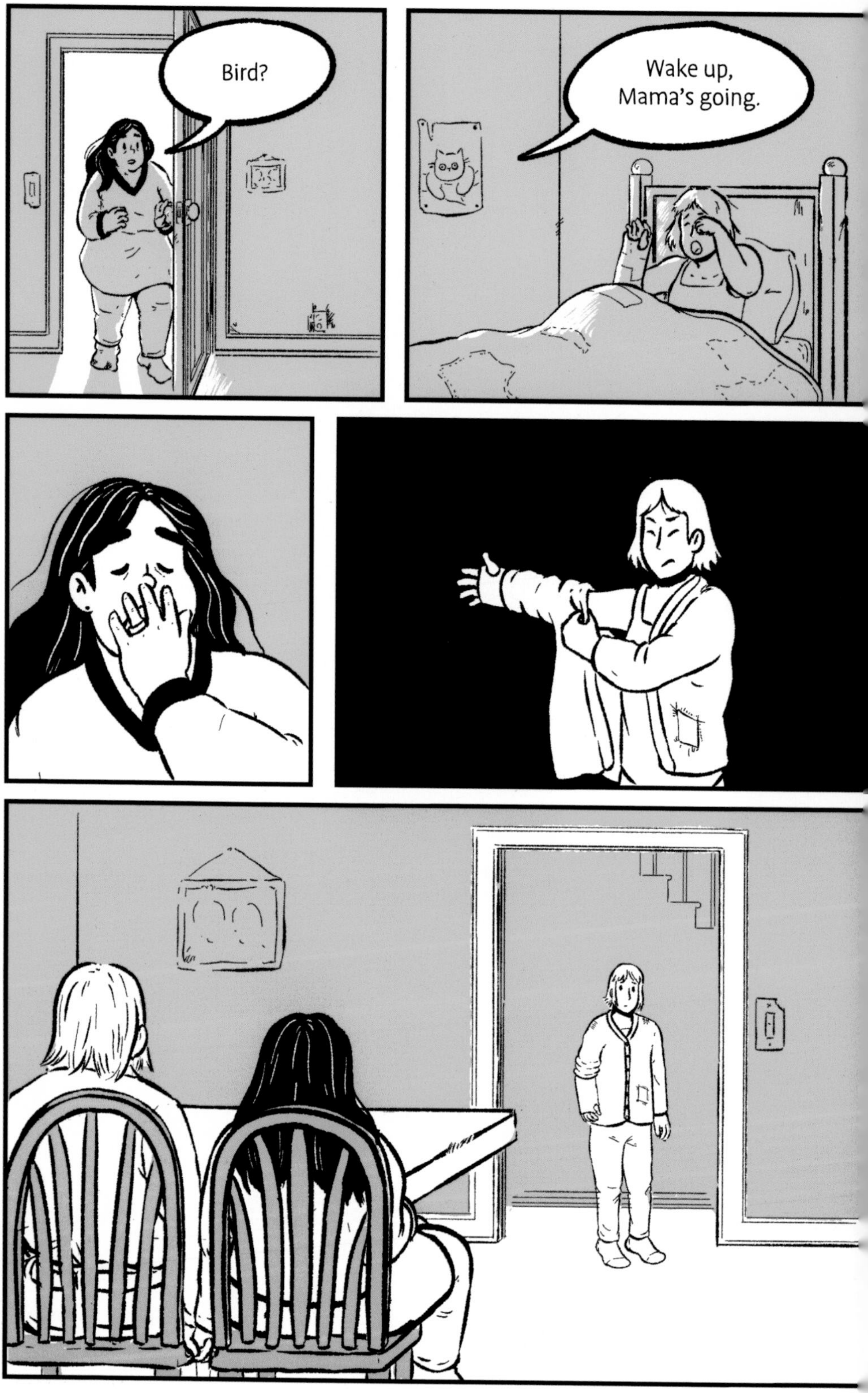
Bird?
Wake up, Mama's going.

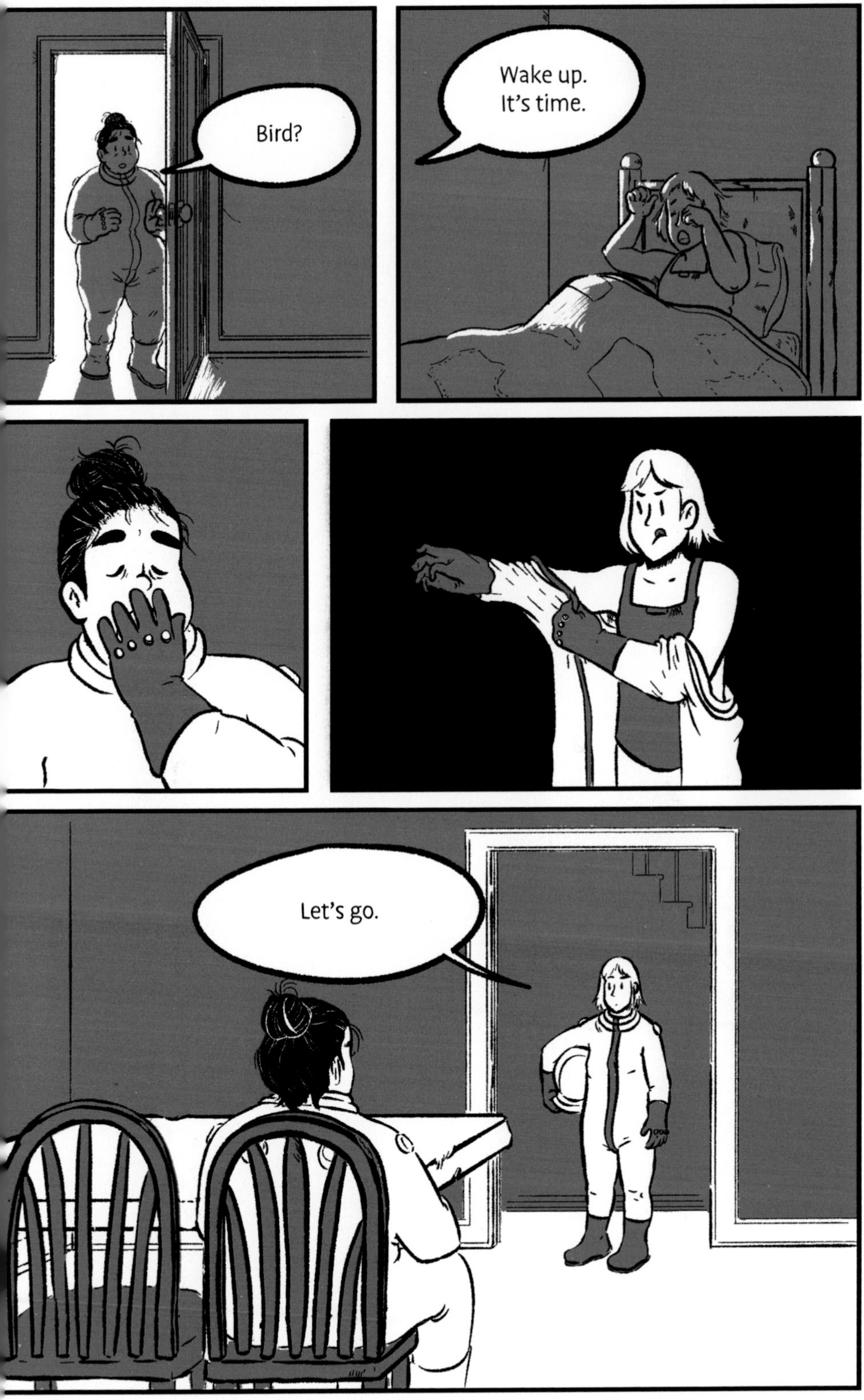
Bird?
Wake up.
It's time.
Let's go.

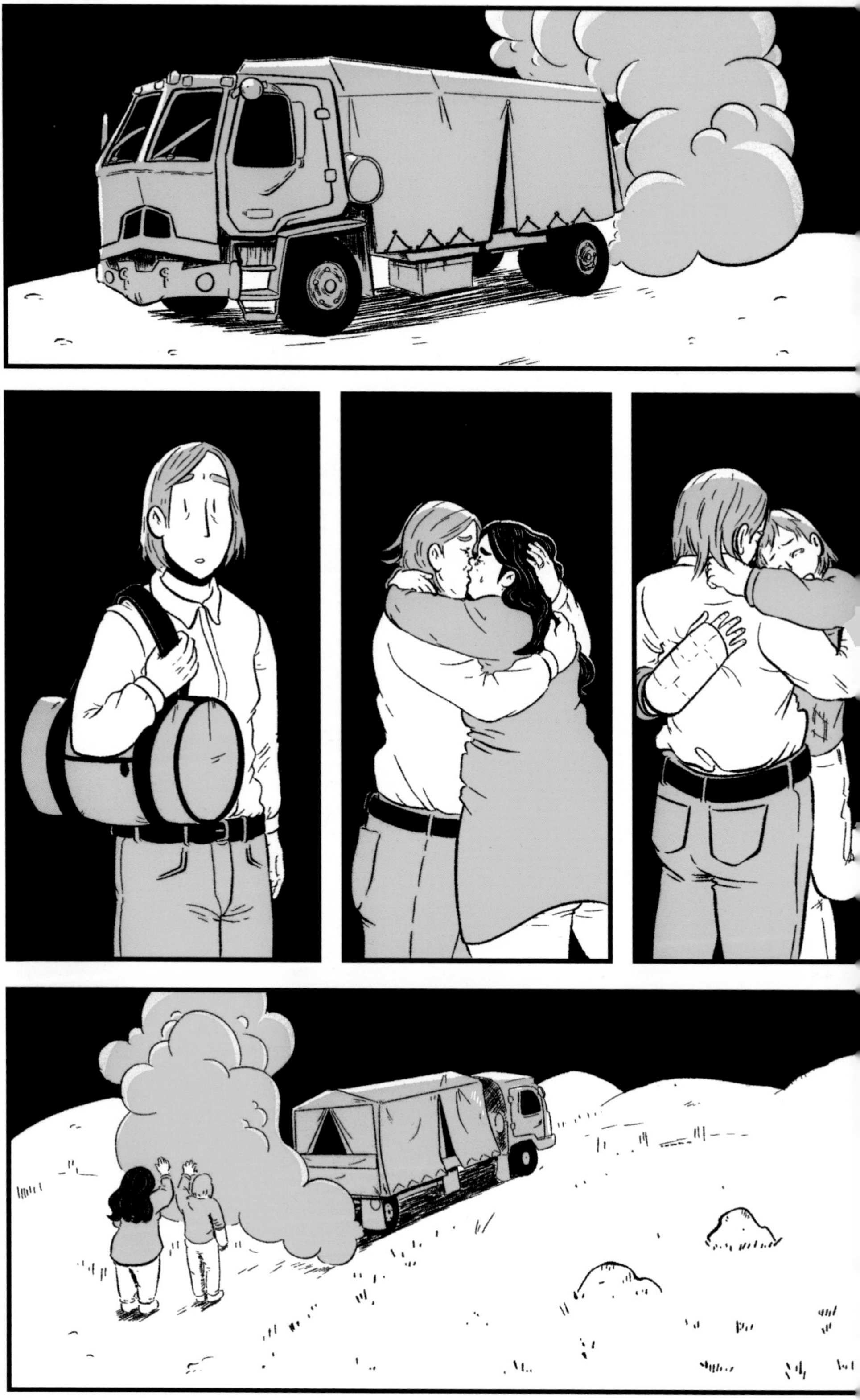

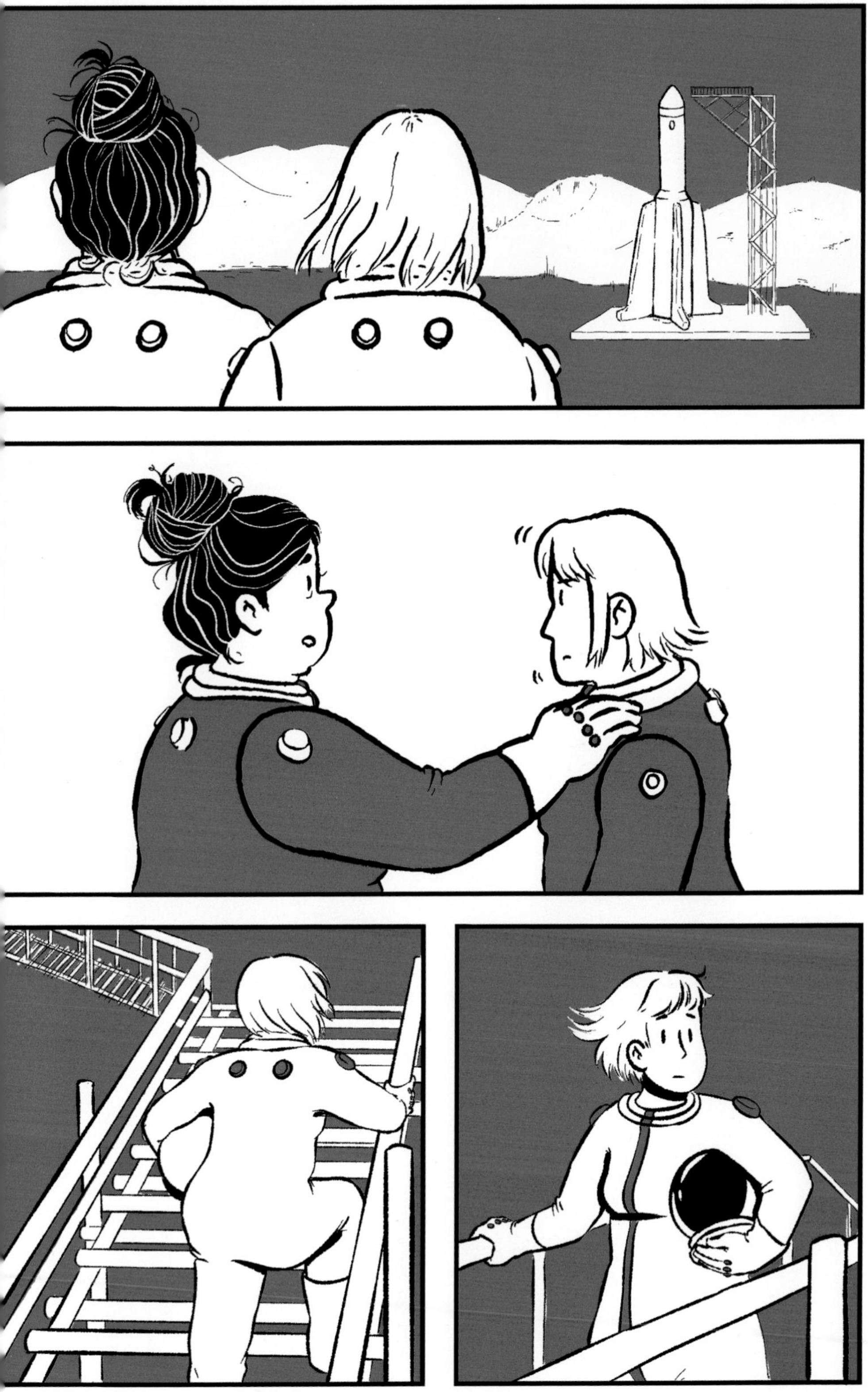

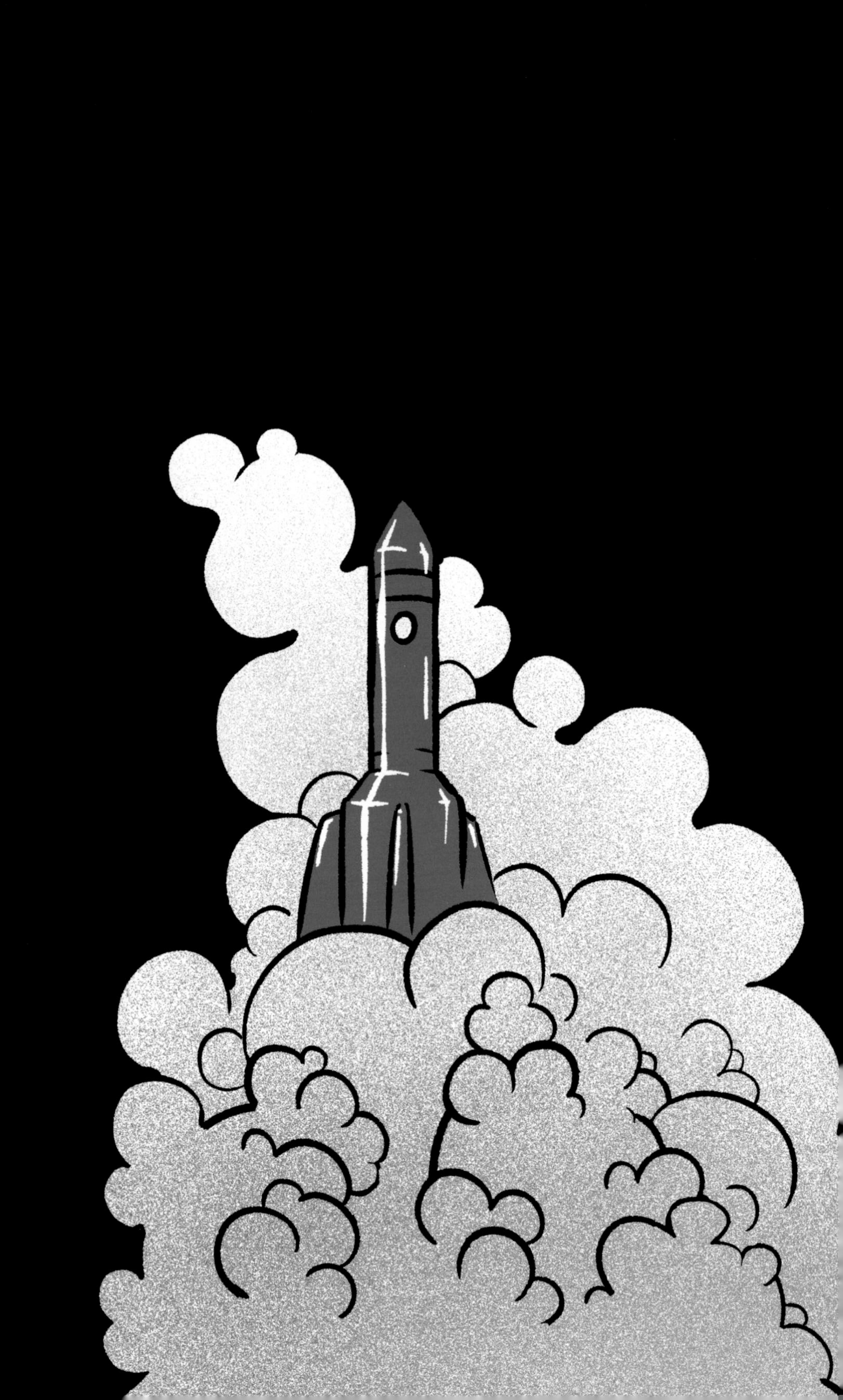

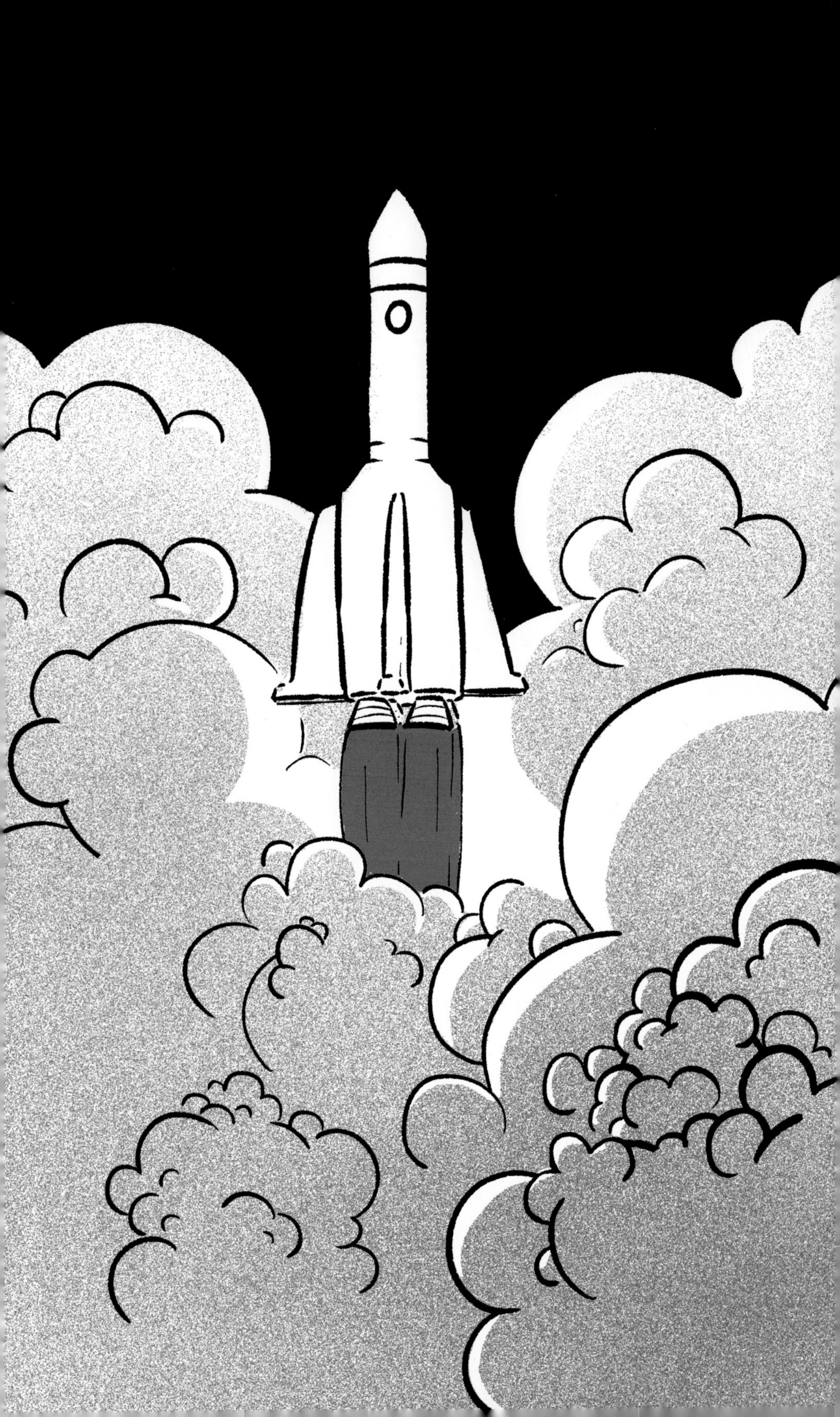

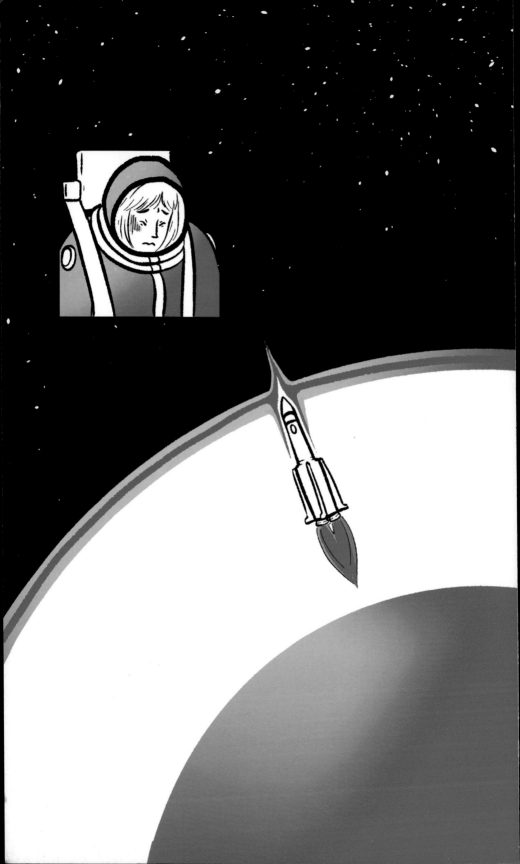

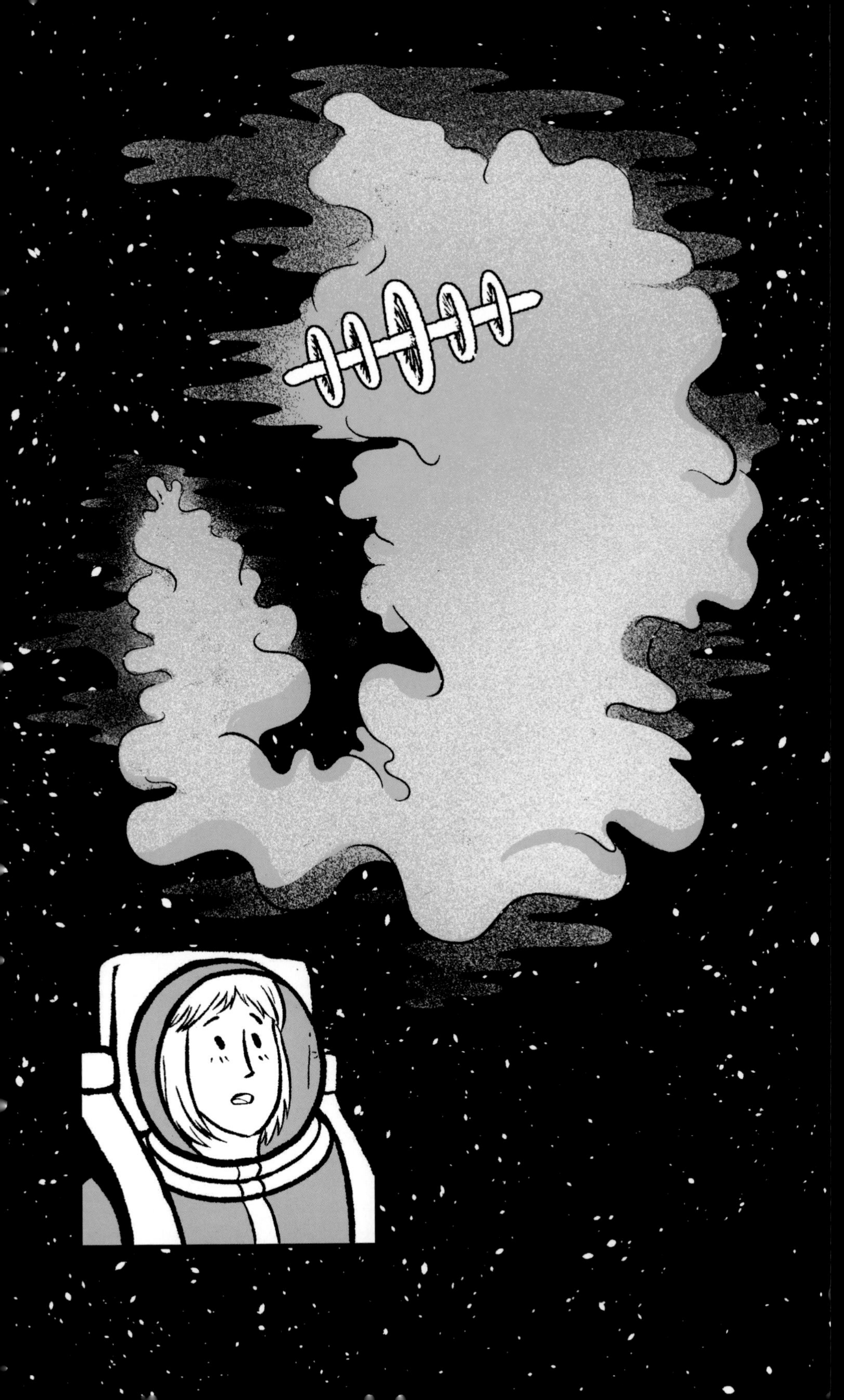

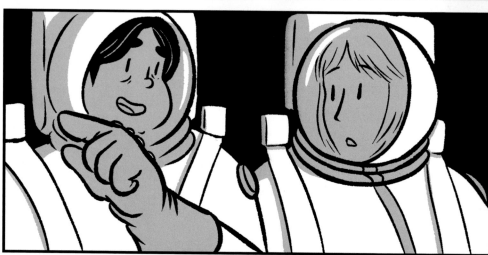

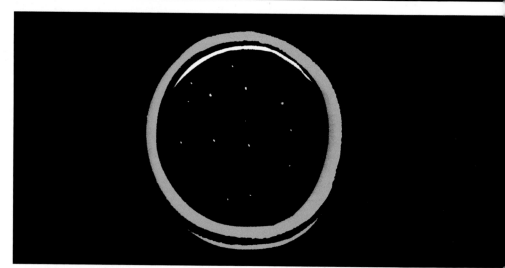

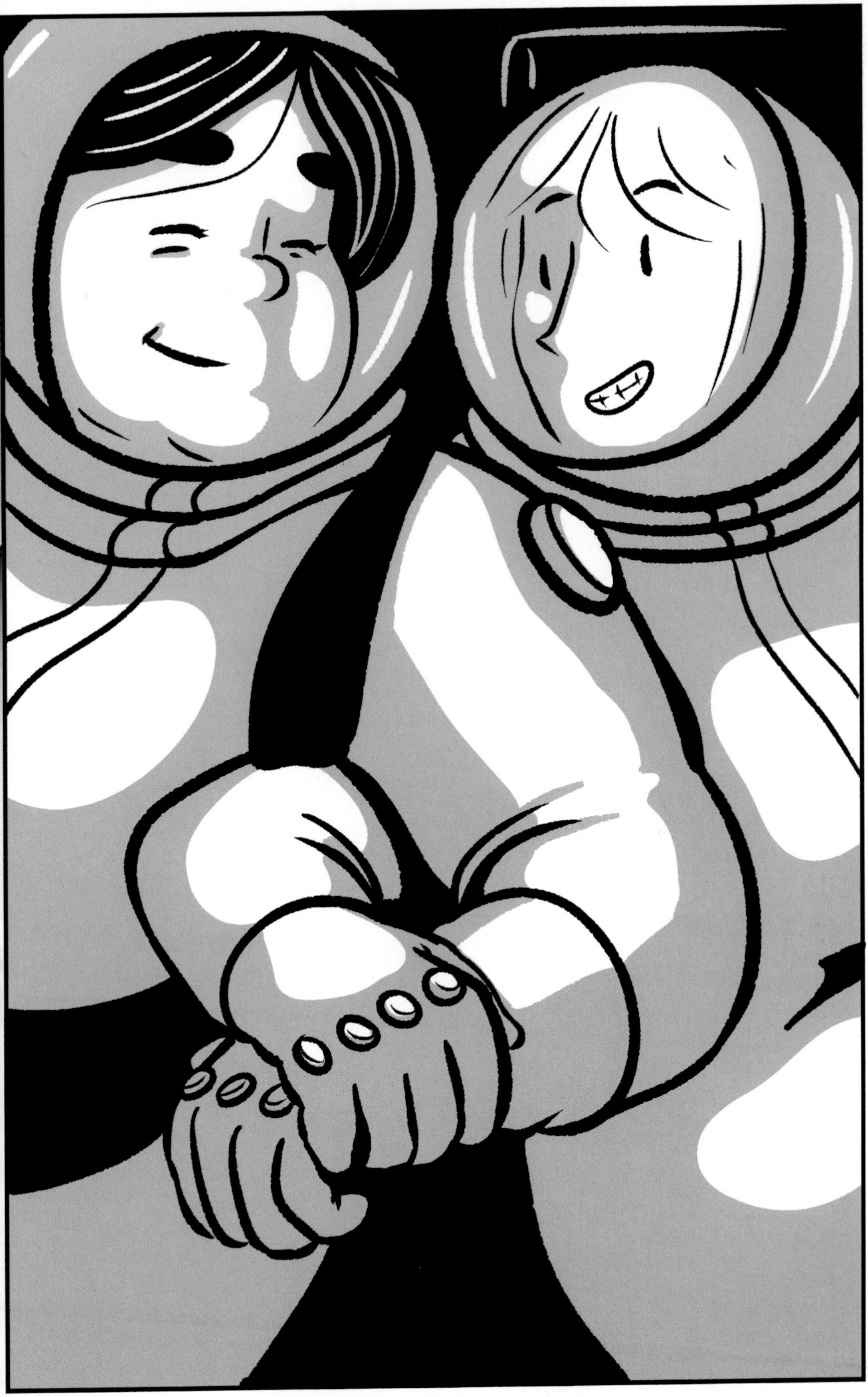

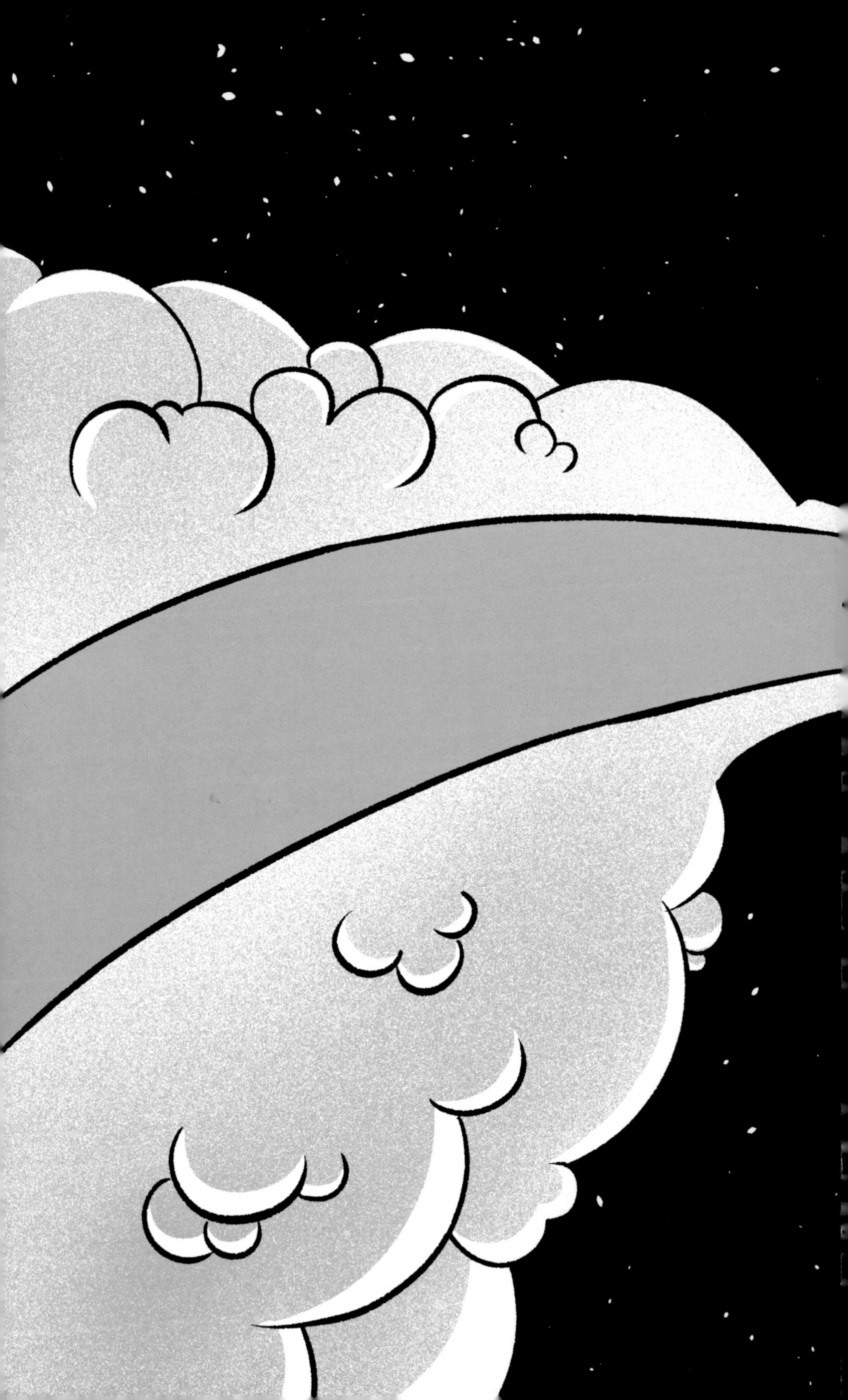

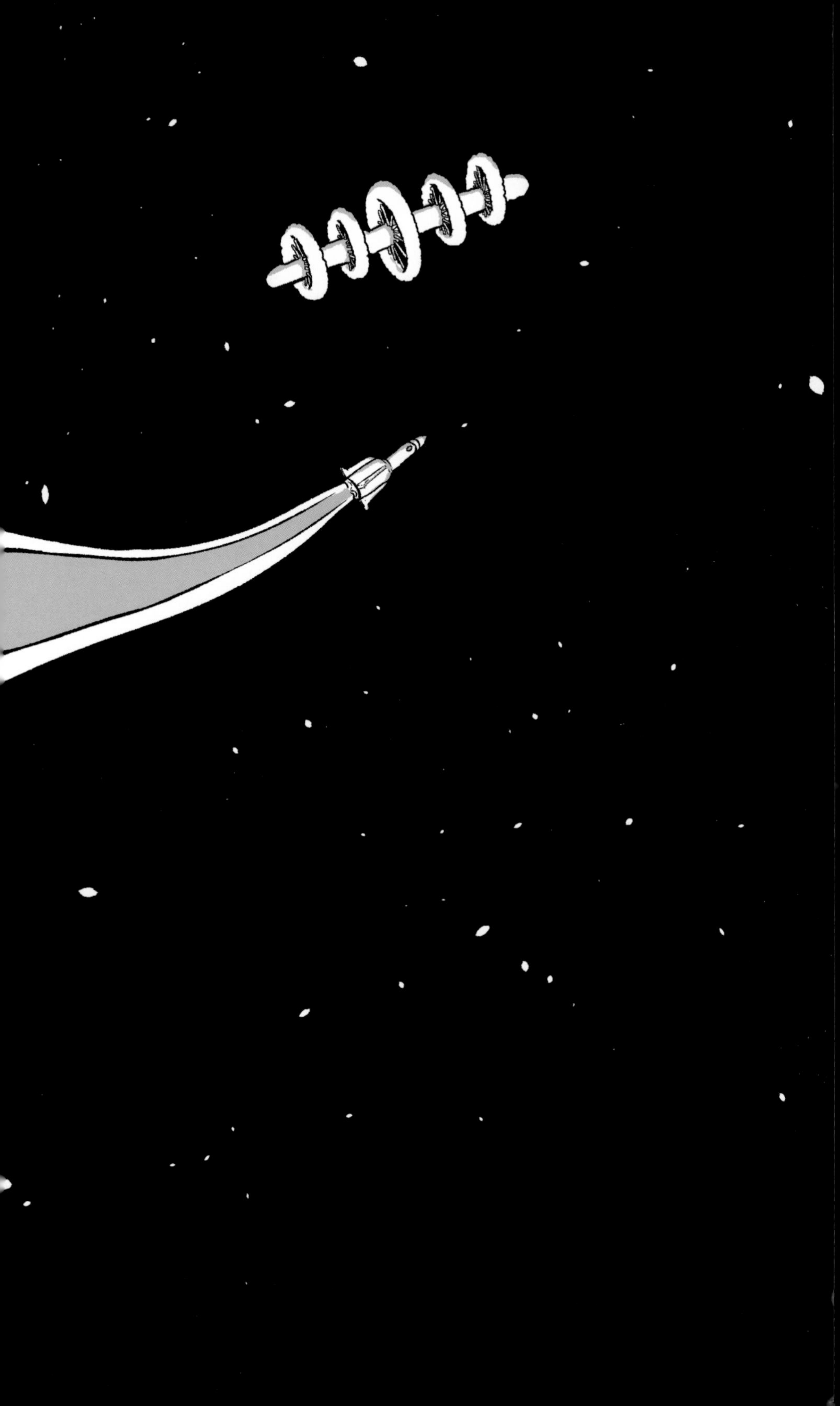

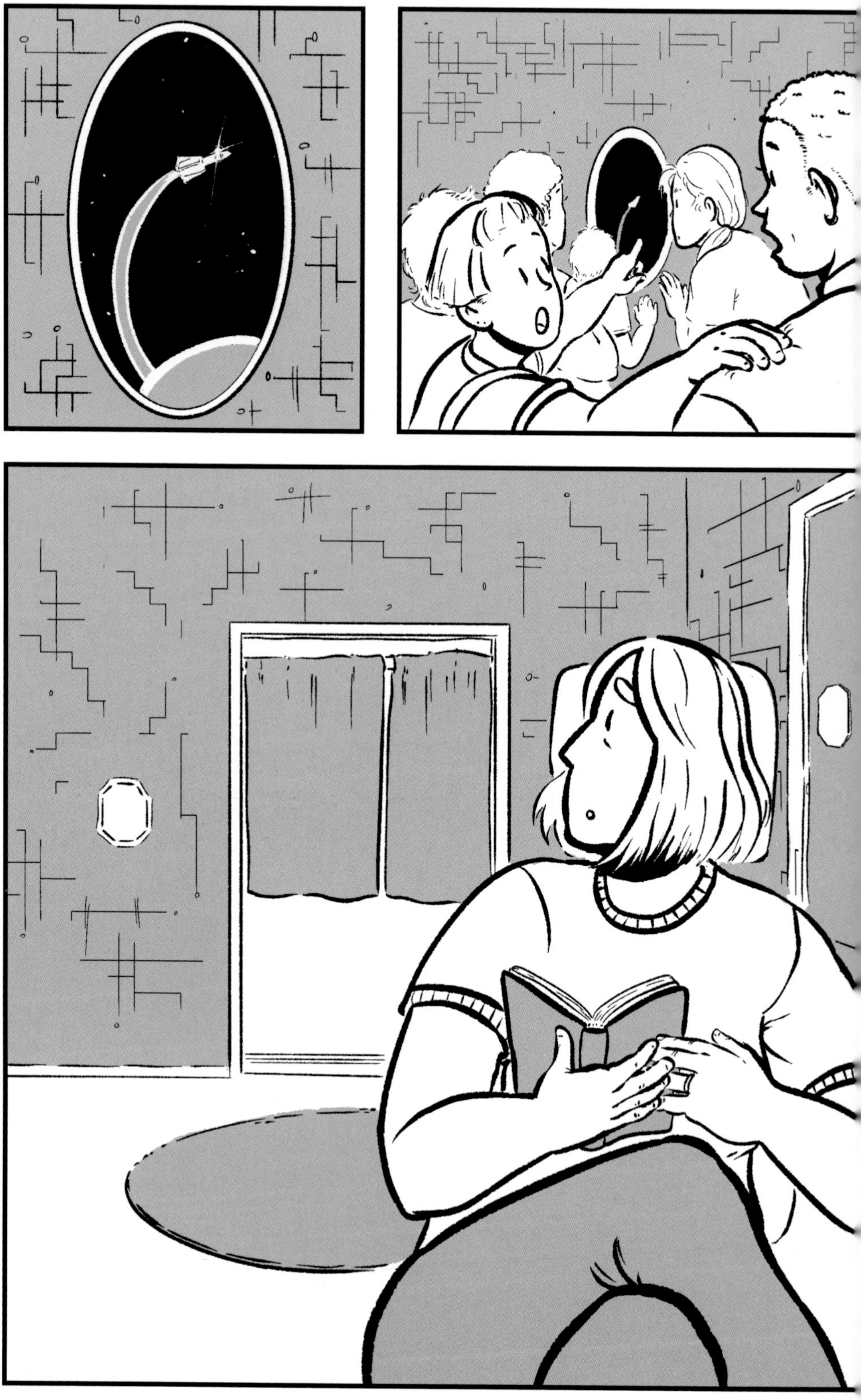

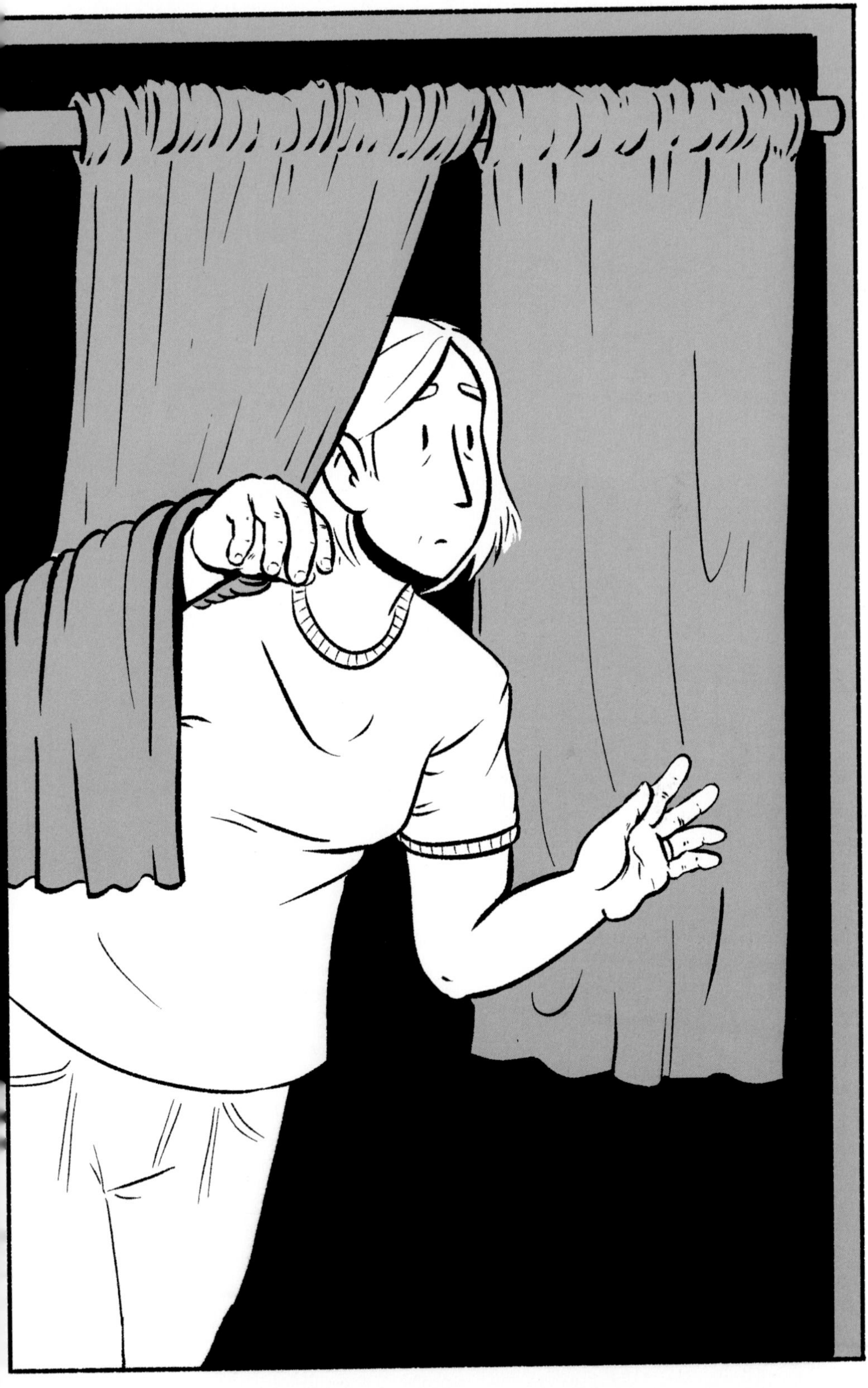

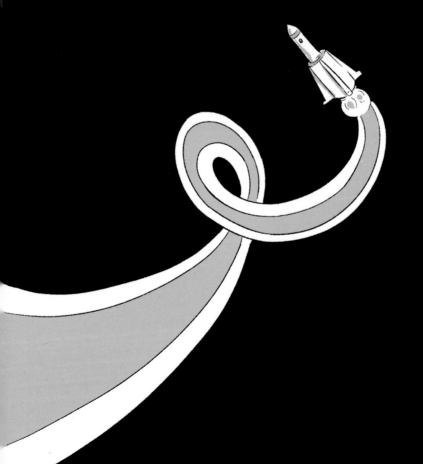

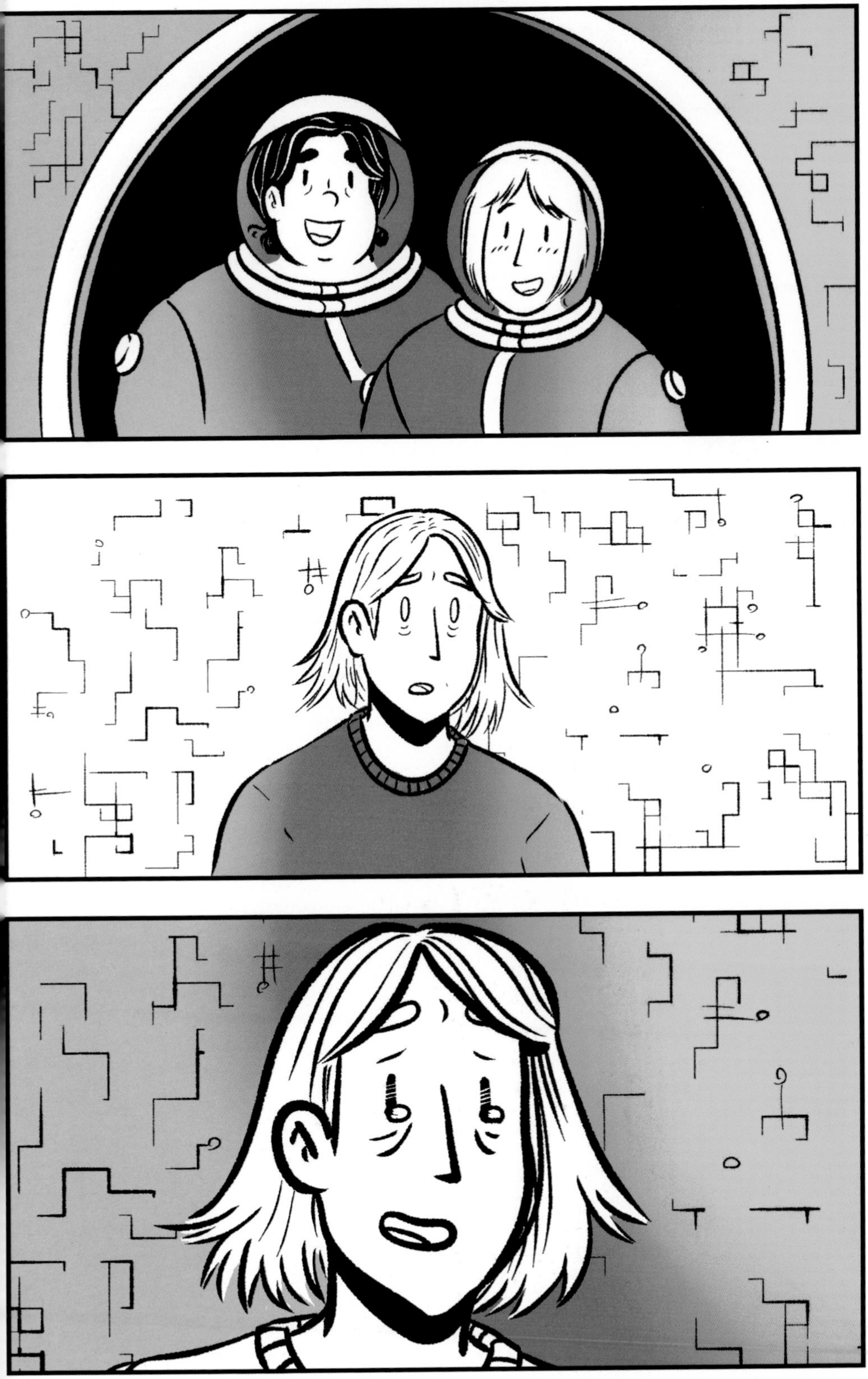

To my parents: I love you so so much.

ACKNOWLEDGMENTS:
I would like to thank: Agent Matt Belford, Jennifer Newens, Olivia Ngai, Rachel Metzger, Micaela Clark, Angie Zbornik, and Alice Wertheimer at West Margin Press for their support.